The period running from the Reformation to the English Civil War saw an evolving understanding of social identity in England. This book uses four illuminating case studies to chart a discursive shift from mid sixteenth-century notions of an individually generated, spiritually motivated sense of identity, to civil-war perceptions of the self as inscribed by the state and inflected according to gender, a site of civil and sexual invigilation and control. Each study centers on the work of an early modern woman writer in the act of self-definition and authorization, in relation to external powers such as the church and the monarchy. Megan Matchinske's analysis illustrates the evolving relationships between public and private selves and the increasing role of gender in determining different identities for men and women. The conjunction of gender and statehood in Matchinske's analysis represents an original contibution to the study of early modern identity.

Cambridge Studies in Renaissance Literature and Culture 26

Writing, gender and state in early modern England

Cambridge Studies in Renaissance Literature and Culture

General editor
STEPHEN ORGEL
Jackson Eli Reynolds Professor of Humanities, Stanford University

Editorial board
Anne Barton, *University of Cambridge*
Jonathan Dollimore, *University of Sussex*
Marjorie Garber, *Harvard University*
Jonathan Goldberg, *Duke University*
Nancy Vickers, *Bryn Mawr College*

Since the 1970s there has been a broad and vital reinterpretation of the nature of literary texts, a move away from formalism to a sense of literatures as an aspect of social, economic, political, and cultural history. While the earliest New Historicist work was criticized for a narrow and anecdotal view of history, it also served as an important stimulus for post-structuralist, feminist, Marxist, and psychoanalytical work, which in turn has increasingly informed and redirected it. Recent writing on the nature of representation, the historical construction of gender and of the concept of identity itself, on theatre as a political and economic phenomenon and on the ideologies of art generally, reveals the breadth of the field. Cambridge Studies in Renaissance Literature and Culture is designed to offer historically oriented studies of Renaissance literature and theater which make use of the insights afforded by theoretical perspectives. The view of history envisioned is above all a view of our own history, a reading of the Renaissance for and from our own time.

Recent titles include

Narrative and meaning in early modern England: Browne's skull and other histories
HOWARD MARCHITELLO, Texas A & M University

The homoerotics of early modern drama
MARIO DIGANGI, Indiana University

Shakespeare's Troy: drama, politics, and the translation of empire
HEATHER JAMES, University of Southern California

Shakespeare, Spenser, and the crisis in Ireland
CHRISTOPHER HIGHLEY, Ohio State University

Discovering the subject in Renaissance England
ELIZABETH HANSON, Queen's University, Kingston, Ontario

A complete list of books in the series is given at the end of the volume

Writing, gender and state in early modern England

Identity formation and the female subject

Megan Matchinske

Assistant Professor of English
University of North Carolina at Chapel Hill

CAMBRIDGE
UNIVERSITY PRESS

CAMBRIDGE UNIVERSITY PRESS
Cambridge, New York, Melbourne, Madrid, Cape Town, Singapore, São Paulo

Cambridge University Press
The Edinburgh Building, Cambridge CB2 2RU, UK

Published in the United States of America by Cambridge University Press, New York

www.cambridge.org
Information on this title: www.cambridge.org/9780521622547

First published 1998
This digitally printed first paperback version 2006

A catalogue record for this publication is available from the British Library

Library of Congress Cataloguing in Publication data

Matchinske, Megan.
Writing, gender and state in early modern England: identity formation and the
female subject / Megan Matchinske.
    p.   cm. – (Cambridge studies in Renaissance literature and culture: 26)
Includes bibliographical references and index.
ISBN 0 521 62254 9 (hardback)
1. English literature – Early modern, 1500–1700 – History and criticism.
2. English literature – Women authors – History and criticism. 3. Women and
literature – England – History – 16th century. 4. Women and literature – England
– History – 17th century. 5. Women – England – History – Renaissance,
1450–1600. 6. Literature and state – Great Britain – History. 7. Identity
(Psychology) in literature. 8. Gender identity in literature.
I. Title.   II. Series:
PR113.M37   1998
820.9′9287 – dc21   97–27259   CIP

ISBN-13 978-0-521-62254-7 hardback
ISBN-10 0-521-62254-9 hardback

ISBN-13 978-0-521-03521-7 paperback
ISBN-10 0-521-03521-X paperback

Contents

Acknowledgments

I would like to thank Louis Montrose for reading innumerable drafts of this project in its infancy, for offering generous and tactful suggestions in its regard, and for sharing with me his vast knowledge of the period. Throughout my graduate study, he gave me the greatest gifts that a teacher can give – encouragement and respect. Page duBois, Stephanie Jed, Cora Kaplan, Masao Miyoshi, and Kathryn Shevelow also deserve note here for their early support and advice; so too, Christina Accomando, Karen Hollis, and Maggie Sale. Many of the ideas put forward in this project would not have been possible without their initial participation in its making.

To my longtime friend, writer Lynn York, who has entered the pages of this book in more ways than she can possibly know. Your interest in this project reminds me that these women lived and breathed and that their stories need telling. To Reid Barbour, Alan Dessen, Anne Hall, Catherine Peyroux, and Keith Wailoo for their suggestions and support at various stages along the way. As my academic "double," Reid has shown me again and again what exemplary teaching and scholarship are all about, and he has done so with grace, with friendship, and with humor. To John McGowan and James Thompson for reading pieces of this project when it was still very much a dissertation, for making me aware of its flaws in time to correct at least a few of them, and for showing by example that political commitment and academic scholarship can and should coexist. Each of you has enabled me to see in different ways and has demanded that I act on those insights in my work.

Within the larger community of scholars writing on early modern English women, I owe several additional debts of gratitude. Thanks are in order to Esther Cope, Barbara Lewalski, and the Folger Shakespeare Library. Having participated in two of many seminars offered at the library – the first, "Preachers, Prophets, and Petitioners in the Age of King Charles I," in 1991, and the second, "Contextualizing Writing by Early Modern Women," in 1994 – I cannot emphasize enough how such dialogues refresh and enrich academic scholarship. As seminar leaders,

Esther and Barbara illustrate profoundly that good teaching need not end with one's students. I am honored to have had the opportunity to experience first-hand their insights and to share with them in the continuing process of critical discovery.

Fran Dolan and Betty Travitsky have suggested sources and offered fact-finding advice at key junctures in this project; Betty Hageman and Sara Jayne Steen, counsel on academic etiquette and scholarly diplomacy. Olga Valbuena continues to provide contributions on all fronts; I value her scholarship and her friendship. I am grateful as well to the members of my writing group, the North Carolina Research Group for the Study of Early Modern Women. Their combined brilliance, inspired conversation, and exceptional cooking have remained reassuring constants throughout the trials and tribulations of revision and re-revision. Within that group Judith Bennett, Jane Burns, and Barbara Harris deserve additional and heartfelt thanks. All three have given me a sense of intellectual rapport that extends beyond the boundaries of my department. As friends and mentors they continue to provide me with support and encouragement, strategy and stamina. Their dedication to junior women across Chapel Hill's campus serves as a constant reminder of what an academic women's community really ought to mean.

This book would never have been possible were it not for the technical and scholarly expertise of several people. Thanks are in order to my readers at the Cambridge University Press for their tactful suggestions and politic nudges; this book is stronger thanks to their critical eye; Nandra Perry for her careful bibliographic work; Leigh Mueller for guiding me through the unfamiliar terrain of book production with ever the hope of coherent prose as an end; Josie Dixon for navigating the intricacies of press schedules and the like; and finally, Stephen Orgel for having faith in this project from the very beginning and the willingness to stick it out. I could never have finished without your combined and generous assistance.

On a personal note, I must ultimately pay homage to all of the friends and colleagues who have made Chapel Hill feel like home and my work worth pursuing. To Pam Cooper, Jane Danielewicz, Bethaney Dale, Robert Dowling, Ritchie Kendall, Susan Navarette, and Dale Traugott, I am grateful to have you in my life. And to my San Diego family, especially those who continue to press for my return, Eve Morris, Scott Rand, Valerie Steele, and Nan Sterman, thank you for your support of my academic passions even though they have carried me across the country. I want to thank my sister and best friend Melinda Thompson for offering me unflagging emotional and technical support on those many occasions when things have seemed too baffling to proceed, and my second mother, Margaret Brehmer, for scrutinizing my work with a keen critical eye and an unwavering moral ethos. Finally and most importantly, I want to thank my parents, Marilyn and Dolph Matchinske; it is your unparalleled faith in me, your absolute and unselfish acceptance of all that I do, that has given me the courage to trust in myself and to take risks that I have. The best parts of this book are your doing; the mistakes are all my own.

I dedicate this project to my partner, David Brehmer, who has weathered it all with humor and patience, who has spent more years with me than without, and who shares with me in the most important part of my life, our two daughters, Erin and Marin. The three of you make me complete. This book is yours.

Permissions

Portions of chapter 3 appeared in different form in "Legislating 'Middle-Class Morality in the Marriage Market: Ester Sowernam's Ester hath hang'd Haman,'" *English Literary Renaissance* 24: 154–83. © 1994. Reprinted with permission. An abbreviated version of chapter 4 appeared in "Holy Hatred: Formations of the Gendered Subject in English Apocalyptic Writing, 1625-1651," *English Literary History* 60: 349-77. © 1993 by the Johns Hopkins University Press. Reprinted with permission.

Introduction

Margaret Cavendish, first Duchess of Newcastle, opens her memoir by recounting a crisis of conscience she faced in her courtly duties at Oxford in the early years of the English Civil War. She writes:

> My brothers and sisters seemed not very well pleased [with my mother's decision to allow me to wait upon the Queen at Oxford], by reason I had never been from home . . . for though they knew I would not behave myself to their . . . dishonour, yet they thought I might to my disadvantage, being very unexperienced in the world . . . [As a result of their warnings and because] I had heard the world was apt to lay aspersions even on the innocent . . . I durst neither look up with my eyes, nor speak, nor be any way sociable: insomuch as I was thought a natural fool . . . And indeed I was so afraid to dishonour my friends and family by my indiscreet actions, that I rather chose to be accounted a fool, than to be thought rude or wanton. In truth, my bashfulness and fears made me repent my going from home to see the world abroad.[1]

In these lines, Cavendish reminds her readers that her demeanor at court depends on several things. In order to accommodate cultural imperatives that demand the absolute innocence of women and aware that even a flawless performance on her part will not guarantee success, she overplays her role. She bows her head and shuts her mouth, withdrawing from social contact of any kind. At the same time, Cavendish realizes the repercussions of her actions. In carrying them out she will be thought "a natural fool."

Cavendish's anecdote illustrates the historical contingencies of Englishwomen's social negotiations in the middle years of the seventeenth century. In her account, Cavendish recognizes the effect of her conduct – the way that her behavior will make her appear to others – yet she reminds her readers that her actions are her own. Hers is a conscious decision to play the fool. Cavendish apparently chooses this tactic in order to avoid charges of rude or wanton behavior: "I was so afraid to dishonour my friends and family by my indiscreet actions, that I rather chose to be accounted a fool." That Cavendish makes a choice, albeit a choice circumscribed by a clearly defined and narrow set of options, is

1

key to the construction of identity – of feminine identity – in her work. Her rhetorical frame presents the subject of this narrative as both active, in determining the shape and course of her life, and reactive, in making her decisions on the basis of a set of cultural directives external to her.

Cavendish's decision to demur, dependent as it is on factors outside of her control, and politically troubling as it may appear to modern readers, nevertheless empowers her. Later in her account, she tells her readers that it is her fool's act that secures her a high-status marriage: "for my lord the Marquis of Newcastle did approve of those bashful fears which many condemned and would choose such a wife as he might bring to his own humours." Cavendish's choice, perhaps much like her husband's own, offers her leverage within a culture that is materially different from our own. Her account and the actions she describes within it are based on seventeenth-century assumptions about women's cultural status – about what is permissible and what is not, in *1641*, in *Oxford*, for *maids of honour*. Accordingly, for modern readers to talk of closed lips and bowed heads as evidence of Cavendish's surrender to normative culture would be inaccurate and unhelpful. The logistics of her eventual title bear this out. As a married duchess, Cavendish will be able to speak her mind more openly than many of her social and economic inferiors, both women and men, despite and because of that earlier silence. Of this, the sheer volume of her published poetry and prose offers substantial proof. Within *her* cultural context, playing the court fool makes sense – strategic sense. What I want to stress here is the material specificity of Cavendish's negotiation and our critical responsibility in attending to it. Reading Cavendish's text within a frame that considers both the range of her options and the kinds of relationships she is able to forge within them complicates and enriches what we are able to say about her. It allows us to talk about how identity, here aristocratic feminine identity, accommodates cultural imperatives at one and the same time that it actively sets about sabotaging them.

Within the above anecdote, Cavendish recognizes the differences for women between a life at court and a life at home.[2] She understands home as a place of retreat, separate from and safer than "the world abroad." When Cavendish publishes her account in 1656, home is where she belongs, a place she "repent[s]" ever having left. At the same time, she understands that her own best interests may be in conflict with those of her supporters. While her narrative recognizes "friends and family" as the recipients of any dishonor that may accrue should she conduct herself improperly, Cavendish claims responsibility for maintaining that honor herself. *Her* discreet behavior will secure their reputation; *her* wantonness, their disgrace. "Friends and family" would feel the effects of her "dishonour" – a dishonor that is here explicitly feminized – in lost privilege, lack of preferment, and aristocratic scandal. In contrast, the "disadvantage" that she describes is all her own. Her social inexperience may secure for her an advantageous match; the duke wants a wife whom he can "bring to his own humours." But her inexperience will also render her foolish. The criteria for appropriate behavior, the ways that various readings of that behavior both impinge on others and determine the self, are multiply inflected. They have different repercussions in different social situations. Privileging one set of options – in this case, home/ family/husband – creates dislocations in another. Cavendish's actions are unacceptable at court and in the world abroad.

Between the English Reformation and the Civil War, the space dividing private identity from public persona, personal history from state archive, is widening. So too, the cultural markers that separate women from men and status from status are becoming more discrete. Writing her memoir in the aftermath of civil upheaval, Cavendish understands her place within these categories in a markedly different manner from her Reformation and Counter-Reformation predecessors. Not only would earlier women of similar status have been incapable of drawing the sorts of distinctions between home and court, between self and society, that Cavendish does in her memoir (largely because those categories did not exist in quite so discrete a form), but the literal forum for those pronouncements – the personal memoir – also would likely have been unavailable. Indeed, writing a "life" for purposes other than religious exposition was largely unthinkable in Henrician England.[3] Early sixteenth-century writers and readers knew their place in terms rather different from those used by Cavendish.

In the pages that follow I would like to exaggerate the dislocations – historic, political, economic, and religious – that eventually shaped Cavendish's notions of the permissible within the early modern English state. In order to do so I will attend to two interrelated and historically unstable terms: "gender" and "state." During the hundred years following Henry VIII's break with the Roman Catholic Church, England was in the process of constructing its national identity by recasting current sites of authority into new and more diverse forms. Where people in early sixteenth-century England had depended for moral guidance (and its attendant behavioral coercion) on church and monarchy, the increasingly diverse economic, political, and religious circumstances of the Reformation required additional and more disparate forms of social regulation. Printing presses, changes in market and land use, revisions in church policy and practice, redistribution of property and title, a bureaucratization of royal government and civil service, all of these allowed for and insisted on a multitude of differing registers within the "state" to monitor behavior and determine acceptable codes of conduct for the English people.[4]

Where earlier versions of private identity and selfhood had been almost uniformly associated with the spiritual, with conversations between priests and penitents,[5] those spaces too change in shape and form during the Tudor and Stuart periods. They become broader and more secular in scope.[6] It is my contention that the domain of the private is, by 1640, concrete, defined, and invasive. Spiritual interiority and religious conscience have been joined by a variety of other private spaces. In addition to singular relationships between private sinners and their God, between secret thoughts and their public ramifications, notions of a secularized civic conscience also begin to gain cultural weight. Accordingly, we can document during this later period an increase in personal litigation;[7] a privatization of political, economic, and familial responsibility;[8] a specialization in business and government skills;[9] as well as a more overtly consumer-based notion of goods and services.[10] As the domestic acquires authority, its purveyors become more carefully defined as well. Women begin to replace priests as regulators of conscience and bearers of secular *and* spiritual morality. Indeed, this transformation marks one of the most significant, powerful, and disturbing cultural upheavals to occur for early modern women like Cavendish.

Where the roles distinguishing women from men were less carefully articulated (if equally restrictive) in the years preceding the English Reformation, by the beginning of the seventeenth century[11] legislation has been set in place, suggesting both a more general anxiety about gender difference and a need to document its various permutations. In the 1520s, both middling-rank and aristocratic wives might work beside their husbands as shop keepers, candle makers, and estate owners; by mid-century, laws that restrict and segregate such employment have been enacted. Some of the most telling legislation to suggest this dis-ease over gender categories can be found in the regulation of labor. The Statute of Artificers of 1563 included, amongst its other provisions for servants, compulsory and gender-specific employment – men in husbandry, women in domestic service.[12] Guild regulations limiting membership and eligibility for women also came into play, though to a far lesser degree than on the continent. Property law, marriage licensing, and inheritance regulation prove sites of intense redefinition as well, in both protecting and undermining women's rights.[13] These qualifications have the joint effect of both specifying and gendering appropriate identity for English men and women by the 1640s.

In this book, I juxtapose the construction of a private and always gendered self to another construction, that of the emerging English state.[14] Tracing the intersections between subject and state across several textually and historically discrete moments, I chart a discursive shift from early sixteenth-century understandings of private conscience as individually generated and spiritually motivated, to civil-war perceptions of interiority as state-inscribed and gender-inflected – a site of civil and sexual invigilation and control. Mapping the proliferation of competing cultural arenas within early modern England as well as the increasingly restrictive nature of each, my analyses not only illustrate the relationships between state and local identities, but also, and perhaps more evocatively, reveal what happens when gender determines those developing identities differently for women and men. The narrative frame that Cavendish employs in scripting her own identity suggests to what extent those refigurings have taken place by mid century. It situates the points of contest – her ability to articulate competing identities – within a carefully prescribed, gender-specific opposition between home and the world abroad, between private disadvantage and public dishonor for women. It is the connection between gender and statehood, largely unexplored by critics of social and cultural formation, that the following chapters will foreground.[15]

Material contexts: theirs, mine, and ours

There is, or should be, a sense of community-building at the beginning of academic pursuits – an acknowledgment of others who grapple with the same questions and concerns, exploring the all-too-familiar terrain of one's own enthusiasms. Since the 1980s, a number of scholars sharing an engagement with and investment in the study of women's history have come together in a collaborative effort to understand England's past in terms of its impact on women. In recent years, this community of scholars has grown enormously. So too has the range and sophistication of critical strategies used in investigating its myriad questions. Less than a generation ago, the task before critics of women's literary history was largely one of recovery. Scholars like Katherine Usher Henderson, Elaine Hobby, Elspeth Graham, Germaine Greer, and Betty Travitsky, began the difficult task of compilation, gathering together manuscripts and out-of-print texts by women poets, diarists, playwrights, and pamphleteers.[16] Their efforts to make sixteenth- and seventeenth-century women's writings accessible to a wider audience were in large part responsible for the almost geometric increase in critical studies that focus on these texts today.[17] Several essay collections bring together a vast range of methodological and interdisciplinary frames from which to consider early modern women's writings.[18] Other book-length studies investigate the cultural dynamics of gender construction across economic, generic, and religious lines.[19]

Where early critical works necessarily focus on introductions, supplying biography and historical context, recent studies have begun to diverge from that model. As more and more scholars have become actively involved in reinterpreting the early modern period in terms of a wider reading of its various voices, the direction of critical research is beginning to change as well. No longer content to see women's voices either subsumed by established texts and histories or kept in isolation from them, recent scholars are more likely to rethink Elizabethan and Stuart institutions and ideologies in light of these works than to insert them into existing categories of masculinist thought or to essentialize them as a separate study altogether.

Before the recent rediscovery of women's writings, much of the standard literature of the early modern period offered little critical legitimacy for making claims to feminine authority. This problem was compounded by the fact that critics were largely dependent on that literature to write female identity.[20] Early analyses that took as their focus male writers such as Shakespeare and Jonson were frequently framed in one of two ways. They opted either to promote some sort of proto-feminist bias that had little connection to the material circumstances of early modern women, or conversely to disallow agency altogether in a reiteration of women's absence of choice and restricted domain. Less "canonical" texts, many of them authored by women, can offer insights into early modern women's cultural roles and obligations, especially when critics attempt to consider them within a wider range of textual traditions. Extending the boundaries of study, however, is not, in itself, sufficient.

"Paramount to a more informed cultural project is a willingness to interrogate these writings within their material contexts, to forestall our own critical (sometimes feminist-inspired) impulses to label them as either successful or failed as a result of their negotiations."[21] Margaret J. M. Ezell explains that the problem with much women's literary history results from "certain models of historiography which have been imported into women's studies without [adequate] scrutiny of the assumptions they contain about the nature of authorship and the generation of literary history."[22] This problem is compounded when we bring to bear on these texts aesthetic perspectives (our own as well as those of early modern readers) that are not sufficiently interrogated. In the analyses that follow I want to explore the ways in which early modern women's individual articulations and negotiations collide with, negate, and support more pervasive, frequently masculine-based, cultural directives. I also want to imagine how those intersections might create multiple narratives that evolve over time. Most women writers of the early modern period did not question dominant masculinist literary modes of production. They did not defy generic expectation. Nor did they altogether reject the assumptions on which those ideas depended. Such acts were untenable. There were, nevertheless, an increasing number of women writers who were inserting themselves into established dialogues, negotiating positions from which to claim authority or define self, and changing the very forms that identity would take (Matchinske, "Credible Consorts," 435).

All of the writers whom I consider here claim affiliations very different from my own.[23] Most of their writings imagine women to be inferior to men and accept as given women's secondary cultural status as wives, mothers, and daughters, dependent for financial, intellectual, and physical support on others. The majority of the works that I consider espouse religious and political beliefs that deny or limit women's public voice and know a woman's place in society according to standards that have little in common with current feminisms or the positions from which they speak. The prophetic Lady Eleanor Davies, writing in the throes of civil war, advocates a program of religious intolerance and militancy that many find unnerving, particularly given its similarities to recent fundamentalist agendas in the United States. While there is little about her value system that modern feminists might admire, it is precisely Davies's distance that I think merits further study.

"How do the often restrictive and seemingly self-deprecatory rhetorical stances that early modern women assert serve the authors who write them? What sorts of prompts encourage them?" (Matchinske, "Credible Consorts," 435). How do they come to represent legitimate and powerful sites for female authority and voice for women in sixteenth- and seventeenth-century England? In each of the following explorations I will attempt to decipher the particular modes of legitimacy and/or articulation available to early modern women writers, always bearing in mind that their articulations, however successful, frequently serve contradictory agendas and policies.[24] Finally, given that the majority of English narratives that remain for us as modern readers and critics are predominantly masculinist in make-up – that the bulk of cultural directives charted to date are "woman-blind" – how can we account for women's voices and choices in surviving these conditions?

While women have been denied standing in politics and government throughout English history (with several rather notable exceptions),[25] many less well-placed sixteenth- and seventeenth-century women entered into debates on political rights, on religious freedoms, and on women's investment in each. "These were women who, in responding to and rewriting current directives and available ideologies, *did* make choices, many of them astonishing in light of their insights and courage" (Matchinske, "Credible Consorts," 436). What I am interested in charting is how these various choices have been historically-coded, how they fit into wider social norms and policies. "In a culture that . . . [was] announcing subject definition (both masculine and feminine) in ever narrowing and specific spheres of influence," these women continued to articulate identity, defining their own lives in that process (Matchinske, "Credible Consorts," 436).

In the studies that follow, I consider the construction of state and gender formulations chronologically, around temporally discrete sets of historical variables and constraints. I take, as the centerpiece to each micro-discussion, the writings of early modern women – women who as a result of their social, religious, political, and chronological positions navigate place in strikingly different ways. Each of the women I have chosen illustrates an effective program of self-definition and authorization. Each negotiates problems central to her own cultural environment. And all four of the women who make up the narratives within this book share their concerns with scores of writers, both female and male, writing contemporaneously with them. As authors and subjects of the various discourses I consider, these women actively recast as well as react to boundaries imposed by those in positions of power. Anne Askew, religious reformer writing in 1546, is tried for heresy; Margaret Clitherow, 1580s recusant butcher's wife, for treachery. Ester Sowernam, women's legal advocate in the early years of the seventeenth century, demands marriage security; and Eleanor Davies, high-born civil-war prophet, active defiance of England's monarch. Yet all four do more than simply counter the opposition. Each rewrites the criteria of her confinement.

In the early years of the Reformation, Anne Askew questions the interpretive and doctrinal boundaries of England's changing religion. And in doing so, she realigns many of the social strictures imposed on her as a woman. Forty years later, in the midst of an intense English nationalism, Margaret Clitherow redefines her allegiance to country and to queen. Deploying religious and domestic obligations in opposition to state policy, Clitherow establishes for herself a forum for voice and choice. Ester Sowernam, in turn, attends to concerns over women's marital opportunities at a moment when those opportunities are being directly challenged and constrained. She neutralizes anxieties inherent within her culture about changing notions of marriage and status by embracing those changes in full. Finally, like those who precede her,

Lady Eleanor Davies enters into one of the principal discursive debates of her time. In writing the apocalypse and charting the downfall of the king, Davies engages in state-making; she navigates a multiply-inflected field of social allegiances only to find that despite notoriety, priorities do matter, especially when one is a woman. These women's material engagements – religious, national, domestic, and political – touch nerves central to the English state and to definitions of the self as gendered. In each case they carry within them the dynamic for social change.

Theorizing the terms

While early modern state practices are both contradictory and mutually reinforcing in the way that they gender subjects, it is nevertheless possible to construct from them a theory of gender- and state-formation that implies both direction and intent. This theoretical construct, incomplete and heuristic though it must be, can allow us to consider the connections – culturally realized in such varied events as the successes of ruling bodies or the stability of local economies – between individual desire and social law, between an understanding of the self as gendered and a belief in the inviolability of nation or national cause.

Before I map such a theory, however, I want to remind my readers that the following explorations are always textually bound, in terms both of the narratives I encounter and the framings I impose on them. In my discussion I will necessarily look to language, to the words and voices that these and other writers have left behind. The only access I have to the histories of these women is textual. Accordingly, genre and style must provide the matter for discussion. As my task is explicitly rhetorical, I will be interested in attending to the discursive questions that such narratives introduce. How was each writing received? In what contexts were individual texts legitimate or open to attack? How were they transmitted and in what forms were they made available? Certainly, my own training as literary critic requires me to engage these writings intimately – in a way that reveals their strategies and illustrates their literariness. As a close reader I intend to encounter them, then, in terms of their particulars and look to the slight shadings of tone that direct our attention and engage us as readers. I hope in addition to read as closely in social formation as in textual nuance, exploring the rhetoric of contexts as well as the intonation of words. Such a redirection insists that I pay equally close attention to the cultural discourses within which these women and their writings circulated.

When I speak about early modern women's writings, I am locating that point of reference materially – in the lives of the individuals who wrote them, as well as the discursive trail they have left behind. The lived politics of Askew's, Clitherow's, Sowernam's, and Davies's material experiences do matter, and they are evident in the texts that survive them. Accordingly, while over 300 years separate the historical moment of these women from my own, I hope to describe an agency that extended beyond the writings I discuss (no matter how elusive) and a repressive environment (no matter how distant) that affected what could and what could not be said within them. That one of the women whom I will consider, Margaret Clitherow, was a recusant butcher's wife from Lincoln with two children and a house in town does matter; it does have consequence, both for the choices she was able to make and the choices that were made for her. That she left no written account of her experiences (her life is recorded by her confessor, Father John Mush) necessarily and absolutely limits what can be said about her and the way such speakings must be framed. But it cannot and should not preclude discussion entirely. Theories of discourse that occlude that material experience are historically incomplete and politically irresponsible.

Probably one of the most freighted and troubling sets of variables that I consider centers on questions of subjectivity and the formation of a gendered social identity. The social construction of gender categories results from material policies and practices that privilege certain behaviors, carry certain expectations, and demand specific obligations on the part of their participants. Accordingly, to talk about a particular writing as qualitatively different in voice or intent from another, simply by virtue of the supposed gender of its author, appears to make little sense. Despite this apparent determinism, I will discuss the following texts as revealing a woman's perspective or negotiating women's concerns in their handling of materials and issues. While I would be loathe to assert direct correlations, I do, nevertheless, want to argue for a textually announced gendering. Laying claim to female identity can be rhetorically powerful – both as policy and as strategy. Linda Alcoff reminds us that "women can take up a [gendered] position, a point of perspective, from which to interpret or (re)construct values and meanings."[26] "Gender is not natural, biological, universal, ahistorical, or essential," she writes, "and yet . . . gender is relevant because we are taking gender as a position from which to act politically" ("Cultural Feminism," 433). Women make choices throughout their lives that announce gender as a category of self-definition and of action. Acknowledging themselves textually as wives, mothers, daughters, and sisters, the women that I write about take up this politics of gender in order to articulate relationships to both self and state. In identifying themselves as women, they locate their textual authority; they gender their authority and authorize their gender. To refuse that essential difference flattens the historical narratives we are able to script about them. It also silences them as finally and effectively as over 300 years of masculinist history.

In exploring concepts of resistance for these women I do not mean to suggest that they are cultural rebels, actively and consciously inserting themselves into an antagonistic historical narrative. I do not mean to imply that theirs is a unified front, a subjectivity that will remain consistent and whole over time. Nevertheless, I refuse to imagine them as completely suborned by their environment, subjected by social structures and cultural constraints over which they had no control. One of the most vexing dilemmas that we face in social theory derives from the inherent dualism of western intellectual traditions: the one focused on subjects, motives, and actions, the other on the institutions and social systems that they inhabit.[27] Trying to integrate notions of individual agency *and* structural control without essentializing a total subject who exerts a single and consistent consciousness or imposing some sort of social determinism is a difficult but necessary endeavor. What is key here is a willingness to complicate *both* moments of mediation – and to attempt to dismantle the binary in doing so.

The women that I will be discussing in the following pages, both those who write and those who are written about, are always constrained by particular ideologies and beholden to established institutions and policies. Their writings are always to some extent a function and effect of the ideological and the systemic. Nevertheless, their participation in any single ideological principle or paradigm is at best fragmentary, their social responsibilities, forever divided, always in some sense compromised by the multitude of ideological and institutional positions and discourses that they embrace. While culturally determined, "subjects" do not maintain the kind of control which the word "individual" might suggest, "neither do they remain consistent or coherent in the passage of time: both they and the discourse[s] they inhabit have histories and memories which alter in constitution over time. Additionally, the interplay of differing subject-positions will make some appear pleasurable and others less so; thus a tension is produced which compels [people] to legislate among them."[28] Each of the women I study has a history that is individualized. Their experiences are never identical or absolutely defining. At the same time, each must maneuver within/choose between a wide range of available positions and possibilities.

Because these negotiations are shaped by an almost infinite number of external factors, they are also shape-less. Yes, decisions to act are ideologically implicated, but they are never absolutely so as the sheer number of ideological variables prohibits linear regimentation or single-issue politics. People's actions are beholden to an infinite range of nebulous and often far-reaching conditions, effects, and possibilities: "Dialectically implicated in the social, but also turned in upon [themselves, people have] to be questioned to [their] capacity for decisions, choices, interventions, and the like which are not specifically or solely determined by such categories as class or economics – however much they may be at the behest of ideology in general" (Smith, *Discerning the Subject*, 24). If we see identity as "a series of moments produced in the course of social life," and agency as a set of variable qualities that are taken up as a way of negotiating those moments and thus of understanding and coping with social relations, we can avoid the theoretical impasse inherent in many discussions of subjectivity (*Discerning the Subject*, 24). Within this more careful view, it would no longer be adequate to posit a social being as "'always-already' a 'subject.'" Rather, we can talk instead of "an over determination in the . . . process of [subject] construction . . . a continual and continuing series of over-lapping subject-positions which may or may not be present to consciousness at any given moment, but which in any case constitute a person's *history*" (*Discerning the Subject*, 32).

If we begin to account for the range – temporal as well as geographic – of possibilities available within culture at any given time, then we can talk about agency, constraint, and compromise. In the following accounts, the women who describe their lives and articulate their beliefs necessarily respond to and adjust from *earlier* inscriptions and *previous* lived histories no less than they do to, and from, more immediate social factors. Their identities are ideologically implicated, but they are also multiply inflected. Their discursive subjectivities can be seen, then, as the consolidation of numerous and always-changing subject positions, positions that make possible unique negotiations within differing ideological registers. Their writings are a result of the various structures and discourses that surround them and those they have encountered within their own specific histories. Looking at subject formation in this manner allows for the possibility of numerous and contradictory dialogues – of gaps or fissures where moments of subject mobility can be mapped.

Resistance is one of the subject's chief means of definition. It is also the stuff of cultural change. The process of constructing social identity asks that subjects navigate between a multitude of positions, some selected, others imposed, some conscious, others involuntary. In each of these various maneuvers, subjects necessarily come into contact with a vast number of positions that for one reason or another are untenable. Thus, despite what must be an over-determination in the process of subject construction, with an infinite number of apparently advantageous positions from which to choose, there are always, simultaneously, conflicts – antagonisms between positions and between the various ideological apparatus that support those positions. When subjects encounter untenable subject positions (e.g., because those positions do not appeal to or include the subject), those positions in turn mark subjectivity, constructing its boundaries by virtue of their opposition to it, and are themselves remade in that confrontation. Resistance, then – the point of contest within subject negotiation – provides a blueprint for cultural formation, and it is in the dynamic interplay between contradictory subject positions where such articulation occurs.

In order to foreground articulation and its concomitant construction of identity, I would like to stress the justificatory aspects of subject negotiations and the inevitable pull between positions that such justifications generate. The subject/individual relies on a multitude of institutional, ideological, and personal affiliations to justify her right to belong – to construct herself as *a* subject. She requires ideological criteria to legitimate her actions, even when those criteria are in reaction to *a* dominant (I do not say *the* dominant) ideology. Subject articulation, then, the ability to change the environment or to act within it, comes in the multitude of justifiable positions available within a cultural moment and in the relatively free movement between them. Those subject positions exist within history and take shape within certain literary forms. They are determined by the particular material circumstances of their moment, by available resources, vested interests, contemporaneous epistemologies, political influences, local incentives, etc. To compound this process, subjects are but rarely aware of these positions as discrete, identifiable options. What this means is that negotiations have messy histories. They alter over time, and those changes can be mapped within the sixteenth and seventeenth centuries, both historically and materially, in a recognition of narrowed options and a need for more careful and overt claims to selfhood and agency as the English Civil War approaches.

I want to complicate further this already complex process by reminding my readers that the material events and circumstances implicated in any subject/individual's history are gender-specific. They vary according to a wide range of cultural imperatives that include, but are not limited to, different behavioral codes for women and men, different social obligations and expectations, different subject status, as well as discrete biological functions that serve as cultural reminders of those differences.[29] As I show in the following chapters, the process of gendering subjectivity becomes more codified within the proliferating discursive realms of the sixteenth- and seventeenth-century English state. The ever-multiplying textual trail is, in part, the result of an increasing availability of presses and writers who publish within them, but it is simultaneously evidence of an elaborate system of checks and controls that is coming into being as English social interactions become more complicated and interconnected.[30]

Early modern subjectivity is often imagined in terms of its ritualistic focus outward – on concepts of the self that construct identity in performative terms, terms that emphasize the specular (externalized) nature of subject formation in the sixteenth and seventeenth centuries, not its interiority.[31] This focus underscores the transitional nature of identity during the hundred-year period between the English Reformation and the Civil War. Public invocations of private identity (on stage, in court record, in state policy) begin the process of an internalized subject interrogation and revision. These outward voicings of interiority also indicate a dramatic re-negotiation of and proliferation in places of privacy within early modern culture.[32] Announcing the singular self, in public forums, as self underscores a growing attention to private identity within early modern English culture. Accordingly, we can trace, during this time, an increasing attention to questions of the subject/self in all facets of public voice, from literature to law. We can also see a revision in who and what controls those aspects of identity that are becoming interiorized. Of central importance to my argument is the way that the space of the interior self, the space of secret thoughts, *genders* during this period. As I see it, women's and men's perceptions of interiority become more discrete as each comes to imagine her- or himself as an individual with different needs and obligations. A first consequence of this gendering is that women, themselves written into a newly articulated private realm – the domestic home[33] – inherit the task of ordering that private space in men's minds; they become purveyors of conscience and moral regulation.[34] A second and perhaps more disturbing consequence of this gendering is that moral processes themselves particularize, eventually cordoning off the civic from the familial, the utilitarian from the representational, and, of course, men's minds from women's.

So far, I have spoken in some detail about constructing individual subjectivity for early modern women, about negotiating a gendered and singular identity in sixteenth- and seventeenth-century England. It is through this focus on singularity, in fact, that we can trace changing definitions of the English state.[35] That individual subjects are internally regulated – obedient, responsible, and guilty – not only attends to current institutional needs but also generates different configurations in a continuing dialectic. The development of a variety of distinct cultural domains that independently monitor subject behavior and demand their own specialized forms of surveillance enables an extension of state function in extra-governmental directions. Accordingly, though I have, of necessity, used blanket terms like "state practices" to describe the increasingly disparate cultural fields (domestic, religious, economic, legal, and moral) that attend to questions of behavior in early modern England,[36] I also want to stress the informality of those practices.

While notions of state intervention may seem to indicate a centralized intelligence at work creating nationhood and documenting its numerous operations, I want to reiterate that the material representatives of the state (monarch, parliament, star chamber, etc.) are not necessarily desirous or cognizant of the ways in which a multitude of practices and policies come to stand in for *The State*. "In large part an ideological construct . . . 'the state is at most a message of domination – an ideological artefact attributing unity, structure and independence to the disunited, structureless and dependent workings of the practice of government'."[37] When I am talking about "state practices" that regulate behavior and conduct, then, I am not imagining a univocal or methodologically pure program of compliance for *all* English subjects. I am not describing a single controlling vision of state development. Rather, I am referring to a far more ambivalent process. This process is evidenced in a wide variety of different and often competing "state" agendas (some of them recognized by government representatives, many of them not) – agendas that follow trajectories outside and beyond any single or cohesive set of principles or national formula.

Accordingly, I shall talk about state policies, practices, and interventions only to extend the scope of subject negotiation into additional cultural arenas, many of them only marginally connected to the material representatives of the "state." Within this broader definition, the fulfilling of marriage obligations and the construction of personal identity both function as legitimate (and effective) sites of "state" regulation, despite their apparent distance from governmental decree or royal intervention. While "lower-casing" my notion of the state allows me to discuss traditionally un-represented or under-represented state subjects in terms of their involvement in and transformation of civic authority, it unfortunately relativizes the consequences of different kinds of authority, rendering their effects identical. Certainly, an action that is frowned upon by one's neighbors is hardly the same as one that can be criminally prosecuted. Although the state as I have defined it may intervene in both instances, taking equal advantage of the frown and the penal system to control civic behavior, the repercussions of each will no doubt differ in severity and degree.[38] A careful attention to differences between state practices can alleviate some of this unintended blurring but not all. In addition, we must generate a more historically precise discussion of state making that will point to shifts in power – realignments between institutional and local interventions that recognize and foreground distinctions between them.

Theorizing an understanding of the early modern state in terms of process is of practical importance particularly when who and what constituted that state metamorphose so frequently and completely during the period I will be investigating. While the Stuart monarchy in 1642 had much in common with its Henrician ancestor, we can also identify substantial differences. Indeed, a centralized "modern state" as we know it was not historically viable in either the sixteenth or the seventeenth centuries. While Henry VIII assumed a great deal more centralized power than did his predecessors, as revealed in the increasing density of governmental machinery during his reign,[39] the real material effects of such an announced power were remote and fairly localized. In the late fifteenth century numerous power holders could lay claim to different obligations from English subjects. A wide variety of requirements were levied and fulfilled on behalf of offices and authorities far removed from those of the English monarchy. These included economic remuneration in the form of land taxes (to manor or shire); military support in the form of manred (to baronial lord), and spiritual obedience in the form of community responsibility (to parish or archiepiscopal province). Probably the most visible and potent alternative to monarchical power could be found within the pre-Reformation church. Prior to King Henry VIII's separation from the Holy Roman Empire, a substantial portion of England's property was in the hands of the Catholic Church, and so, too, much of its revenue.[40] Because of the multitude of different wielders of authority, and the countless hierarchies of obedience beneath them, a fully functioning centralized government was, in the first years of the sixteenth century, inconceivable.

As the English monarchy began to consolidate power after dissolving ties to the Holy Catholic See (multiplying both its economic and political assets in selling off church land for profit and parlaying payment due into civic obligation from its people), there was far more likelihood that royal decree could be carried out and that vested interests would coincide and not hinder one another in either policy-making or policy-enforcing.[41] While these changes were significant from the point of view of amassed capital and political leverage, they were still a far cry from an autonomous and internally cohesive power center (or, to be more precise, the perception of such a centralized authority by English subjects). The gradual (and often sporadic) impetus toward a modern definition of statehood (a unified body of authority with a perceived totality of power emanating from a single source) metamorphoses government over the course of the next hundred years when, as the result of additional changes in political structure, social and economic regulation, and religious perspective, perceptions of civic authority begin to shift onto English citizens themselves. Once English subjects can imagine themselves as representatives of the very authority they are required to obey, not simply obedient to a crown outside and above themselves but beholden to an idealized concept of a state that includes them,[42] once they become purveyors of state authority themselves as its constituent members (again, if only fictively), then the lines of power that the "state" is able to control become more invasive and successful. Accordingly, "state practices," as I have defined them, infiltrate bodies as well as operate around them.

The English Civil War did not all at once create the possibility for subjects to imagine themselves as part of the state; rather, that civic upheaval was a dramatic enactment in what had been and would be a long and fragmented history of gradual transformation. As parliament and other constituent bodies of government control begin to assert greater authority on behalf of the monarchy, those same underlings, hierarchically organized in terms of their proximity to or distance from civic center, embrace smaller and smaller populations until they subsume the individual. Accordingly, when I talk about a proliferation in state practices that included the formation of explicit gender roles, what I mean is that while men and women no doubt embraced separate social functions *prior to* a more centralized notion of state authority – functions that were marked by a wide range of ritual and political assumptions – it was not until the idea of a single civic authority ("the state") both multiplied and particularized to include individual members of its constituency, and crystallized in a central and totalizing notion of its government (i.e., monarchy, protectorate, prime minister, or president) that "gender" could become an effect of the state – an aspect of its civil control.

The parameters

While my primary focus in this book is on women writers of the early modern period, and I attempt to chart the ways in which constructions of feminine subjectivity intersect with processes of state formation in the sixteenth and seventeenth centuries, explorations of gender construction cannot be limited to a study of women alone. The processes that I discuss affect men, determining acceptable forms of behavior for them as well as for women. Looking at Askew's *Examinations* without considering their history at the hands of male Protestant reformers would be an incomplete endeavor. To neglect that dialogue is to erase much of the historical specificity of our encounter with her work. By the same token, relying absolutely on an announced authorial gendering to direct these analyses would be unnecessarily restrictive, if only from a critical standpoint. Because part of this project is devoted to considering the range of relationships that occur when gender and state norms intersect and to recovering the erased histories that are its legacy, it is important not to refuse those understandings in whatever form they come. Forgoing a discussion of recusancy, gender, and the state in the 1580s because there are few Catholic women's voices left for us to hear is to fall into the trap of our own historical pre-narratives. Accordingly I have intentionally and perhaps vexingly introduced the problem of gender ambiguity into three of the five chapters in this book. Askew's account of her trial in chapter 1 comes to us mediated by the men who take up her cause, and yet I assume that narrative as legitimate. In chapter 2 I hypothetically imagine the conditions of writing and subject articulation for a 1580s, middling-rank, Catholic, butcher's wife, using another representative female-authored text as a point of comparison and creating additional proofs to support that reading. In chapter 3 I look to a pamphlet written pseudonymously in order to test the boundaries of what can be said and not be said about an essential gendered voice.

In each case I look at early modern women – Askew, Clitherow, Sowernam, and Davies – in terms of a constellation of other writer/ subjects grappling with the same or similar sets of problems. I consider how writers of differing status and gender negotiate voice and place differently. It is my contention that only by juxtaposing disparate materials can we construct a culturally based subject articulation for these women. Only by trying to imagine the variety of responses possible can we understand how their writings come to be employed by the state in monitoring behavior for its citizens or rewriting its policies to accommodate changing sets of civic concerns.

Accordingly, in what follows I will de-emphasize the formal concerns of genre to consider cultural issues that extend across genres and encompass a multitude of intents and audiences. While this kind of analysis locates texts squarely within their material histories, fore-grounding their embeddedness within a wide range of cultural problems, positions, and possibilities, it can generate problems of its own, particularly when it fails to acknowledge generic differences and their profound cultural influence. Chapter 1 takes as its point of focus a published court examination and a religio-historical encyclopedia that was a required possession of every member of the clergy.[43] Chapter 2 adds to that mix a spiritual biography in manuscript form. Chapter 3 connects court and popular drama to the gender debate; chapter 4, parliamentary sermon to vanity-press apocalypse. The formal differences between these texts *do* determine their trajectories. They frame the ways in which these authors are able to construct and negotiate their materials; they influence when and where materials are published or whether they are published at all; finally, they affect both the make-up of a particular audience and the kinds of responses that audience is willing to consider.[44] I have tried to be careful in calling out the dynamics of this blending and to account for its manifold possibilities, but again the very process of theorizing insists on simplification and redirection. It is my hope that later studies will contribute to a more complete evaluation of subject formation by attending to questions of status and reception more particularly than I have done here.

An overview

One of the aims of this exploration is to determine some theoretical understanding of the ways in which the cultural gendering of the subject is affected by, impinges on, and transforms the coming into being of the state, and the way that both terms, "gender" and "state," are themselves reflected through discourse. To do so, however, I must necessarily focus closely and particularly. Each of the following chapters will revolve around different pieces of this theoretical construct. The narratives that run through these discussions then will not be chronological. Rather each will posit different understandings and explore local concerns. It is my hope that the insights that each provides will in turn offer us a place to begin imagining the larger structures of gender- and state-formation that inform the whole project.

I begin my discussion with the historically loaded narrative of the early English Reformation. Chapter 1, "Resistance, Reformation, and the remaining narratives," illustrates what is at stake in embracing one of sixteenth-century England's central paradigms. Documenting the kinds of erasures that occur once Reformation narratives take over, I suggest the consequences of such narratives in discussions of agency and cultural change for women. Anne Askew's recorded martyrdom – the scripting of her saintly sacrifice – announces the layer upon layer of historical forgetting that makes up the English Reformation. More significantly, however, the supposedly selfless religiosity encoded by reform narratives de-emphasizes the secularly motivated aspects of Askew's initial participation in those dialogues; it downplays the potentially transformative circumstances of her encounter outside reformist polemic and the narratives that remain. I argue, in a rather different discursive scenario, that Askew's *Examinations* do not attend strictly or solely to reformist doctrine; they do not announce their own "glorious" self-martyrdom. Instead, her accounts of her trials gesture toward a secular interiority and self-sufficiency that acquire their definition through a material grappling with female identity. It is in fact precisely because Askew as a woman must face obstacles that deny her access to legitimate voice that her writings necessarily gender as they redefine and privatize as they pronounce.

Chapter 2, "Framing recusant identity in Counter-Reformation England," takes as its point of focus the problem of framing early modern feminist historiography when much of what constitutes legitimate evidence for that historiography is unavailable. Using comparative and non-traditional techniques to situate the hagiographical martyrdom of Margaret Clitherow within the broader terms of Counter-Reformation female identity, I provide both a model for historiographical recovery and evidence of its continued specificity. Moving between and across texts and histories, between the first two of the four subjects under investigation – Askew (1546) and Clitherow (1586) – and across the disciplinary boundaries of historical and imaginative writing, I reveal how cultural valences shift from historic moment to historic moment and how those shifts anticipate different navigational strategies for each writer. As a result of shifting ideological criteria, earlier and later claims to female spiritual authority acquire vastly different configurations. In 1546, Askew's construction of a subject-self responds to and develops out of a proliferation of religious possibilities – possibilities that allow her autonomy and voice. But the ideologies available in 1546 London – ideologies that permit Askew to write – recast and recenter later options. They narrow and codify the spheres of access available to Elizabethan women like Clitherow.

Although Clitherow may share with Askew similar convictions concerning her faith, those convictions are both announced and received differently. Accordingly, we can see a more particularized and emphatic voicing of gender as we move into the later years of the sixteenth century. Clitherow's articulations, however they are imagined,[45] simultaneously acknowledge their connection to the domestic and to the regulatory. Her claims to authority are now deemed legitimate by virtue of their relation to her private duties as wife and mother. It is her outward conformity to custom, her decorous behavior and speech, that will offer her leverage within the community. Because Clitherow claims her authority through established "state" channels (chastity, silence, and obedience), she is free to negotiate a space for female identity that actively defies the state (i.e., is treasonous in terms of its religious affiliations).

In chapter 3, "Legislating morality in the marriage market," I explore a later construction of the domestic (1617), this time from a more overtly secular point of view. Here I consider the relationship between a by now largely privatized female subjectivity and the expanding legal, economic, and moral domains of Jacobean culture. Within this chapter, I illustrate the ways in which Sowernam's *Ester hath hang'd Haman* turns marriage into a system of fair market exchange, demanding financial obligation from men (itself charted in market terms), and promising in return the construction of an internalized code of conduct for women. Sowernam's text stresses the growing importance of labor division and market value to secure status and determine worth. Drawing parallels between contract law and marriage practice, Sowernam's account reveals current cultural anxieties about marriage as a reorganization of middling-rank property and also foreshadows a later concretization of those anxieties in emended civil legislation.

While Sowernam's tract loosely parallels other early Jacobean texts in its recognition of English marriage law as a site of cultural instability, it reinterprets those predominantly masculine-centered accounts, among them William Shakespeare's *Measure for Measure* and the anonymously written comedy, *Swetnam the Woman-Hater*. For Sowernam and other seventeenth-century women of the middling ranks, marriage is an only option, its stakes all or nothing. Accordingly, her valorization of female chastity as an obligation in marriage necessarily rewrites much of the masculinist ambivalence that occurs simultaneously, securing for women a real and saleable value in pre-nuptial negotiations. It also anticipates a reordering of moral regulation within domestic circles, placing questions of chaste conscience squarely within female provenance. But Sowernam's success is double edged. In a contractual catch-22, her tract advocates a programmatic chastity that codifies greater and more precise behavioral categories for women, categories that are called to service as the English state begins to embrace the private and the domestic as sites of potential invigilation and control.

Chapter 4, "Gender formation in English apocalyptic writing," re-aligns intersections once again, looking this time at the connections between female subjectivity, religion, and politics in the early years of the Civil War. In the religious writings of the 1640s, preachers and prophets were demanding that people look inward for spiritual direction, to the particular and the individual. At the same time they were also calling for uniformity in church doctrine, for a broad and unified national outlook. In order for these two seemingly contradictory impulses to coexist, these writers had to create a value system that would rank each in terms of its relative importance; they had to find a way of connecting and ordering both spheres. That the first was eventually remanded into service for the second was hardly arbitrary. In fact, it is this hierarchical movement from individual to totality that seventeenth-century apocalyptic discourse manages to chart so graphically – at least within its masculine versions. Unfortunately, women's and men's access to regulation differ as a result of separate mid-century cultural requirements and obligations. A consequence of this unequal positioning is that feminine subjectivity does not always or perhaps ever fit the patriarchal norms of state and subject regulation as they were generally conceived in the religious and political discourses of the 1640s.[46] It is already disruptive, even in the way that it articulates *legitimate* behavior for women. In Davies's more than sixty apocalyptic tracts, contradictory female subject and state regulation are literalized in an unavoidable doubling of expectations and requirements. Her writings construct a subject status that can never be fulfilled.

Gender and state

Gender and state are the crucial terms in these analyses. Constructions of "women" carry what Denise Riley calls an "extraordinary weight of categorisation,"[47] And this element of subject formation has yet to be considered adequately or effectively. It is my belief that situating women materially, within specific histories, can alleviate some of the pressure that results from absolute gender definition, and it can reinsert multiple concepts of female identity back into state formation. Women and women's writings exist in history not outside it. Women feel the effects of patriarchy, of law, of public policy, of religion, whether they will or no. There is a tendency in much post-structuralist thought to construe an avant-garde text or a rebellious female subjectivity – one that is disruptive of readers' expectations and conventions – as politically viable in and of itself. This tendency neglects history – the history of the human agent, the reader who may simply miss the point or who may be too caught up within dominant paradigms to recognize in difference anything but failure.

Given the teleological incentive of western culture, its focus on where we are going, it is essential that we reveal its originary points as non-originary and demystify the aura of "History" that covers the past. Historical paradigms will not shift unless there is a basis from which to begin contesting them. If we are to decode "History," we first need to reveal the absence of any single universal vocabulary defining it. The past is not simply an unmarked template conferring power on dominant ideologies. We carry its traces not only in how we construct society now, but also in assumptions we make about society in the future. Obviously, charting a viable theory of female subject formation will be of crucial importance to continued research on early modern English women as will the historical particularity in which that theory is framed. I envision the same sort of shifting perspective, the same sort of variable focus,[48] in identifying the multiplicity of our own articulations and their all-too-inextricable ties to "nation" and "state."

1   Resistance, Reformation, and the remaining narratives

In 1546, awaiting death by burning in Newgate Prison, Anne Askew wrote an account of her court examinations, in which she justified her behavior and defended her Protestant beliefs. Her writings, taken up by two of England's foremost reformers, were printed with interpretive glosses and circulated in England and abroad for the next hundred years. As material evidence of both the constancy of Protestant believers and the unbroken history of a doctrinally pure religion in England, Askew's *Examinations* have outlived her, securing for her a place within the history of the English Reformation. A recent biographical entry announces the terms of that abbreviated celebrity specifically: "Anne Askew's learning and steadfastness made her an exemplary martyr in the eyes of sixteenth-century Protestant England, and her story, based on her own account of her examinations and torture [has been] powerfully retold, first by John Bale and later by the Elizabethan martyrologist John Foxe."[1] In the sketch, the salient moments of Askew's career are simple and few. She is an example of English Protestant fortitude, fortunate enough, in retrospect, to be powerfully narrated by writerly men who count.

I begin with a dictionary entry on Askew, not to be flippant, though flippancy here is tempting, but rather to talk about two related issues: first, the inevitable thinning out of meanings that results from recorded history, and, second, the misperceptions that such brevity inevitably supports in discussions of agency and cultural change. Askew's martyr-status underscores the layer upon layer of historical forgetting that makes up the English Reformation. More importantly, it camouflages the impious and secularly motivated aspects of Askew's initial participation in that dialogue; it masks the potentially transformative circumstances of her encounter outside reformist polemic and the narratives that remain.

Anne Askew died "an exemplary martyr" for the English Reformation, or so we are told.[2] Indeed, Bale's narrative of her last few months in London contains all the dramatic elements of a good martyr story –

heroics, villainy, personal sacrifice, and historical payoff.[3] If ever we could find a direct correlation between individual agency and cultural effect, between the actions of one religiously inspired woman and the course of English Church history, then Askew's story might be just the place to look.[4] Most if not all of the reforms that her cause came to represent were eventually embraced. In its transformative tidiness, then, Askew's tale is almost too good to be true. In any event, it is certainly too anomalous to be useful as a template for modern theories of resistance. How many of us, inspired by the same sense of political or religious unjustness, would sacrifice so much and at such mortal cost? How many of us, in the right place at the right time, could validate the national and historic course of events in standing up for our convictions? Not many. Narratives such as the one handed down about Askew generally provide temporal absolutes – divisions that are hard and fast, scenarios that can be charted in terms of befores and afters. In following the storyline, we create binaries and calculate our understandings of social change in those terms, a move from point "A" to point "B," an understanding of "this" but not "that." Even when we introduce complications that attempt to focus outside the teleological, we forget that basing our sense of "historicity" in concepts like religious resistance or reform politics forecloses a consideration of any number of additional incentives that may have been at work in shaping English lives.

Yes, the religious rewriting of England's history via martyrs like Askew did change forever the configuration of the English Church, of that we can be sure. Still, in drawing lines, we forget important elements in the mix, failing to note what does not fit within the familiar connections. The Reformation offers a particularly powerful and seductive example of this kind of analytical predestination. Indeed, from its earliest moments, the Reformation began to narrate itself as linear history. Reformers, motivated at first by a pressing need to separate themselves from all things novel and new – to establish in Protestant doctrine a consistent and long-lived religious presence – repeatedly asserted their own historical and spiritual foundations, their own connections to the past.[5] They spoke of common ground and shared heritage, of unity of purpose and institutional backing. Indeed, one of the most successful methods for establishing normativity and verifying the "truth" of the Protestant faith was in the recreation/recitation of an unbroken line of Protestant religious martyrs, all of them hailing from the same "Catholyck" (i.e., universal) church. While John Bale and John Foxe, Askew's narrators, may have been two of the most ardent and copious polemicists writing in those early years, they certainly were not the only men to construct a timeline of religious persecution.[6] Protestant martyrologies and historical patterning can be found from the 1520s, in the writings of Luther and Tyndale, to the final decades of the sixteenth century in works such as *Les Tragiques* by the Huguenot poet Théodore d'Aubigné.[7]

Even more telling, however, in terms of established progress narratives and recorded meaning, was a shared, humanist-inspired association of English religious reform with historical *telos* – a sense of Reformation-destiny. In his opening address to "The True and Faithful Congregation of Christ's Universal Church," Foxe situates the historical narrative of his book, *Acts and Monuments*, within an apocalyptic frame that ends with an English national church and the second coming of Christ. He writes,

but yet because God hath so placed us Englishmen here in one commonwealth, also in one church, as in one ship together, let us not mangle or divide the ship, which being divided, perisheth; but every man serve with diligence and discretion in his order, wherein he is called . . .

The God of peace, who hath power both of land and sea, reach forth his merciful hand to help them up that sink, to keep up them that stand . . . that we, professing one Christ, may, in one unity of doctrine, gather ourselves into one ark or the true church together; where we, continuing stedfast in faith, may at the last luckily be conducted to the joyful port of our desired landing-place by his heavenly grace. To whom, both in heaven and earth, be all power and glory, with his Father and the Holy Spirit, for ever. Amen.[8]

Foxe's sense of mission here mirrors the chronology of his account; the one replicates the other. In a constant iteration of timelines and causal certainty, of oneness and direction, *Acts and Monuments* anticipates the narrative frame that much English Reformation history will take in the centuries to come. Looking at Foxe and others like him we see replayed again and again a move from specific example to universal outcome, from martyrology to methodology.[9]

As one of England's central historical paradigms, the Reformation has, more than most, been charted in terms of a Foxian storyline: it is cause-based and to a large extent teleological. In its scripting we can witness tremendous change – social and religious upheavals that have reshaped the way that we think about English history. It would seem then that Askew's case, situated as it is only moments after Henry VIII's initial break with the Roman Catholic Church and voiced by some of England's most formidable polemicists, might provide evidence of successful resistance and agency – an appealing thought for those of us who would like to see our actions as political and potentially transformative. Such a formulation, however, is also naïve and at best only minimally accurate. Askew's account is full of narratives, many of them unrecorded and long forgotten. These other dialogues necessarily complicate and befuddle the neat causality that her martyrdom might initially suggest. While that fuzziness does not mean that we have to forgo altogether concepts of individual agency, it does demand a more careful accounting of incentive and outcomes. Resistance need not presuppose absolute personal sacrifice or effective marketing strategies. Nor must it take as its end result the reconfiguration of a national religion. High drama and high stakes are perhaps not where we ought to begin looking. What if those moments in the Askew narrative that are locally resistant, that are immediately transformative, have less to do with defending reformist theology, than with scripting something else – another definition of conscience, perhaps, or a notion of private identity that accommodates gender differently?

I would like to frame this discussion in terms of personal incentive and desire – in precisely those spaces where records do not exist. The historical *telos* of the Askew example, its place in Reformation history, makes it a perfect vehicle for such study in that its reformist storyline has so effectively and profoundly covered those tracks. As a narrative of Protestant belief, Askew's account illustrates the all too frequent divide between intent and effect and our reading of both. Despite what her persecutors or promoters tell us her words mean, despite the appended narratives that have come to determine her for future readers, Askew, in her *Examinations*, continually gestures toward the unmarked, toward notions of interiority and self-sufficiency that may be Reformation-inspired but are hardly "reformist" in allegiance. At the same time, her account genders those spaces in speaking them, and again, this move is not simply reformist in lineage; Askew's *Examinations* explore ideas of subjecthood that acquire their definition through a material grappling with female identity. It is precisely because Askew as a woman must face obstacles that deny her access to legitimate voice that her account necessarily genders as it resists and secularizes in announcing its spiritual allegiances.[10]

Traversed by a multitude of different desires and debates, Askew's accounts finally have *nothing* and *everything* to do with the way that they are eventually read. The secular and gendered subject/self that she ultimately defines in these accounts is a by-product of that mixing. Askew's resistant voice, then, is not simply hidden from but also bolstered by institutional hegemonies, by the narratives that remain. In fact, it is this discursive ambivalence that makes concepts of resistance so difficult to trace – the cultural changes they provoke so impossible to map. In the discussion that follows, I would like to suggest a few of the forgotten discourses and resistant moments within this massively over-determined encounter – the writing and publication of Anne Askew's *Examinations*.

Forgotten discourses

Separated from her husband and two children and seeking an annulment to her marriage, Anne Askew, second daughter of a wealthy Yorkshire knight, moved to London in her twenty-fifth year, alone. For the greater part of her ten-month stay in that city prior to arrest, Askew attended prayer meetings and openly discussed passages from the New Testament, making a name for herself throughout London as an outspoken interpreter of biblical texts. This much we have been told from the documents that have survived her.[11] Labeled sacramentarian, Askew's radical Protestantism was punishable,[12] at the end of Henry VIII's reign, by burning on charges of heresy. After two trials, a supposed recanting of her religious beliefs, and at least one purported episode of physical torture, Askew was convicted and executed according to the first article of the Act of Six Articles (1539).[13] Article I dealt with the theological question of transubstantiation.[14] To Askew, the sacrament of communion recalled the Last Supper and Christ's Passion but did not relive them. The bread remained bread; the wine remained wine; and the faithful received both in spirit not in body as Henry VIII's newly formed Church of England would have it. Because of her refusal to accept the definition of the Eucharist as outlined in the Act, Askew died at the stake in the summer of 1546, before a large crowd at Smithfield.

Askew's unsupervised presence in London, her familiarity with a Bible she had no legal business touching, and her temerity in acknowledging both no doubt contributed to the vehement reactions against her under English law.[15] She was also in the wrong place at the wrong time. And it is to this unfortunate set of circumstances that I wish to direct our attention first. Askew's arrest and execution were not part of a sweeping response to reformist ideology or religious disobedience in England; rather, they represent an isolated example of a court-specific threat about the problem of reform for Henry VIII's politically unstable government. That positioning, despite the real and lasting impact that it had on Askew (she suffered death because of it), was also fortunate as it permitted the very conditions that would make Askew's framing of self so persuasive. Specifically, it enabled the public presentation of a resistant discourse (reformist, personal, gendered) outside the immediate context of its voicing (court conspiracy and conciliar debate), and provided reformists – Bale and later Foxe – with an opportunity to script the woman and her writings as a *cause célèbre*. Even more significantly in terms of this argument, however, the combined [in]attention that Askew's voice was to receive at the hands of persecutors *and* promoters alike allowed for a highly visible and largely uncontested forum for both secularizing and gendering private identity.

The two court examinations of Anne Askew and the execution that followed occurred at the end of King Henry VIII's reign, a little over a year before his death. At that time, and literally since Cardinal Wolsey's overthrow in 1530, conciliar allegiances were both multiple and divided, with strong and fluctuating factions promoting the ideas of Tyndale and Calvin and equally powerful and outspoken opponents to them.[16] For conservative and reform-minded council members alike, the religious fallout of the English Reformation threatened personal standing, both economically and hierarchically, in the awarding of key positions, estates, and monies to political and religious rivals.[17] Of the more traditionally minded royal advisors, the most active within the Askew trial and the most odious according to Bale was Stephen Gardiner, Bishop of Winchester.[18] In marked opposition to Gardiner, others like Thomas Cranmer, Archbishop of Canterbury, sought additional reform and greater autonomy for English churchgoers.[19]

The almost equally weighted rift between traditional and reformist sympathies at court ensured constant factionalism and conspiracy, with each allegiance attempting to discredit the other. Henry VIII, whether by strategy or inaction, often encouraged these debates, transferring his allegiance and support from one side to the next. Despite numerous vacillations that saw Cromwell's execution (via Gardiner's faction) then Howard's (via Cranmer's), the king followed a middle, if somewhat conservative, administrative path through all of this.[20] In fact, as the repercussions from Henry VIII's initial actions against the Catholic Church were felt more and more forcefully, both in popular reaction against the newly proclaimed royal authority and in perceptions of a divided and unruled England from abroad, damage control became increasingly imperative.[21] Askew's death warrant, the "Act of Six Articles," was itself verification that the king perceived many of the continental reforms as too disruptive of established institutions and traditions to embrace in any holistic way. In consequence, at Askew's death and in the last years of Henry VIII's reign, the monarchy seemed intent on qualifying many of the religious changes it had set in motion twenty years earlier.[22]

Despite the king's obvious and continued conservatism, traditionalists did in the end have cause for worry, and it is their last bid for power that figures in the Askew trials so specifically and so dramatically. By 1543, reformist sympathizer Katherine Parr had become Henry VIII's sixth wife. By 1545, the king, plagued by growing ill health, had become increasingly unwilling to involve himself in affairs of state. Accordingly, political and religious lines were redrawn once again, this time along specific geographic divides – between an insular and largely reformist royal household and a traditionalist Privy Council with limited and sporadic access to an unwell king.[23] The threat of a growing imbalance between inside (Privy Chamber) and outside (Privy Council) factions upped the ante for conservatives and directed heresy charges into the royal household, against Henry VIII's servants and intimates. Hence, it was in the arena of "domestic" politics where religious outspokenness posed the biggest threat and garnered the bloodiest response.[24] It was also to those offenders that Henrician policy proved the most punitive.

Askew was no exception. Household connections, court conspiracy, and questionable colleagues were all to work against her. Archbishop Cranmer had recently recommended her brother Edward for a position at court. Her eldest brother, Sir Francis Askew, had already been knighted for serving under the Duke of Suffolk.[25] At the same time, a half-brother, Christopher (d. 1543) had been a gentleman of the king's Privy Chamber.[26] While reformist patronage would be slim grounds for inciting direct antagonism by council traditionalists, there were other more egregious offenses that Askew had to her credit, the first and most damaging being her proximity to official scrutiny and the royal ear. Askew's proselytizing was literally too close for comfort, feeding directly into questions of royal succession and magisterial control. In fact, the outcome of the Askew trial and the information divulged within it proved pivotal in determining who would hold the reins to power upon Henry VIII's eventual demise.

According to Askew's account, Lord Chancellor Richard Rich questioned her as to her involvement with several women of high standing, women *within* Katherine Parr's inner circle, including Lady Suffolk, Lady Sussex, Lady Hertford, Lady Denny, and Lady Fitzwilliam.[27] Not only were these women potential targets for traditionalists by virtue of their access to the queen, but they were also linked by marriage to key officers in Henry VIII's court.[28] Rich's concerns as they are framed within the *Examinations* attempt to elicit from Askew a list of co-conspirators – co-conspirators who by their own admissions of guilt could discredit reformist members of both the Privy Council and the royal household, including among them Sir Anthony Denny, Chief Gentleman of the Privy Chamber, controller of the Privy Coffers and Dry Stamp, and the man directly responsible for Henry VIII's signature as it would appear in his last will.[29] While Askew discursively refuses to divulge the names of her supporters, it is the possibility of that confession that so appeals to her persecutors. In fact, Askew's potential access to and interaction with political and religious dissenters *within* Henry VIII's inner circle – *within* household chambers – likely proved far more damaging to her case than the mere fact of her religious radicalism.

Add to that connection still another, this time personally antagonistic to Gardiner, and the trial's outcome seems a foregone conclusion. Almost immediately after her arrival in London, Askew met and joined forces with another household insider, John Lascelles, sewer of the king's chamber, a man with whom she would correspond while in prison and share in eventual martyrdom. Askew's religious companion was the same John Lascelles who secured Catherine Howard's fall from grace, by supplying evidence of her extramarital affairs to the council.[30] That Gardiner might have felt some direct animosity to Lascelles seems likely. The bishop had, after all, introduced the king to Howard, played go-between in the marriage negotiations, and lost considerable prestige in Howard's undoing. Threatened by a growing inability to gain audience to the king, and certain that the connections between Lascelles, Askew, and others of the Privy Chamber, including one of the king's own physicians, Dr. Robert Huick, might prove the opposition's undoing, Gardiner would have been foolish to let the Askew case go unnoticed.[31]

Askew's decision to seek restitution in London for her locally refused marriage annulment undoubtedly proved fatal. If she had remained less markedly visible to the Privy Council's eye, it is likely that her "gospelling" would have gone ignored. Anxiety over reformist sympathizers was, in 1546, hardly "national" in scope. Most English subjects were barely cognizant of the doctrinal aspects of the religious debates, much less actively rebellious in their behalf.[32] At the same time, local ecclesial courts were far less willing or able to try a person, particularly a woman, of Askew's standing on the charges set forward in the Act of Six Articles. Her presence in London and among the ladies-in-waiting to the queen placed her within the same acknowledged sphere of treachery, heresy, and political intrigue as such central figures as Cromwell and Howard and precipitated a surprisingly personal and excessive form of retribution from Henry VIII's ministers. Her trial and execution were not then the result of a conscientious and thorough sweep of the English countryside in search of Protestant dissidents. They were instead, at least partially, the result of sporadic forays on the part of a divided power bloc in Henry VIII's last years – a split between chamber and council, between inner and outer, that sought to address political, social, and personal problems in terms of England's new schismatic religion. In the last years of Henry VIII's reign, there was a willingness, a pressing need, to reveal punitive authority within the gentried ranks of a divided English court and more particularly to do so in the immediate vicinity of London and its environs.

So what do these motivations suggest? Askew's accusers were not actively tackling the problem of reformist doctrine; they were not in their interrogations making a last stand for all things Catholic. At the same time, they did not focus on gender as *the* central component of Askew's transgression. Nor were they considering overly her views on justification and conscience. What seemed to matter more in this case was Askew's involvement, intentional or accidental, in a court-specific battle that resulted from and took its bearings in a struggle over authority and who had the right to wield it. Yes, religious belief was perhaps *the* dominant feature of the English social landscape and as such was inextricably embedded within a wide network of relationships including politics and place, but it did not determine absolutely the course of English jurisprudence. Yes, the fact of Askew's sexuality did work against her in the framing of court evidence (as a woman she was not supposed to be offering up biblical exegesis under any circumstance, and certainly not in public contexts). But neither of these positions, in and of themselves, would have been cause to initiate such vehement retribution. Askew's persecutors took action – directed, brutal, and spectacular action. They burned a woman at the stake for any number of reasons, to warn their opponents perhaps, to suggest to an ailing king the unwisdom of his confidences, to balance old accounts. But the threats that Askew's gospelling posed were far from uniform or absolute and so too were the motivations that secured her conviction. Given that certain aspects of Askew's social identity were called out as transgressive while others were not (her crimes were London-based and court-affiliated), only those *announced* boundaries were open to public scrutiny. Less obvious resistances – resistances not so actively policed or carefully defended – went unpublished and, more to the point, unattended.

Askew's accusers did not in all likelihood anticipate an idea of Askew as national martyr. If they had done so perhaps Bale would have had a harder time defining both woman and event to suit his reformist agenda. For all we know, such an astonishing lack of foresight may even have enabled the publication of the Askew text in the first place. Bale tells us that the *Examinations* were delivered to him by Dutch merchants traveling at that time in England.[33] How might such merchants have obtained Askew's writings? Would they have been able to visit prisoners in the Tower, especially gentlewomen of Askew's standing? Perhaps those guarding her were given the wrong instructions? Perhaps the routes of communication open to her were incorrectly or inadequately monitored? If authorities were most interested in observing the comings and goings of high-status court visitors, they may have let slip these less *visible* foreigners. I do not mean to supply biographical evidence here or to presume that Bale's potentially fictive merchant narrative could provide us with such documentation. What I do want to suggest is what might happen to the story and its telling when motivations are multiple and agendas unidentified.

The incentives at work in generating Askew's persecutions were both messy and divided. Was she being punished because she was a heretic or because she stepped into the middle of a battle over the very terms and offices of government that Henry VIII's separation from Rome had allowed? Was she persecuted because her trial would provide a dramatic example of the lengths to which defenders of the realm were willing to go to save it or because she was caught associating with the *wrong* sorts of people? These questions do matter. Their answers, skewing the material weight of these encounters in one direction or another, have tremendous impact on historical event and historical making, but also on the very shape and substance that resistance would take in the years to come.

And the word was God

If any single element of the English religious debate could be said to be ideologically central in 1546, it would have to be the scriptural primacy of the written word. With reformists demanding the right to interpret the Bible independently and traditionalists calling on the authority of biblical scholars and hundreds of years of historical glosses for their own readings, Bible exegesis became at mid century a point of contestation in itself – a site for persecution and resistance. The introduction of additional scriptural perspectives temporarily opened up a more flexible set of interpretive standards in religious discourse. This flexibility was not so much the result of the Protestant availability of the Bible for all English subjects (already limited in 1543 by the "Act for the Advancement of True Religion") or a unique and unparalleled moment in interpretive availability, but rather the result of a historically specific forum for disagreement – the written exegetical text – between separate and competing strains of religious "interpretation."

A 1547 letter from Bishop Gardiner to the Lord Protector, included in Foxe's *Acts and Monuments*, reveals the historic ambivalence that the religious debate generated in disrupting linguistic certainty for both sides.[34] In a post-trial attack on the published *Examinations*, Gardiner purportedly writes,

I have seen of late two books [the *Examinations*] set forth in English by Bale, very pernicious, seditious, and slanderous [they are] . . . to note a woman to have suffered under [my late sovereign lord and master] as a martyr; and the woman therewith to be . . . and is boasted to be, a sacramentary . . . Certain printers, players, and preachers, make a wonderment, as though we know not yet how to be justified nor what sacraments we should have. And if the agreement in religion made in the time of our late sovereign lord be of no force in their judgment, what establishment could any new agreement have? and ever uncertainty is noisome to any realm. And where every man will be master, there must needs be uncertainty. And one thing is marvellous, that at the same time it is taught that all men be liars, at the selfsame time almost every man would be believed; and amongst them Bale, when his untruth appeareth evidently in setting forth the examination of Anne Askew, which is utterly misreported.[35]

Gardiner focuses on the perceived general threat to the realm that reformists like Bale embody.[36] In condemning them, he disallows the possibility of "uncertainty" and interpretive variation. Gardiner's nervousness, however, is not simply a traditionalist fear of total participation for the religious community.[37] He posits misrepresentation as the result of writing, speaking, or acting "without authority" – a problem which he sees manifested in all "printers, players, and preachers." Gardiner locates the potential for radical misrepresentation in writing and reading, talking and listening. It is after all these same "printers, players, and preachers" who have the power to persuade others to believe in their untruths. Gardiner's nervousness identifies the site of threat explicitly in the power of the word – printed, performed, preached – to influence and direct popular opinion, to secure the ear of a now-dead king or be denied that access in a conspiracy of misreportings. It also recognizes the inherent duplicity that language will afford to its speakers. Words need not be true, but, once said, they will make truths.

The debate over discursive interpretation operated within a multitude of cultural registers – religious, economic, punitive, personal – all of them, to some extent, contradictory. Accordingly, while Askew's accounts of her trial are no doubt religiously inspired and thus instrumental in the furthering of the reformed church in England, her involvement in that debate need not have been motivated solely to that end. For Askew the written word (and the interpretive and performative power that it afforded her) need not have been inspired by a wish to secure doctrine or verify religious belief; instead it may have satisfied other social needs, fulfilled additional subjective desires. And the same could be said for the men who would later appropriate her narrative. Askew's promoters, much like her persecutors, shaped the contours of her historical legacy. It is to those offices and one of those men, John Bale, that I now turn. Yes, Bale saw in Askew's *Examinations* an opportunity to illustrate the word of God and to reveal to the English people the suffering of His true believers. It is easy to see as well that Bale's decision to elucidate the Askew manuscript proved enabling for other reasons. His biographer speculates that the public success of the *Examinations* with its numerous reprintings prompted Bale to write his own autobiography.[38] Be that as it may, Bale's complete works, no fewer than eighty-five productions, succeeded in making him known throughout England and abroad. Countless references to his texts survive among the writings of his contemporaries, including those of the briefly enthroned King Edward VI. Under Edward, Bale was given the rectory of Bishopstoke in Hampshire and eventually the bishopric of Ossory. Both offices were proffered, one would imagine, as a reward for services, particularly written services, rendered to a pro-reformist government. At the same time, to further complicate matters, Bale's texts point to still other interests – interests that certainly reinforce constructions of Bale as Christian believer and defender of the faith, but also announce that self-identity in terms of exile, authorship, and a bitter rhetorical battle between a select group of government men.

Bale and the meta-discursive

Bale's confrontation with Askew was *always* a written one. As far as we know, he was neither her teacher, her friend, nor even her acquaintance. Given Bale's fascination with both the printed word and its power to reach a wide audience (its public availability), and given the centrality of that site for reformers and traditionalists alike, I would like to consider first Bale's comments on writing and reading. Here we can find evidence of *his* intimate authority, of motivations that operate outside, and sometimes at odds with, announced reformist paradigms. And here too, the multiplicity of intents and effects is enabling, not simply in what it permits writers like Bale to accomplish, but also in how those accomplishments in turn promote different configurations of legitimate authority, secularizing and gendering speech, performance, and prayer, for rebellious women as well as reformist men.

While Bale's elucidations circle around issues of authorship continually, calling attention to the satisfactions and resistances that are tied up with the printed word, he rarely alights on Askew as creator of that word in her own right. Instead Askew's accounts provide Bale with the medium to grapple with other writers, established writers of the opposition like William Peryn and Stephen Gardiner, and, on his own side, such notables as John Wycliffe and Martin Luther. Askew's texts offer Bale a "safe" discursive platform from which to antagonize his opponents without risking life or limb – a means of resistance that validates his own status as writer.

Whether Bale speculates on given events or imagined ones, his positioning of self in the midst of Askew's religious debates satisfies the need for an intellectual confrontation with the enemy at a safe and distant remove (across the Channel and in print). Nor need this confrontation be understood solely in terms of a struggle for spiritual truth.[39] One may read Bale's argument as vocational justification.[40] Indeed, distancing as discursive strategy seems particularly apt in its mirroring of Bale's own situation as English exile. Forced to flee England in 1540 after the death of his patron Thomas Cromwell, Bale spent much of the middle decades of the sixteenth century on the continent. Askew's account was first printed and circulated in Marpurg, a community far more sympathetic to Protestant rhetoric and Protestant exiles than the country he had left behind.[41] Bale insists that the *Examinations* are to be read by an international audience. In opening, he promises that Askew's account will ensure that "the glorye and great power of the Lorde ... maye not now perysh at all handes, & be unthankefullye neglected, but be spred the worlde over, as wele in Latyne as Englysh, to the perpetuall infamye of so wyllfullye cruell and spyghtful tyrauntes."[42] Acknowledging both the continued execution of Protestant martyrs and the increasing censorship of reformist texts, Bale repeatedly insists that geographic distance will provide reformists with both perspective and numerical superiority:

Nothynge at all shall it terryfye us, nor yet in anye poynt lett us of our purpose, that our bokes are now in Englande condempned and brent, by the Byshoppes and prestes with their frantyck affynyte . . . But it wyll from hens forth occasyon us, to set fourth in Latyne also, that afore we wrote onlye in the Englysh, and so make their spyrytuall wyckednesse and treason knowne moche farther of. (*first examinacyon*, 5B)

Censorship within England will provoke additional labor outside its boundaries in Latin as well as English.[43] More will know and at greater distances.

That Bale envisions an audience within and without England is both a recognition of the global and communal nature of the reformist enterprise *and* an illustration of *his own* exiled position. In an earlier treatise entitled *The Image of bothe churches*, Bale in fact equates his ability to write with that distancing, valorizing the act and exonerating his decision to leave the country at one and the same instant.

In exyle are the powers therof most ernestly proved of them that hath fayth. . . .
. . . The forsaken wretched sort, hath ye lord provided alwayes to rebuke the world of sinne for want of true fayth . . . is it not therfore, that he hath exiled a

certen nombre of beleving brethren the realme of England, of the whych afflicted family my faith is that I am one. Where upon I have considered it no less than my bound deuty, undre peyne of damnation, to admonish Christes flocke by this present revelacion of their perels past.[44]

Again and again in Bale's accounts, his rhetorical elaboration of his "Christian duty" transcends national borders; his proselytizing takes in both English speakers and their more widely scattered Latin counterparts. That positioning reminds us forcefully that while Bale is a missionary, he is also an exile. His faith is proved as his flight is defended. Tying in with mid-century impulses (both Catholic and Protestant) to extend borders and fulfill "prophetic" obligations, Bale's assertions acquire religious legitimacy and justify a life in hiding at one and the same instant; yet the latter incentive effectively drops from the record in discussions of a changing Reformation landscape. So too our attempts to figure resistance get sidetracked; we forget what happens to questions of identity once exile has been legitimized.[45]

In presenting Askew's *Examinations* to the public, Bale can answer his enemies at considerable remove and rewrite personal identity; he can antagonize without repercussion and save face at the same time. When Askew's accusers supposedly misrepresent an event that she has earlier recounted, Bale literally replaces her response with his own, replying in her stead. He writes, "whan she was in the myddes of them, she myght wele have sayd wyth David, Delyver me lorde from the quarelouse dealynges of men, that I maye kepe thy comaundementes" (*first examinacyon,* 32B). Bale's emendations reveal a desire to intervene – to face her accusers himself – under cover of the printed text. He does this by substituting his words for Askew's. In the *Examinations,* Bale reveals his insiderism; he becomes a key player in a debate that is occurring at a considerable geographic remove. Bale's engagement is not simply at the level of word replacement, however. His sense of identity acquires its community status because he is *as well read* as his enemies. On several occasions Bale engages his opponents in a battle of books, and in each rally, Bale reveals an obvious delight in his textual expertise. He calls on author after author to defend one position or attack another. When Askew is asked whether a mouse eating the host receives good (a common point of debate focusing on the efficacy of the sacrament),[46] Bale responds with a litany of informed citations:

Wylye wynchestre answereth thys questyon . . . in hys *wyse detectyon of the devyls sophystrye* . . . "a mouse can not devoure God." Yet reporteth he after, in fo. 21. that Christes bodye maye as wele dwell in a mouse as it ded in Judas. Than foloweth fryre fynke, fryre Peryn I shuld saye. . . .
    Bycause these ii workemen be scant wettye in their owne occupacyon, I shal

bryng them forth here ii olde artyfycers of theirs to help them; Guimundus
Aversanus a bishop, to helpe byshopp Steven, & Thomas walden, a fryre, to
helpe fryre Peryn . . . But now cometh Algerus, a monk, more crafty than they
both. (*first examinacyon,* 8B–9A)

Quoting from each author and literally manipulating them like puppets,
Bale ends his commentary with a promise to continue the debate outside
the frame of this discourse. "More of thys shall I wryte," he insists, "in
the answere of their bokes" (*first examinacyon,* 10A). Here, the text
become stridently sarcastic: "if we wolde attende wele unto Christes
dyvynyte," he suggests, "and lete these oyled dyvynes dyspute amonge
olde gossypes, we shuld sone dyscharge myce and rattes, weake sto-
makes, and parbreakynge dronkardes, of a farre other sort than thus"
(*first examinacyon,* 9B). Bale's mastery in written debate invariably
insists on the last word. As the ultimate interpreter within this multi-
voiced text, Bale will be victorious. He will situate himself within a
hierarchical community of writers by powerfully retelling both his
opponents and Askew.

Another instance of Bale's authorial self-definition that says as much
about him as it does about reformist doctrine can be found in his
insistence on being in on the secret – this time, a written secret. He
promises his audience,

I coulde write here of manye other mysteryes, concernyng the observaunt fryres
& other rangynge Rome ronners, what newes they receyve wekelye out of
Englande from the papystes there, & in what hope they are put, of their returne
thydre agayne; for I have seane ther braggynge letters thereof, sent from Emeryck
to Frisland, & from the cuntraye of Coleyne into Westphalye. (*lattre examinacyon,* 42A)

Bale's anticipated audience undoubtedly consists of opponents as well as
supporters. While the information that Bale provides may enlighten
fellow reformers of papist intrigue, it will also remind writerly "Rome
ronners" that their correspondence is being intercepted and that Bale is
privy to its secrets. "I have seane ther braggynge letters," he boasts.
Bale's continual shifting back and forth from a position of attack,
responding to potential detractors, to a position of support, agreeing
with "gentyll readers" (*first examinacyon,* 42A), indicates that the
confrontational and strategic aspects of writing are part of its appeal. It
also extends Bale's readership into both camps. It is as likely that his
words will be read by his opponents as by his supporters. At one point,
he directly addresses the recanting Nicholas Shaxton.[47] At another, he
reminds displaced priests, "A warnynge myght the turnynge over of your
monasteryes have bene unto yow, if ye were not, as ye are altogyther
blynde" (*lattre examinacyon,* 25B). Bale recognizes the written word,

particularly *his* written word, in terms of real effect, and so, to a certain extent styles himself an "author."[48] "Moche are . . . [papists] offended with [our] bokes, for that they so playnelye do manyfest their myschefes" (*first examinacyon,* 21B), he writes, and "I dare boldelye saye unto them, that by burnynge Anne Askewe and her, iii. companyens, they have one thousande lesse of the popysh beleve than they had afore. They thynke also by condempnynge and burnynge our bokes, to put us to sylence. But that wyll surelye brynge double upon them, if they be not ware" (*first examinacyon,* 42B-43A). Later he insists, addressing his assertions to "tormentours and tyrauntes abhomynable": "I promyse yow, so to dyvulge thys unsemelye facte of yours in the latyne, that all christendome over, it shall be knowne what ye are."[49]

Bale's authorial involvement in the text reveals itself as a desire for engagement with other "bokes" – men's "bokes." While Bale addresses Askew's writings in much the same fashion that he does the scriptures,[50] using her words to elucidate arguments of his own devising, the commentary he chooses from her accounts almost always comes from the questions leveled at her by her inquisitors – questions raised by Gardiner, Bonner, and Wriothesley. Within Bale's elucidations, then, resistance means upending established and familiar texts – all of them authored by men and all of them focusing on the religious debates of his times. Bale's writings are set in opposition to texts by Peryn and Winchester. They are also positioned within a history of already-valorized, and hence legitimate, reformist works that precede them. In one incident Bale accommodates himself to that history overtly, relating his attacks on the Henrician belief in the remission of sins to a host of reformist texts that precede them:

thys most devylysh blasphemye with soche other lyke, provoked the seyd Johan wycleve, the verye organe of God, and vessell of the holye Ghost not onlye to replye than agaynst them at Oxforde in the open schooles, but also to write a great nombre of bokes agaynst that pestylent popysh kyngedome of theirs. lyke as Martyne Luther hath done also in our tyme. (*first examinacyon,* 30A–B)

To this litany of reformist authors, Bale adds his own name. He writes, "the devylyshnesse of thys newe doctryne of theirs [the popish Mass], shall be refelled in my bokes agaynst fryre Peryn and Wynchestre" (*first examinacyon,* 30B). The *Examinations* serve as an index to a number of Bale's more recent texts. He mentions "*the mysterye of iniquyte,* fo. 33" and later a forthcoming work: "what other ghostlye frutes it hath," he insists, "I shall more largelye shewe in my boke called, *The myracles of the Masse agaynst Peryne.*"[51]

Bale's representation of self as reformist author allows him a direct line to God. Like Luther and Wycliffe before him, he becomes a vessel of the Holy Ghost. The occurrence in Bale's account of repeated allusions to the offices of writer and text suggests a formulation of the subject/self which offers religious support, safe distance, and satisfied desire, all within the actively resisting political platform of religious exile. Bale's framings also illustrate a definition of the self that takes its bearings from community and place, not in opposition to them. Bale is who and what he is precisely because he can situate himself and his works *within* a network of other writers and texts on either side of the debate.[52] Obviously, the secular gratification that Bale receives as author, exile, and political strategist, cannot be separated from a real commitment to theological principle. But to allow the doctrinal aspects of his discussion – the reformist narrative – to subsume other incentives is to forfeit the possibility of mixed loyalties and to deny the often useful and resistant divisions between them in charting social transformation. What is striking to me about the history of this articulation is its inherent duplicity – the messiness of its making versus the tidiness of its telling. As we have seen, its positioning within the Reformation never acknowledges the particular arguments within its pages or the personal agendas of its writer. Both are absent from the narratives that remain.

Extending the boundaries: Askew and the written *Examinations*

Askew is the ostensible subject of Bale's account. In the *Examinations*, responses are discussed and actions revealed that purport to shed light on the life of this historically framed woman. Yet, for the most part the discussions that occur within the pages of Bale's text are highly reflective. Bale's elucidations only marginally interact with Askew's initial court responses, revealing instead Bale as writer, exile, and as written subject within a particular cultural moment in English history. The publication of Askew's account had as much to do with drawing Bale into an elite community of writers and justifying his flight from England as it did with reforming the English Church. Yet those affiliations are largely unreported in the historical transcription of this text. Askew's *Examinations*, as they are printed, then, are inevitably texts about Bale and the fulfillment of his desires or Askew and hers, but they are read and engaged as something entirely different – about martyrdom and reformist doctrine or about still other sets of intents and subjectivities its readers bring to them. The break in the chain – the separation between the satisfaction of one desire and the illustration of another – points to the almost infinite number of redirections possible within a single text, redirections which may be deflected back into familiar and ideologically stable positions but which need not be.

The same proliferation of intents and outcomes occurs in Askew's own construction of the trial, but here they are of a uniquely different tenor. In fact, one of the more intriguing aspects of Askew's and Bale's shared "reformist" discourse is how radically dissimilar both constructions really are, in form as well as function. If martyrdom meant toeing the party line, an exemplary martyr Askew was not.[53] Throughout her account, she refuses to locate her responses solidly either inside her accuser's camp or outside its confines. Obviously, rhetorical evasion would prove politic within court before judges who will use her words against her. Remember, however, this account is not a court transcription; it is not a reenactment of an actual trial. Rather, it is an autobiographical narrative that is meant to be read. Accordingly, Askew's evasive ambiguity is not a means to avoid punishment, nor is it simply a written vindication of her faith.[54] She does not write this account in order to be let off the hook or to reveal the consistency of her religious convictions. In either case, clear statement and solid assertion would seem better suited to the task. Instead, the opportunity to maneuver simultaneously within and between a number of different contexts opens up the possibility of legitimate and resistant voice outside those venues.

Askew can, in writing her account, extend the boundaries of one set of limitations by replacing them with another. This cross-over is literalized textually in the frequent exchanges that Askew makes between her role as female subject, beholden to institutional mandates which demand her obedience and verify her lack of education, and her role as religious subject, required to obey God's commands. Challenged by her accusers to clarify her reading of a statement made by St. Paul concerning transubstantiation – a reading that could secure her conviction – Askew recognizes the need to realign her affiliations – to move to diplomatically safer ground. Calling on additional scriptural support, she re-negotiates the space available to her, abandoning her status as a religious subject and taking up her status as a woman to deflect the brunt of their attack. "I answered," she writes, "that it was agaynst saynt Paules lernynge, that I beynge a woman, shuld interprete the scriptures, specyallye where so manye wyse lerned men were."[55] Defined doctrinally as a disobedient religious subject, Askew calls on gender to avoid entrapment, but the binary that she sets up here is hardly unidirectional. She will have no scruples in disavowing it when need be. Askew is not solely interested in a reformist agenda. Indeed, it is Askew's continued willingness to change allegiances, to hedge her bets, that marks that different motivation unquestionably.

Rebuked earlier in her account for uttering the scriptures in contradiction to those same commands of St. Paul, that women should not speak the word of God, Askew easily reverses the conditions that confine her as a woman, pulling this time to her prerogative as a religious subject. "I answered [my accuser], that I knewe Paules meanynge so well as he, whych is. . . that a woman ought not to speake in the congregacyon by the waye of teachynge" (*first examinacyon,* 10A). Relying on her religious authority, Askew now *interprets* the definition of the scriptural "congregacyon" to mean pulpit, avoiding the penalty that her persecutor lays before her. "I asked hym, how manye women he had seane, go into the pulpett and preache," she explains. "He sayde he never sawe non. Then I sayd he ought to fynde no fallt . . . except they had offended the lawe."[56] No longer obedient woman, in this second instance Askew becomes an interpreter of the scriptures and an active Protestant reformer. She knows "Paules meanynge so well as he."

Within the religious contradictions separating the reformist and traditional positions, Askew has equal room for engagement *and* transferal, for resistance *and* redirection. While these kinds of rhetorical evasions illustrate at a fairly explicit textual level a movement between subject positions that are in conflict with one another, that conflict need not be limited to the terms of the debate as reformists and traditionals have set it up. Askew can admit to other readings which may, in fact, accommodate neither position overtly, and which have the secondary effect of reconstituting both. This tendency, repeated throughout her account, to refuse crucial definitions and labels, seems to gesture toward additional sites of interpretive power. Askew's authority here results from the freedom to "read" the Bible as she chooses. Clearly the presence of two, already articulated, and culturally sanctioned readings (reformist and traditional) eventually necessitates a direct address; she will have to take a stand on one or the other sooner or later. But the availability of more than one option suggests the possibility of movement between them, and allows for a temporary recognition of some sort of subjective and resistant authority in having to make a choice.

Where reformist debates, including Askew's own, assert the public nature of God's word, its availability for all Protestant believers, Askew continually describes meaning in possessive and singular terms, recognizing the amorphous nature of all potential interpretations of the text. "Thys was *my* sayenge," she explains at one point.[57] "I answered hym *my* meanynge," she promises in another.[58] Askew keeps her meanings intentionally diffuse; they are not necessarily anyone else's. Within her particular historical moment, a moment when reformist doctrines are still being introduced to English audiences, when interpretive flexibility is as yet relatively legitimate in and of itself, Askew's "resistance" supplants the notion of a shared religious community with individual and privatized scriptural interpretations. That the interpretations are celebrated as reformist, persecuted as conspiratorial, and unmarked as autobiographic ought hopefully to remind us of their potential value in cultural transformation. In the conflation of intents and effects, pieces can and will fall through the cracks.

Askew's call to a resistant self-focused identity is hardly arbitrary; it makes valid material sense, both within the broader context of the Reformation and within the particular circumstances of bible-reading women. Askew cannot, like Bale, enter into a discursive debate that has acknowledged participants and positions. To speak from such a perspective would be both unthinkable and unacceptable. As a religious believer newly free to interpret the scriptures for herself, Askew can legitimate her right to understand differently, but to situate herself in relation to established writers, or to place her voice in the same general sphere of sermonizing as that of Luther and Wycliffe has no institutionalized platform of defense, at least not at this historic moment in time.[59] Even scriptures will not help her here. The validity of Askew's claims to religious freedom exist only so long as she remains outside restricted forums of masculine discourse, as long as she stays at a considerable remove from the domain of the public pulpit.[60] Her resistances, accordingly, turn to singular truths, to individual certainties.

Even the format of the *Examinations* reiterates a recognition of appropriate female voice as separate from and dependent on masculine prerogative.[61] With or without Bale's validating elucidations, Askew never speaks unless she is spoken to.[62] She never reveals her beliefs until she is told to do so by the authorities. While the scripting of her narrative necessarily includes both a recounting of the questions asked by her inquisitors and her answers to them (she believes herself authorized to speak for her enemies, documenting her replies in terms of commands that she herself has framed), she announces her own voice only in response: "I answered," "my answere was styll," "non other answere wolde I make hym." Yes, Askew's meanings and her ability to make them enable her to evade her accusers; yes, they enable her to write an account of her persecutions, and recognize in both actions *some* sort of cultural legitimacy, but that legitimacy acquires its privatized shape via *the very institutional restrictions and gender hierarchies that are already in place.* The resistant interiority that Askew's text proclaims, an interiority that will, in fact, become synonymous with later Reformation paradigms for *both men and women* finds at least one of its early voices in an institutionally framed definition of acceptable, reformist, *female* exegesis.[63]

Askew offers a particularly evocative example of resistant woman's voice in the following scenario. Here the conflation of public and private, of speech and silence, illustrates both Askew's renegotiation of existing restrictions and a certainty that she will be able to bypass them. Askew obviously believes her oratory capable of convincing others, but she refuses to initiate it herself; she will not publicly converse unless pressured to do so. Responding to an accusation that she has been spreading rumors and embellishing on her own importance, Askew describes her confrontation with the whole of the Lincoln ecclesia (no fewer than sixty priests according to her account). Here Askew relishes in the opportunity to argue doctrine with her opponents:

Then he rebuked me, and sayd, that I shuld report, that there were bent agaynst me, thre score prestes at Lyncolne. In dede (quoth I) I sayd so; for my fryndes tolde me, if I ded come to Lyncolne, the prestes wolde assault me and put me to great trouble, as therof they had made their boast. And whan I hearde it, I went thydre in dede, not beynge afrayd, because I knewe my matter to be good. More over I remayned there. vi. dayes, to se what wolde be sayd unto me. And as I was in the mynster, readynge upon the Byble, they resorted unto me by ii. and by ii. by v. and by vi. myndynge to have spoken to me; yet went they theyr wayes agayne with out wordes speakynge. (*first examinacyon*, 32B–33A)

In this passage, hearing that her notoriety precedes her and certain of her claims of truth, Askew instigates a direct confrontation: "because [she knows her] matter to be good," she goes to Lincoln "to se what wolde be sayd unto [her]." Once there, however, Askew waits until she is given permission to display that knowledge appropriately. Because she is given none, no exposition occurs.

The image conveyed through the text, of Askew reading in the "mynster," literalizes the power of the scriptural word to arm her against her enemies, but it is a private arming. Her presence, actively interpreting, not her public discourse, will silence the opposition. She will not preach in congregational terms but will wait until her encounters have been personalized – "by ii. and by ii. by v. and by vi." That Askew recognizes herself as justified in taking an interpretive stand against the Lincoln priests, in opposing their numerical authority with her own "individual" presence, suggests the legitimacy of her "matter" to extend and subvert traditional gender requirements – it announces the site of her resistance – but it also relies on those same traditional strictures to validate its claims. Askew will resist in obeying; she will defy only as long as she defers.

While Askew frames the substance of her confrontations in private terms, celebrating her separation from others, her words suggest that she is all too aware of the profound effect that isolation must have on sustained dialogue. She recognizes the power of communities and the *men* within them who refuse to listen:

Then my lorde asked, if there were not one that ded speake unto me. I tolde hym, yeas, that there was one of them at the last, whych ded speake to me in dede. And my lorde than asked me, what he sayd. And I tolde hym, hys wordes were of so small effecte, that I ded not now remembre them. (*first examinacyon,* 34A)

Singularity promises Askew a certain kind of leverage that would be unavailable to her within established (and masculinized) hierarchies of community. She can dismiss or forget what does not suit; she can deflect potentially damaging accusations by refusing to understand them. Unfortunately, isolationist strategies work two ways. In claiming a position of singular identity, Askew necessarily loses listeners herself. Within the materially specific terms of her own resistance, Askew cannot be heard *in her own terms* and be heard *by men*. Unlike Bale, she cannot "have her cake and eat it too."

In an attempt to accommodate both frames at the same time, Askew moves from general statement to singular proof. She proclaims, "I wolde wyshe, that all men knewe my conversacyon & lyvynge in all poyntes, for I am so sure of my selfe thys houre, that there are non able to prove anye dyshonestie by me. If yow knowe anye that can do it, I praye yow brynge them fourth" (*first examinacyon,* 34B). Askew's combined wish for "all men" to know and "anye" to prove illustrates the double bind that private female identity necessitates at this historical juncture. Askew is not yet part of a community of individuals who can recognize singular claims as legitimate in and of themselves. Still, her assertion is both significant and profound in the nature of its voicings. When responding to her accusers Askew does not say, "I am so sure of my status as a gentlewoman that I speak these things." Instead, the focus is on the individual nature of her certainty and her separation from others: "I am so sure of *my selfe* thys houre, that there are non able to prove anye dyshonestie by me (my emphasis)." Askew's proclaimed singularity directs the way that her text demands to be noticed.[64] Not just a piece of propaganda for the reform movement as a whole, her account asks to be read as a personal justification.

Askew's desire to keep the substance of her exchanges with the inquest amorphous, diffuse, and singular can be seen in the careful voicing of her own declaratives. Throughout her account she responds in a manner that privileges individual perception over communal assertion – private process over shared resolution. She either believes something to be the case or perceives that it is not. Responding to a priest sent to her in the prison adjoining the court, she admits, "I wyll not . . . [answer the question], bycause I perceyve ye come to tempte me" (*first examinacyon*, 13B). Earlier, her inquisitor at Sadler Hall elicits the same type of reply: "non other answere wolde I make hym, because I perceyved hym a papyst."[65] What I think is interesting here is the juxtaposition of Askew's own speculative discourse with the certainty of that of her accusers and her elucidators. Within the body of the recitations themselves, Askew's respondents continually demand straight speech, plain text, and shared meanings. "The Byshopp of wynchestre bad me make a dyrect answere" (*lattre examinacyon,*, 16A), Askew writes in the beginning of her second account. "The Byshopp sayd, I spake in parables" (16B), she later adds. Askew's responses, even the confession that she signs after her first inquest, all fall short of that mark; they are not clear, closed, or Catholic.[66]

Askew's tendency to select words that imply uncertainty and variable meaning may simply reflect a rhetorical caginess on her part or indicate a written proclivity for disclaimer. What is striking nevertheless is how, in both her account *and* in Bale's appended elucidations, Askew's gestures are erased by solid assertion and inflexible interpretive closure.[67] Askew's speculation concerning the confessor sent to her in prison, "I perceyve ye come to tempte me," is summarily dismissed by Bale as already proved papist deceit. "Lyttle nede shall other men have to manyfest their blasphemouse folyes," he writes, "whan [the priests] do it so playnelye their selves" (*first examinacyon,* 14A). Within Bale's readings of the Askew text there are no moments of uncertainty. Temptations are never "perceyved"; they are revealed "playnelye."[68]

Bishop Bonner is equally adamant in his positioning of Askew. When he questions her on her faith concerning the sacrament, Askew reiterates the singularity of her beliefs by announcing them as "beliefs":

I beleve as the scripture doth teache me. Then enquired he of me, what if the scripture doth saye, that it is the bodye of Christ? I beleve (sayd I) lyke as the scripture doth teache me. Then asked he agayne, what if the scripture doth saye, that it is not the bodye of Christ? My answere was styll, I beleve as the scripture infourmeth me. And upon thys argument he tarryed a great whyle, to have dryven me to make hym an answere to hys mynde. (*first examinacyon,* 17A–B)

Askew's refusal to assert specifics allows for a multiplicity of options; it does not accommodate the either/or binary that Bonner demands (is it the body of Christ or not?). Askew's statement of "beleve" is instead open-ended. All three, Askew, Bale, *and* Bonner, believe in the "truth" of the scriptures. It is Askew's response, however, or perhaps her failure to respond adequately, that underscores the multiplicity of available scriptural interpretations within the traditional/reformist debate. Her refusal also recognizes the impossibility of a substantive (closed) answer unless it be in private terms. Askew's assertion of *any* univocal reading of the scriptures will drive her "to make [Bonner] an answere to hys mynde," or Bale to his, or Askew to hers, but never to all three within the same church. Askew instead hypothesizes an understanding that denies the binaries with the brotherhood. In calling on the righteousness of making an answer to her own mind, she expands her options, solidifying her separation from both reformists and traditionalists alike.

Perhaps the most telling episode of this private voicing to occur in the *Examinations* comes in the form of a fictionalized conversation that includes Bale. Recalling an attempt by the inquest to have her shriven, Askew describes an analogy comparing her conscience to a wound and offers her response. She tells us that her accuser

brought . . . fourth thys unsaverye symylytude, that if a man had a wounde, no wyse surgeon wolde mynystre help unto it, before he had seane it uncovered. In like case (sayth he) can I geve yow no good counsell, unlesse I knowe wherwith your conscyence is burdened. I answered, that my conscience was clere in all thynges. And for to laye a playstre unto the whole skynne, it might apere moche folye. (*first examinacyon*, 23B–24A)

The religious issue in question here concerns the act of confession itself. The reformed platform denied the efficacy of the sacrament of penance, insisting instead that in spiritual offenses the only legitimate avowal of sin must be unmediated – direct communication between the penitent and God. The Henrician position insisted on priestly intervention as the only acceptable recourse to forgiveness. The priest's spiritual office, his theological training and ordination, ensured that the path of communication would be open. Without priestly intercession, penitents would have no access to the Lord *or* to salvation.

In Askew's text, her accuser's analogy posits the act of confession as the healing of a wound, the uncovering of the disease of sin. Her reply, however, effaces the doctrinal nature of his analogy (in either traditional or reformist terms) to assert "individual" prerogative. "My conscience was clere in all thynges," she writes. As she is without wounds and of unburdened conscience, her positions as accused woman, as accused Protestant, and as accused English subject, are all thrown open to contest. Ideologically, her assertions here suggest a surprisingly secular definition of the self – a definition that, in 1546, relies on a marginal, and as yet flexible, notion of Protestant privacy. In embracing such a notion, Askew can abandon traditional positions of gender and religious belief and begin, in their place, to articulate herself as a singular "self."

Even in its earliest stages of transmission, the Askew document is framed to support ideological positions that ignore Askew's claims to selfhood. It is not that such statements are flatly refused; rather they are simply unrecognized. This is certainly the case in Bale's scripting of her text. While his textual resistances satisfy a multitude of antithetical subject positions, his readings of Askew – her placement as object of his reportings – deny her the same scope. She becomes for him a univocal representation of reformist polemic. Indeed, Bale's refusal to acknowledge Askew's voice is due in part to her skirting of the religious binaries before her. Again and again her responses – the information that she includes and omits – fail to align themselves neatly within the traditional/ reformist debate. For Bale Askew's answers are inappropriate. In his elucidated *Examinations*, her evasions become meaningless because they have no useful interpretive value. Accordingly, Bale focuses on only those questions leveled at her by her accusers, responding to each appropriately and matter-of-factly.

In Bale's reply to the encounter that I have just described, he turns to Bishop Gardiner, Askew's inquisitor, for religious support. He writes, "hath not he now (thynke yow) moche nede of helpe, whych seketh to soche a surgeon. Uncircumspect is that pacyent, and most commonlye unfortunate, whych goeth to a commen murtherer to be healed of hys dysease" (*first examinacyon,* 24A). Like Askew's accusers, Bale assumes the legitimacy of Gardiner's metaphor; he assumes her "dysease." For him it is the treatment itself (the confessional) that is most suspect. Indeed Askew's protestations of guiltlessness are, in and of themselves, *heretical* to the reformist platform as Bale constructs it. "The nature of these [priests] . . . is not to make whole, but to persecute them thou hast smytten, and to adde woundes unto wounde, Psalms 68," he promises (*first examinacyon,* 24A). As *reformed* or *traditional* believer, Askew should already be "smytten," already be "wounded." To lobby for clear conscience is, on a literal level, to deny original sin. Askew's call to clear conscience then ought to be read as a truth claim operating outside the familiar domain of religious discourse. The assertion asks readers to pay particular attention to the temporal and to the material in its framing – to the here and now. That Askew is locating that certainty *secularly*, in an understanding of conscience that is, at this moment, separate from though dependent on religious belief, seems likely.

While an emerging conception of the individual subject has long been associated with the Reformation and no doubt can be traced back further still, that formulation comes to represent markedly different understandings throughout English history. The voicings of self that occur in Askew's *Examinations* are specific to and unusual for her period. They are striking, both in their constant and unabashed naming of "me" and "myne," and in their sense of that identity as authorized and empowered. Askew did not invent the individual subject, nor did the

Reformation. Events – political, economic, and religious – and people – empowered, persecuted, and persevering – together shaped those definitions, forming, in their combined influence, our understandings of English culture and of the numerous identities that inhabit it. Askew's skill in evading her inquisitors, in one-upping them rhetorically, then, is evidence of singular capabilities *as well as* shared religious righteousness, of personal resistance as well as church Reformation. In the *Examinations*, she gestures toward a singular definition of "self" (materially required as she is a woman), and she explores an as yet open and oddly a-religious creation of private being – of conscience – that will eventually discursively announce female interiority as synonymous with both family and the domestic.[69]

Narratives in the making

The *Examinations* ask to be read from a number of different perspectives, including that of personal justification. The interpretive space that opens up as a result of conflicting ideological and text-based platforms allows for a proliferation of available subject positions – positions which are for Askew and Bale literalized in reading and in the written word. Despite their eventual recuperation as reformist polemic, then, the *Examinations* focus on multiple constructions of the self, constructions that are not defined solely in terms of conventional or established economies of religion. In Askew's text, this framing takes shape in a privatized representation of self; Askew constructs a separate and interior space from which to imagine her subjectivity. It is this internal mechanism of behavioral choice that contributes so directly to the active redefinition of a culture by its members. Individual agency is never removed from ideological or institutional underpinnings, but it is malleable in that it operates, is able to operate, at cross-purposes to a dominant ideology or institution by legitimate and "justifiable" intransigence. The subversive potential of such a cross-over ensures occasional and, in some cases, immediate transformation of the cultural requirements around it.

The point that I am making here is that the criteria that we recognize in identifying successful resistance, if they are to be accurate and accountable, must be extended to include a whole range of potential contradictions and deflections, some temporary, some permanent, some successful, and ultimately some failed. Resistance, given these complications, is never pure – in terms either of its motivations or of its outcomes. No doubt it is this messiness that is partly responsible for a general tendency to discount agency all together. Because resistance can never be traced back to a single source, because it never succeeds in isolation or offers results that are absolute, mapping resistance in terms of straight lines, altruistic motives, or single-issue politics is impossible. Instead, resistances are continually refigured, given different status, and accorded additional restrictions in the creation of new sets of ideological requirements. Despite this unavoidable entanglement in existing cultural forms, resistances are never simply "contained."[70] They do not neatly reinscribe ideologies already in place. Redefinitions occur constantly and at times comprehensively. Indeed, the very institutions that would seem to deny agency enable it. The family, the church, and, in some cases, the state itself, all participate in this justifying process.

If we are to attempt to refigure or document strategies of resistance, we need to get a better sense of what makes action acceptable, transformable, local or global, and we need to recognize in those patterns some sense of history and temporality. Given the multiplicity of discursive resistance, what is it that directs the historical trajectory of a given act of intransigence? What factors determine prosecution or preferment for those who resist? Clearly from the distant perspective of the cultural critic there is a flattening of narrative possibility in any reconstruction of historical events. Creating sound-bites for future generations necessarily presupposes simplistic political solutions, but that alone cannot account for the uneven nature of culture's listenings. Words and texts do affect bodies. They further careers, memorialize voices, and direct religious reformations. They also sentence prisoners to death. And the cultural weight of each action is determined as much by the source of its speaking as by the substance of its conversations. Telling stories and signing death warrants, we must remember, are not the same thing at all.

When Askew finally does fix her responses within these debates, when she finally decides to defend the reformist position *and* accept status within that political binary, the story is over. In the narrative that makes up the last weeks of Askew's life, this assertion ensures her conviction, and she is punished accordingly. Askew's decision to admit to a single scriptural reading (the wrong reading according to her captors) insists on her alignment with institutional authority – the king's council – even if only by negation. As an opponent to state-sanctioned religious control, she is subject to all of its legislative penalties – most particularly, execution for heresy: "I answered that I was no heretyke . . . But as concernynge the faythe whych I uttered and wrote to the counsell, I wolde not (I sayd) denye it, bycause I know it true. Then wolde they nedes knowe, if I wolde denye the sacrament to be Christes bodye and bloude: I sayd, yea" (*lattre examinacyon,* 31A). Askew's profession of her religious beliefs calls for the full condemnation of English law. In her account, spoken "resistance" is directly linked to eventual martyrdom and to the cost in human life that such opposition entails. "What enables people . . . to resist the Gulag?" Michel Foucault wondered. "What can give [them] . . . the courage to stand up and die in order to utter a word or a poem?"[71] In a chilling precursor to Foucault's famous question, Askew eventually prefaces her own execution. She answers with the following: "and upon these wordes, that I have now spoken, wyll I suffer deathe" (*lattre examinacyon*, 59A).

Askew lost her life *because* she was a religious dissident, *because* she was a woman, and *because* she had gained the notice of influential and potentially persuadable women around Katherine Parr, but I want to repeat that her execution was not part of an endemic sweep of the English countryside for female religious dissenters. Rather it was an isolated example of a court-specific threat involving the problem of reform in the highest echelons of government – a problem that might be usefully illustrated in a dramatic and gender-specific form, but that was not specifically attentive to gender or privacy or to the potential upheavals that religious reform might eventually precipitate within the conventionalized hierarchies that shaped English identity. Accordingly, what Askew is saying in this account about individual female identity is only of moderate significance to her accusers (her claims in that regard are still largely disregarded). Some of the most resistant moments of this text then are inconsequential to the immediate focus of its debate and survive it unexamined.

This text was also multiply appropriated, first by Bale, then by Foxe, and finally by something as epic and inclusive as the English Reformation. Accordingly, it is getting read by an endless cycle of readers – readers who bring to their encounters with this text and this woman any number of additional priorities and positions. What all of this means is not that Askew's resistant voice is only resistant now, when we are attending to it explicitly, or that she herself was recipient to many of its redirections in the months leading up to her death, but, rather, that the positions that she was able to occupy at a particular juncture of cultural history were multiple and multiply comprehensible. It also means that her voice did participate in a resistant construction of singular conscience and shifted the bases of definition regarding what gender and religion might have meant to her culture as a result of that participation. That her voice would have listeners, indeed, an almost limitless array of listeners over the course of the next century, suggests as well the possibility of others hearing and remembering outside the master paradigms.

With an infinite number of subjects and ideologies at work in justifying and directing choice, the possibility of informed agency or unified resistance is, at best, illusory. This problem is compounded geometrically in an institutional hegemony of selective listening. Some voices will be heard and many will not. At the same time, we can never account for and anticipate the myriad combinations and influences that will promote successful or advantageous ideological transformation. Accordingly, it is crucial that we familiarize ourselves with the "processes of change." Paying careful attention to the materiality of our cultural restraints – the limitations imposed by seemingly normative categories of gender, status, education, age, and ethnic origin – we can begin to discover or imagine patterns of choice. Decisions to resist, then, whether they be written, spoken, or acted, involve a multitude of shifting subject positions, positions that *do* have effect – positions, finally, that offer the possibility for resistance and the promise of cultural transformation.

2　Framing recusant identity in Counter-Reformation England

The daughter of a Thomas Myddleton, wax chandler, Margaret Clitherow married a butcher in her thirteenth year, converted to Catholicism sometime after that marriage, and bore at least three children who survived. According to her only modern biographer, she was an "ideal Elizabethan wife" and an exemplary Catholic, a woman who spent the bulk of her time caring for family and house and trying to rekindle the faith in her community.[1] Clitherow ran into trouble, however – religious trouble – when local authorities began to monitor attendance at church and levy fines against those who failed to appear. Clitherow was finally tried for priest-harboring, a treasonous crime punishable in the 1580s by death. During the course of her trial, Clitherow literally refused to plead; she refused to answer the charges against her, responding to her inquisitors instead with silence. Clitherow was executed because of that refusal; her sentence fell in accord with her voicelessness. Accordingly, in 1586, Clitherow was pressed to death.[2] She died leaving no record of her life, no personal account of her ordeals – nothing, not even a letter. Instead her narrative was written after the fact, by one of her confessors, Father John Mush.[3]

Clitherow's narrative is included in this study precisely because of its compromised lineage. In the account that is her life and martyrdom, she is the mother of three children, the wife of a butcher, and the would-be woman-saint of a confessor who is also and always her author. The identities that define Clitherow – mother, wife, and written saint – necessarily shape what we can know about this woman. Her story is also reflective of many Elizabethan accounts in this compromised construction, especially accounts that focus on England's middling rank women, women who have had little if any formal education, much less the leisure to put that learning into print themselves. It also represents one of the most common forms of early modern women's history available to us – a man writes a woman's life after the fact and without her consent. Mush's narrative is, like most of its ilk, an unauthorized biography.[4] Nevertheless, I include the hagiographical account of the martyr Margaret

Clitherow in this study of gender construction and state formation because to refuse it as a legitimate source for that history is to repeat the initial absence.

The 1580s have left behind surprisingly few recusant women's voices, this despite their prevalence within the unique circumstances of the English Catholic mission.[5] Of course, recusant women did speak and act during the Catholic persecutions – women like Clitherow who have much to tell us about Catholic life in a by now largely Protestant Elizabethan England.[6] How to attend to that absent presence? How to do justice to narratives that have all but disappeared? Using Mush's "Life of Margaret Clitherow" as a point of departure, we can imaginatively reconstruct the circumstances in which Clitherow was asked to perform and attempt to understand her motivations for doing so. We can illustrate, through Mush's narrative, some of the complex subject negotiations marking the last years of the sixteenth century. Mush's narrative can supply the broad strokes necessary to document Clitherow's life; it can outline the woman and her religious insubordination in explicitly Catholic and masculinist terms, but is it enough? Will it answer the questions that we want to ask? It seems to me that additional narratives must be called on to improve our chances of "getting it right," to enhance the likelihood of defining female subjecthood outside those terms, and to reveal once again women's active participation in the process of gender construction and state making. One strategy is to consider comparatively, to juxtapose Clitherow's missing voice with available, albeit historically discrete, counterparts. Anne Askew's 1546 detailing of her own criminal prosecution can provide one such an alternative. A second and perhaps equally compelling alternative is to write Clitherow's voice into being – to create it anew.

It seems to me that the success of historical recovery work, especially such tenuous recovery work, relies on two complementary tasks. We need to historicize difference, documenting the unique circumstances of Clitherow's struggle in terms of its similarities to and distances from other religious and gendered persecution. We need simultaneously to consider some of the more pronounced ideological shifts that have taken place via that historical difference, exploring the impact of those shifts on identity formation and subject negotiation. Supplying specific and often disparate detail to the events of Askew's 1546 heresy trial and Clitherow's 1586 trial for treason can remind us usefully of the very real effects of subject articulation in reorganizing social and religious roles, in enacting cultural change.[7] What was possible in Henrician London may in fact be untenable forty years later. At the same time, a heightened emphasis on behavioral regulation in the last years of the sixteenth century may provide Elizabethan subjects with leverage where none previously existed. Accordingly, I want to stress in this chapter the importance of tracing shifts in subject construction and articulation as we move from mid to late century, from London to York, from Protestant to Catholic, from gentlewoman to butcher's wife, each with its different contexts and concerns. Generating a cultural model that can account for difference will allow us to talk about avenues for female authority in history-specific terms and to hypothesize future configurations politically. It will offer us a fuller sense of how state and local identities were and are variously shaped.

Clitherow's success in navigating conflicting ideological, institutional, and official authorities derives in part from earlier forays like Askew's, but it also develops out of the paradox that was Counter-Reformation England. In the peculiar circumstances of illicit Catholicism that were to occur during the later years of the sixteenth century, the middling-rank household itself became a privileged and contested site. As a result of this restructuring, recusant mothers and wives gained considerable religious and familial leverage, redefining the limits of both ecclesial and patriarchal control in conducting Catholic service, supervising priestly behavior, and acting as spiritual stand-ins for outwardly conforming husbands and sons. Clitherow's participation in Catholic household chores secured for her a means to sainthood; it also brought her mobility, local success, and separation from her peers. That shaping was double-edged, however, in that Catholic definitions of the domestic saint/martyr further reified boundaries between inner and outer, between a spiritualized domestic space and the secular world outside its domain. Performances like Clitherow's would only count as long as they remained discrete/discreet, and it is that separation and silence that become so telling in 1580s female subjectivity. In a combined focus on religiosity and good housekeeping, on conscience and conduct, Clitherow's social navigations will, like Askew's, have direct and sometimes deleterious consequences for later constructions of gendered identity and state control.[8]

Defining the particulars of subject negotiation can supply historical context, but it is finally so much detail unless it is considered to some end. Of rather more significance is a theoretical awareness of how and why such comparative projects matter. Sometimes it is not enough to depend on available narratives to rethink and rewrite women's history. While we as scholars need to make use of established discourses and to consider them as thoroughly as we can, we must on occasion be willing to recast our notions of acceptable historiography and legitimate proof. This may mean inventing stories as well as rediscovering them, relying on historically disparate voices and events to get at the unrecoverable, creating historical fact at one and the same moment that we are contesting it. While such undertakings necessarily involve immense risk, to refuse them as options is to leave much unwritten and unexplored. I ask that, in paying careful attention to available voices and texts to frame our understandings, we consider not only contemporary discourses like Mush's but also cross-period/cross-genre discourses like Askew's.[9] I want to suggest as well that our refigurings may on occasion require additional help in a literal re-imagining of historical record.[10]

Forty years and four separate monarchies

Ideologies of gender and state are fluid, and their fluidity depends as much on the possibility of individual subject articulation as on the likelihood of group conformity. As I see it, the potential for *directive* political action (action that precipitates change) is both historical *and* transhistorical; it operates within a set of always available discourses which nevertheless present themselves in different spheres and with different degrees of momentum depending on their particular historical location. In the following discussion, I hope to illustrate and particularize the historical adaptability of subject articulation as we move from 1540s fledgeling Protestant court circles to 1580s, middling-rank, rural recusancy. One of the most significant elements of such a comparison lies in an understanding that events, circumstances, locations, and people *do* generate difference.[11] At the same time, movement between historical vantage points is not arbitrary; rather it evolves through what can best be described as a negotiation of conflicting tensions within cultural perspectives. Because situations vary over time, what is possible or desirable in one instance may in fact be precisely what is most expendable in another. Accordingly, historical shifts, sometimes subtle, sometimes dramatic, redefine both the subjects who inhabit them and the kinds of articulations that each is able to enact within that framing.

At the time of the Clitherow trial and Mush's writing of her biography in 1586, England presented a far more unified and politically reactive front than it did in the last years of Henry VIII's reign. The religious controversies that beset the earlier period, though still present, were masked by Elizabeth I's direct refusal to allow free discussion of religion in parliament – her only persistent qualification of Parliamentary freedom.[12] The queen's solution to the "religious" problem – "the Elizabethan Religious Settlement" – generally let English subjects alone, provided that they obeyed English law outwardly.[13] Where Henry VIII had been committed to no single course of action or individual councilor after Wolsey, Elizabeth I depended heavily on one man, William Cecil, Lord Burghley, to carry out her policies. Unfortunately, Burghley's political connections were both conservative and of a strongly Protestant cast. As the queen's chief advisor for most of her reign, Burghley oversaw much of the anti-Catholic legislation set up in England.[14] At the same time, thanks to Burghley's political longevity, Elizabeth I's Privy Council remained surprisingly stable. Relatively few positions changed hands, for reasons other than death, after 1570.[15]

Given the veneer of religious uniformity at the highest levels of government office, the penalties and punishments for failure to accept "the Elizabethan Settlement" tended to fall *outside* those ranks, most visibly on the northern Catholic gentry, and the yeomen, husbandmen, and tenants who came under their rule.[16] "Surviving" (and that is a crucial term here) evidence in the form of letters, bills, commission statements, etc., suggests that the "perceived" problems were situated most heavily in rural areas. London certainly had its share of religious intransigence once continental seminarians began to make their way back into the country,[17] as did the south, in and around Canterbury, but the most pressing problems of recusancy and priest harboring, according to surviving records, seemed to lay at a distance from court, in the north where subjects had been less exposed to articulations of the Queen's Settlement and where university-trained Protestant ministers were few and far between.[18]

The focus on persecution directed at people and politics removed from court had a two-fold effect: first, in augmenting and perhaps exaggerating parliamentary fears of the potential dangers of unchecked recusancy – rumors of sedition and possible revolt took the place of acknowledged personal retribution or vendetta – and second, in persecuting middling-rank Catholic non-conformists in place of their wealthier and better-positioned neighbors.[19] The court's real fears about Catholic nonconformity seemed to manifest themselves most forcefully after 1575 when arrivals from the English College in Rome returned to England to begin the task of rekindling Catholic belief and practice.[20] Until this point most Catholic nonconformists managed to avoid the few enforced religious restrictions quite successfully.[21] The threats, either perceived or real, from these trained seminary priests brought Elizabeth I's governors about-face in their treatment and prosecution of Catholic offenders. Mary Stuart's presence in England and the numerous attempted conspiracies which directly or indirectly involved her, further increased national fears or exploited already circulating suspicions.[22]

By 1584, the Elizabethans in parliamentary office seemed as a body intensely nationalistic, rallying behind both the queen and her laws. The religion question, when it was addressed at all, had come to represent a primary and direct threat to the queen's person and to the English way of life. In October and November of 1584, during the Parliamentary elections, Elizabeth I's council appealed to all English*men* to join a new association for the protection of the queen.[23] This Band of Association was a sworn brotherhood of avengers, and the adoption of its "Act for the Queen's safety" promised to "pursue to utter extermination all that shall attempt or give consent to anything that shall tend to the harm of her majesty's person."[24] Not only does the drafting of this highly nationalistic policy illustrate an articulated patriotic intensity, but it also literalizes the extent to which perceived threat could direct governmental proclamation or be exploited by it.[25]

The sense at court of the urgency of national unity and religious solidarity also resulted in the establishment of numerous regional ecclesial commissions – commissions which had the secondary effect of augmenting local authority and further bureaucratizing state and local policy. The commission at York, operating as a law court from 1561 on,[26] was indirectly responsible for Clitherow's numerous arrests and gave greater authority to the Assize Judges who ultimately held her accountable for her refusal to stand trial. Local commissions, like the York Commission, were authorized both to try and to convict without final approval from the queen's High Commission. They relied on secondhand and often contradictory information concerning government sentiment on issues of recusancy. In Mush's account of Clitherow's trial proceedings, he laments the lack of communication between regional commissions and the queen's. Had Elizabeth I known of Clitherow's imprisonment – or so he believes – Clitherow would not have been executed.[27]

Despite Mush's faith in the queen's "better judgment," royal statute did implicate English recusants rather more frequently than it did the puritan opposition. While Elizabeth I apparently recognized threats from both Catholic and Protestant extremists, the laws of the land and the religious affiliations of the closest claimant to the throne (Mary Stuart) helped to ensure a far more direct attack on the Catholic community than on its radical Protestant counterparts.[28] A number of statutes passed in the years preceding Clitherow's inquest made it increasingly difficult for Catholics to hear Mass or to follow the various rituals of their church. From general restrictions and mild punishments to more directly coercive legislation, the government and its local affiliates sought to control and subdue the Catholic side of nonconformity.[29]

In 1581 a £20 per month fee was levied on convicted recusants.[30] As encouragement to prosecution, common informers as well as church wardens were allowed to bring charges of recusancy to authorities, occasionally receiving remuneration for their services. Goods and land were subject to seizure by the crown for failed payments. One ruling, authorized by parliament in 1581, promised the penalty of high treason for anyone claiming the power to absolve subjects from allegiance to the queen or withdraw them from obedience to the state. In 1582, the queen and Privy Council followed this decision with another that declared first by proclamation and later by statute, that all seminarians in the country were *ipso facto* traitors. Under the new law, priests could be executed or banished because they were priests.[31] With this later legislation came the requirement that would eventually secure Clitherow's execution and martyrdom. According to the statute of 1585, not only were priests considered traitors in and of themselves, but the sheltering of them became a felony punishable by death.[32]

Letters from the Privy Council to various members of the York Ecclesial Commission (particularly the Archbishop of York, Edwin Sandys, and Henry Hastings, Earl of Huntingdon) reveal the "local" particularity of anti-Catholic legislation within Clitherow's district – an attention to community standing and a concern over numbers.[33] In 1580, following a reorganization of the commission and a renewed interest in its proceedings from Elizabeth I's court, the Privy Council recommends an upgrading of the status of recusants summoned. In numerous early letters, the council warns that:

as this Defection is principallie begunne by sundrye principall Gentlemen of that Countrie, by whom the meaner sort of People are ledd & seduced; soe it is thought meter that in the execution of the Commission you begin first with the best of the Said Recusants. For that we suppose that the inferior people will thereby the soner be reclaymed or brought to Obedience. (Peck, *Desiderata curiosa*, 3.9.85)

The focus on people of "higher" standing is particularly significant not only in the government's recognition of threat but also in the purely economic or remunerative side to recusant prosecution.[34] Wealthier merchants and tradespeople brought in more money to government and local coffers, while fines levied on indigent and property-less people became an economic burden that the Elizabethan courts were not willing to support.[35]

Still, the notion of what constituted "higher" standing was itself fairly ambiguous. In one of the first lists from the York Commission delivered up to council members, local recusants are cited in order of property and status. For the Holy Trinity, Christ's parish, Margaret Clitherow – "*uxor*, John Clitherow" – is one of the most prominent names.[36] In 1576 Clitherow's husband declared himself to be worth £6 in clear goods.[37]

The comparatively low figure reveals the double bind that the commission was facing in trying to secure arrest.[38] Elected to the office of Chamberlain, John Clitherow was known in York by the more polite address "Mr. Clitherow"; he was, indeed, of "good standing."[39] Yet his income level reveals the conditional nature of most recusant arrests and punishments in York. "Principall Gentlemen" meant people with enough money to pay moderate recusant fines and prison fees, but it apparently did not mean "gentlemen" in quite the way that the council intended.

With stepped-up demands for results and the commission's attempts to oblige the council's requests for "high-status" recusants, local officers were apparently running into some trouble. Not only were recusant families protective of each other and difficult to pin down, but the few arrests that did manage to focus on affluent gentry invariably met with both local and national opposition. Privy Council members themselves begged for leniency or reconsideration for particularly well-placed recusants, reducing the very same ranks they were ostensibly in the process of increasing.[40] Where Henry VIII's government had seemed to focus the bulk of its heresy persecutions on court familiars, by Elizabeth I's reign that role had been reversed.[41] Government scrutiny, when it was to occur at all, occurred at some distance from London and centered on those with the fewest court connections.

One also senses, via the letters to the York Commission, that the *source* of anxiety has also changed – from print to populace. In 1586, laws are less likely to focus on eradicating the threat of written disobedience (publishing, playing, and preaching). Instead, we can find legislative worry over *physical* disobedience, evoked in the direct actions of the queen's subjects.

The Quenes Majestie finding the daily Inconveniences growinge unto the Realme by the Education of great Number of younge Gentlemen & other her subjects in the Partes beyond the sea's . . . with such Instructions as maketh them to mislike the Government of the Realme, & Soe likelie to become undutifull subjects, soe as returninge have manie of them doe, not onlie themselves refuse to yelde obedience unto her majesties Lawes & Proceedings in matters of Religion established by Parlement, but by there evill Example corrupt such others as are well disposed; the contagion whereof beginneth to extend it self soe farre within the Realme, as if some speidie Remedie be not had for the Preventinge of Mischief that maie in Time folowe thereof, it cannot but be daungerous unto her Majestie & her Estate. (Peck, *Desiderata curiosa*, 3.26.99)

Here the emphasis is on the act of intransigence itself. Elizabeth I's "undutifull subjects" refuse to "yelde obedience" and do so not in writing but by "by there evill Example." Where Gardiner's complaint focused on the unlikelihood of effective law in the face of seditious texts

– "and if the [old] agreement in religion . . . be of no force in their judgment, what establishment could any new agreement have?" – council letters to the commission locate the potential threat as directed against the queen's own person, against the body politic itself. "It cannot but be daungerous unto her Majestie & her Estate," this writer insists. The shift in the focus of persecution suggests not simply a geographical relocation from London to York or a quantitative move from private revenge to public restitution, but a literal transformation in the topos of subject articulation. The body supplants the book as the site of transgression. By 1584, then, the council makes little separation between the recusant population at large and the possibility of royal assassination through foreign conspiracy, between "undutifull subjects" and the literal *act* of regicide.[42]

Where Askew's and Bale's ties to Protestantism were involving them in a still-nascent English movement with its powers located in the highest levels of the monarchy, where the written work of Protestant writers and reformers was only beginning to infiltrate universities and alehouses, and where court factionalism and protection of personal interests directed and even legitimated the course of events leading up to Askew's execution and Bale's immediate publication of her work, Clitherow's and Mush's Catholicism found its bases in substantially different and seemingly more diffuse power centers. The 1580s reveal the public expression of an intense nationalism, a Catholic base outside the country and a small but adamantly stubborn, English, Catholic, recusant population. Where Henry VIII's court was divided with both supporters of and antagonists toward the unfamiliar Protestant teachings, Elizabeth I's government was predominantly Anglican and, hence, opposed in "body" to the Catholic position. Where Protestant reform looked to writing and publication to secure religious conversion, Counter-Reformation Catholicism seemed to depend instead upon active priests and focused on the restitution of once-familiar practices and rituals. Priests were far too precariously placed to risk direct confrontation. Instead they sought established Catholic communities, frequently situated in the north, and attempted to influence only the small but, by 1580, strongly religious recusant populations within them.

Cultural blueprints

Where institutional authorities determine the nature and location of religious persecution in Reformation England, situating the punitive and regulatory according to a wide range of economic and geographic markers, the uneven weighting of ideological perspectives from one historical moment to the next is no less directive, no less determining.[43] Because certain features within ideological formulations predominate at different times and in different places, the blueprints that they provide for acceptable personal and group negotiation vary as well, ensuring access to particular types of subject positions and behaviors. At the same time, political action depends on an overlapping of ideological communities and on the wide range of group and personal definitions that subjects inhabit within them. What is legitimate or justifiable in one context may be inappropriate in another. Identifying historically resonant ideological incentives can further situate and particularize what we can say about subject definition, offering us a more descriptive vantage point from which to consider the processes of cultural transformation. In 1586 recusant circles, three sites of intense discursive interest revolve around discussions of the private, the familial, and the performative.[44] In examining all three, I want to address some of the specific pressures at work shaping late-century subject articulation for Catholic believers. I also hope to reveal the way that ideological systems inevitably rely on earlier formations in rewriting them.

The private

Written forty years after Bale's publication of the Askew *Examinations*, Mush's narrative presents an oddly privatized history. Ordinances systematically set in place during Elizabeth I's reign imposed tight regulation on the printing of heterodox or potentially subversive texts. In 1586, the crown issued several decrees restricting the number of legitimate presses in the country, giving Wardens of the Company wider powers, and devising sharper punishments for breaches in the law.[45] Under Elizabethan rule, clandestine presses were discovered and destroyed, and defiant printers, on occasion, both imprisoned and executed for their misconduct.[46] Numerous copies of orders, demanding that customs officers search cargoes and seize Catholic literature, remain.[47] While increased regulation did not stop the flow of subversive texts into England from the continent or extinguish internal printings entirely, fourth-quarter regulations, both promised and carried out, meant that Catholic texts were more difficult to come by than their Protestant counterparts and had to be physically hidden with other illegal Catholic articles – literally kept within the privacy of the home.[48]

Given the additional restrictions and a markedly different focus in audience and circulation, Mush's manuscript edition of Clitherow's life was not printed until the nineteenth century when the Catholic Parker Society published it and a number of other manuscripts in a three-volume work, entitled *The Troubles of Our Catholic Forefathers Related by Themselves*. Prior to this printing, Mary Claridge traces six extant manuscript copies of the "Life," three of them dating from the sixteenth century (*Margaret Clitherow [1556?–1586]*, 182–83). The earliest of these texts seems to have been written between March and December of 1586, immediately following Clitherow's execution; the second, at least a year later. Clearly, English law discouraged any overt attempts to publish Mush's manuscript in England. Writing at the height of the Yorkist persecutions, Mush may have been too preoccupied in avoiding capture to make many forays in that direction himself. Still, it seems to me that the focus and intent of Mush's account suggests an intimate handling of the text, regardless of risk.

Like Bale, Mush promises that his account will edify in its consideration of the oppressed religious in England, but there the similarity stops. Recounting three of the most recent English Catholic martyrdoms, Mush describes the victims – one a priest, one a layman, and one a woman – "whose godly lives and fortitude in the last conflict of death [he] doubt[s] not but some will publish, to the honour of God and His saints, and for the profitable example of other Christians not free as yet from the like terror."[49] Mush continues his account as follows: "And [I] for [my] small portion of ability, being most willing to set forth so good a work, have attempted to manifest the virtuous life and glorious martyrdom of one of them, that is of the woman" ("Life," 365). Mush's professed authorial scope is far narrower than Bale's, just as his small Catholic community of "Christians not free as yet from . . . like terror" is substantially more circumscribed than the Protestants' "international" and multilingual one.[50] Intended, perhaps, as a spur to lukewarm (outwardly conforming) Catholics and as a model for the more solidly recusant religious in and around York, Mush's work also caters to an elite clerical community that he left on his return to England.

Scripting his text in the familiar format of the saint's biography (only now in the English vernacular), Mush's account may not, in fact, be intended for all eyes and ears. With a focus on reinstating divisions between cleric and lay, the idea of a universal or widely circulated text may be inappropriate. Martyr's lives *must be* duly registered in Rome,[51] and they *may be* distributed locally, particularly among other seminary priests in England who can, in turn, recount them to parishioners; but their focus is not on generating texts or converting the unconverted. Rather, the Clitherow hagiography comes to represent a private (church-specific) expression of Mush's successful Catholic interventions in Protestant England.[52] Mush's account of the "Life" lacks Bale's sense of commercial enterprise or the power in volume production. Where Bale sees himself as a part of a writers' community, a select "we" – "Nothynge at all shall it terryfe us," he insists[53] – Mush is far more circumspect in imagining other Catholic biographers beside himself. "I doubt not but some will publish," he explains, tentatively choosing both a negative construction and a central action that suggest uncertainty and qualification.

The ideological parameters of Bale's and Mush's authorial options, bounded by printing requirements and religious obligations, determine the forms of negotiation available to each. As more or less private correspondences, Mush's writings verify the success of his actions in York.[54] Clitherow's potential sanctity, nurtured by a diligent priesthood, illustrates a job well done and legitimates Mush's active defiance of English law in individual and performative terms.[55] Mush's private text is a record of his equally private actions on behalf of the Catholic Church. In contrast, Bale's public assertions seem to derive their authority from the words that he generates on the page, from the act of writing itself. The more readers that Bale is able to rally to his side, the more valid his own status as exiled writer *and* religious resister. The difference in formulation and execution between private action and public text directs the shape of subject construction and political purpose for these men and perhaps for the moment of their speaking as well. With an ideological focus on the righteousness of the private and active servant of God, on an idea of success that is weighed in terms of singular achievements and local responses, Elizabethan Catholic identity possesses a character substantially different from what has preceded it, allowing subjects to conform and resist for personal reasons and particular audiences.

The familial

The ideological primacy of private action that is foregrounded in Mush's sense of the Catholic mission takes rather different shape in its detailing of appropriate behavior for recusant women like Clitherow. Here it becomes largely synonymous with the domestic.[56] I take as a useful reference point John Dod's and Robert Cleaver's *A Godly Form of Household Governement: for the ordering of private Families* (London, 1598). In this tract, Dod and Cleaver analogize house with commonwealth, outlining the various tasks that are required of each participant within the family. Mush's construction of Clitherow as Catholic martyr maintains these same distinctions, depending for its success on her performance as mother, wife, and homemaker. Clitherow's marital status is in fact one of the first pieces of information that Mush offers his readers. "The Martyr's name was Margaret Clitherow, wife of John Clitherow, citizen of York," he writes. "She was . . . a plentiful mother in children and her husband of competent wealth and ability" ("Life," 368). Later Mush further qualifies that identity by insisting on its singularity – on its uniqueness. He tells us that Clitherow was "inferior to none of her neighbours in any honest, comely, womanly, or decent quality, and worthy to be preferred before them in every point wherein the commendation of a good housewife standeth" ("Life," 375). In matters relating to Clitherow's special resolve, the issue that always seems to pull most heavily on her – that aspect in her life that Mush uses to illustrate the terrible double bind that she is forced to endure – is her domesticity.[57]

First, Mush as Catholic hagiographer must insist that Clitherow "is not any whit inferior" to her husband before God, and second, he must simultaneously insist that in secular matters she is the perfect wife. That these are both concepts generally associated with Protestant doctrine and belief is telling. In one passage that Mush recounts, Clitherow addresses the conflict between family obligation and church requirement directly, revealing Mush's articulation of it as a legitimate problem. When warned by a friend to be more cautious in her religious affairs – this shortly after the 1585 statute penalizing aiders and abettors – Clitherow turns to her spiritual Father for advice: " 'may I not . . . receive priests and serve God as I have done, notwithstanding these new laws, without my husband's consent?' " ("Life," 381). The last part of her question is key. May she act *without* her husband's consent?

Mush wants to assure us that Clitherow's decision to continue Catholic service is not the result of disobedience for its own sake. Her spiritual Father validates her right to receive priests. He justifies her actions: "in this, your necessary duty to God, you are not any whit inferior." He even goes so far as to warn her that "it is [her] husband's most safety not to know these things" ("Life," 381). Mush also believes, however, that family and church should not be antagonistic. Clitherow's obedience to religion should "imitate" and parallel the natural "patriarchal" duty she owes to her family, not oppose it. The topos of familial obligation comes up countless times in the text. In some instances Mush simply reiterates its importance, verifying her perfection in this duty as well as in her spiritual exercises, but in others Mush faces the contradiction head on, acknowledging detractors who fault Clitherow in forsaking her family for God. In both sets of articulations, the primacy of the marital union comes to the fore.

Although Mush's is necessarily a Catholic response to the marriage bond (Clitherow and Mush are both practicing Catholics), the relationship between Clitherow and her husband seems to be defined in terms of its newer Protestant underpinnings – underpinnings that posit woman as equal under God and deny the legitimacy of any alternative lifestyle in that construction.[58] Catholic religious practice in 1586, influenced by forty years of almost unbroken coexistence with state-backed Protestant doctrine, reflects more an unintentional blending of both religions than a return to an unadulterated Roman Church. Clitherow may be a potential "Catholic" saint, but she is also and always a good "Protestant" wife.[59] In fact, Mush continually foregrounds Clitherow's exemplary relationship to husband and family. She will not attend Mass until all of her household chores and obligations have been tended to. When her husband hears that her accusers have condemned her, Mush writes, "he fared like a man out of his wits, and wept so vehemently that the blood gushed out of his nose in great quantity, and said, 'Alas, will they kill my wife? Let them take all I have and save her, for she is the best wife in all England, and the best Catholic also'" ("Life," 418). Mush's inclusion of the statement by Clitherow's husband is significant in that it reaffirms the sanctity of both states simultaneously and exonerates Clitherow's chosen martyrdom in secular terms. Her husband does not blame her for her actions. He is willing to admit that she is not only "the best wife" but also "the best Catholic."

Even Clitherow's last act before death is emblematic of her wifely obedience. Mush writes, "her hat before she died she sent to her husband, in sign of her loving duty to him as her head" ("Life," 432). It appears from Mush's account that he is not only revealing the "exquisite" martyrdom of a good *Catholic* wife, but also reminding us that she is indeed a good Catholic *wife* in her obedience to husband. Most probably, Mush is addressing rumors that begin to circulate after the execution – rumors that throw doubt on Clitherow's "wifely" behavior. On several occasions he faces these reports directly, framing the circumstances of their initiation to weaken the case against her. Reminded of her obligations to family during her trial, "the martyr answers, 'I would to God my husband and children might suffer with me for so good a cause.' Upon which words the heretics reported after, that she would have hanged her husband and children if she could" ("Life," 477). Mush's recovery of the actual address here, no doubt a reconstruction itself, neutralizes the potential assault of the subsequent and now "heretical" report about it.

Returning to the same issue later in his account, Mush is even more emphatic. When Clitherow is warned that she dies "desperately" with "no care on her husband and children," she is made to exclaim:

as for my husband, know you that I love him next unto God in this world, and I have care over my children as a mother ought to have, I trust I have done my duty to them to bring them up in the fear of God . . . I confess death is fearful, and the flesh is frail; yet I mind by God's assistance to spend my blood in this faith, as willingly as ever I put my paps to my children's mouths. ("Life," 426–27)

Again Mush has the martyr affirm the parallel between God and husband. In accordance with her Protestant-inspired role as helpmeet to her husband, Clitherow's duty is now in instructing her children in the tenets of God: "I have done my duty to bring them up in the fear of God." That Mush ends her declaration by metaphorically connecting her martyrdom – her willingness "to spend [her] blood" – with her already performed responsibility as nursing mother to her children, reinforces the parallel still more emphatically. In Mush's account, marriage and the role of wife within it are valorized and paralleled with service and obedience to God.

Relying perhaps on Protestant-inspired values already in place, the "Life" creates an ideal Catholic martyr who is also and most significantly the perfect wife to her husband and an exemplary mother to her children. Mush's insistence on Clitherow's continued domesticity illustrates for us the specific discursive criteria that middling-rank, fourth-quarter, female identity must possess in order to be taken seriously in Elizabethan England. It also announces an effective site for subject definition for women during this period, especially recusant women. Indeed, for women in the middling ranks, illicit Catholicism may in fact be one of the most fluid spaces available, precisely because it is intimately connected to the household and to a domestic religious scene.[60] Fourth-quarter English Catholicism opens up possibilities for women within legitimate and already privileged realms. Oddly enough, it is their very obedience to established ideological norms as wives and mothers to outwardly conforming husbands and sons that enables this mobility.

Divided by forty years and antithetical religious platforms, the ideological requirements of church and family obligation shift in both emphasis and location as they move between mid- and late-century experience. Where Askew's gentried Protestantism promised her a nascent form of secular identity that seemed to recognize individual choice and singular meanings, Clitherow's middling-rank Catholicism in turn emphasized the private nature of her experience, lauding her religious qualifications within the isolated domestic domain of the household. This shift in ideological parameters (the narrowing of gendered options) necessarily altered the means by which both subjects – Askew and Clitherow – were able to articulate identity. The primacy of the domestic circle in 1586 necessitates Clitherow's active employment of it as both a means to legitimate her actions and a site of rebellion from its various constraints. Accordingly it is to her performed duties within the home that we ought to look for signs of her saintly confirmation and outright social defiance.

The performative

In Catholicism's privileging of good works over good faith, the body over the word, we can find justification for both Mush's private correspondence and Clitherow's 1580s helpful homemaking. This privileging is perhaps most evident in the Catholic definition of the Mass. In Holy Communion, the bread and wine become the "true body and blood" of Jesus – the literal crucified Christ on the cross. In contrast, according to reformist doctrine, the sacrament, still evoked through the service of bread and wine, recalls its communicants to Christ's death but does not relive it. There is no literal transubstantiation but rather a spiritual recollection of the account as it has been described in the gospels. The bread and wine remain bread and wine. Both become "signs" of Christ's actions, not the actions themselves.

The emphasis on material act within the Catholic Mass has repercussions in its services and throughout its literature. From the church's innumerable rituals (its censings, vestments, and statuary) to its rhetorical emphasis on graphic representations of "living" acts (its promotion of good works and specified saints' days), the notion of a lived materiality is privileged.[61] Reformist doctrine, in turn, foregrounds the scriptures – the word of God, not the site and performance of its worship. Obviously, Henry VIII's lucrative closing of religious houses and selling-off of church plate and cloth fed conveniently into this second form of religious discourse. The scarcity of church paraphernalia became simply another valorization of text over act, spirit over matter.[62]

Responding to her accusers, Clitherow articulates the Catholic position explicitly. When asked, "'what is the Church?'" the martyr supposedly replies, "'It is *that wherein* the true word of God *is preached*, which Christ left to his Apostles, and to their successors ministering the Seven Sacraments, which the same Church hath always observed, the Doctors preached, and the martyrs and confessors witnessed.'"[63] In this account, Mush is quick to separate the word of God from the literal Church "wherein . . . [it] is preached" – the written scripture from the material building that houses it. Within the Catholic Church the sacraments are actively "ministered," the doctors physically "preach," and the martyrs and confessors materially "witness." Given this definition of the legitimate church, it is no wonder that Mush's account is far more explicit in the descriptions it gives us of particular events and interactions, even those which locate Clitherow in prison or on trial (descriptions that Mush must fabricate given what he has heard about Clitherow's proceedings). Mush is far more likely to "set the scene" or draw a saintly picture than is Bale.

In one episode, Mush describes the martyr's final night in prison prior to her execution:

At twelve of the clock [another prisoner] . . . saw the martyr rise from her knees, and put off all her apparel, putting on a linen habit like to an alb, which she made with her own hands three days before to suffer martyrdom in. Then she kneeled down again, without anything upon her saving that linen cloth, from twelve of the clock until three, at which time she arose and came to the fireside. There she laid her down flat upon the stones one quarter of an hour. ("Life," 429)

Here the martyr's physical movements and actions have become valorized in and of themselves. Even the sewing of her linen habit, or Mush's mention of it, reveals an awareness of the spectacle of her death and the importance of its physical, material presentation. There is no quoting of scripture here, no elucidation. Clitherow, in fact, performs in mime. Her prayers are silent.

As Catholic martyr, Clitherow need not explain her relation to God as much as live it. It is not so much what she says as how she acts. Mush writes:

I also will ever witness the same, how carefully she cast her charitable eye into every corner, where Thy secret servants lay desolate and afflicted, to get them fed with Thy heavenly food in due season, lest, for want of Thy banquet, they might happen to fall from Thee. How also she hath looked to their bodily needs, and procured to every one relief with discretion. ("Life," 384)

Tending "bodily needs" – feeding and clothing her religious charges – Mush's created martyr, Margaret Clitherow, fulfills her duties in performance as Catholic homemaker. The emphasis on intimate bodily acts legitimates, perhaps mandates, the active domesticity of Clitherow's life, insisting that she physically reveal God through *household* Catholic works. It provides a middling-rank woman, with no formal education, a forum for religious authority where none might otherwise be possible.

While Askew displays an informed knowledge of scriptural doctrine in her answers to the court's questions, Clitherow's spoken responses are apparently unimportant. Instead, she is tested in performance. Mush recounts one enigmatic episode where the charges against Clitherow are never aired: "[her spiritual] Father being desirous to make some especial proof of her charity to God . . . moved talk again with her as concerning the same matter . . . feigning himself to have more advisedly considered of it . . . [he] told her that she had offended God in the first doing of it, and should daily sin if she continued to do the same" ("Life," 380). In Mush's presentation of this incident, the "matter" under consideration is never identified – we are never told what the conversation was about. In and of itself, it is not important, nor is the "feigned" offense. What is significant apparently is Clitherow's *demeanor* in responding – the physical performance of her obedience and humility. Her actions constitute the proof that Mush requires to convince his audience of her potential sanctity. Mush explains that upon hearing such "speeches she fetched a deep sigh and said nothing" ("Life," 380). Asked directly what she would do, she finally replies, "rather than I offend God herein any more, I will sustain any temporal rebuke or reproach. Therefore, if you speak the word, I am ready to obey it."[64] Clitherow's "sigh" materially legitimates her sanctity as does her response of active, not spoken, obedience.

Mush's Clitherow is humble, soft-spoken, and obedient. Acknowledging Clitherow's "sincerity and lowliness of spirit," Mush points out that "when she had been reproved of anything, she would mildly have answered to have satisfied them; and if it would not serve, then, without all contention, [she would] keep silence, and return to the comfort of her inward mind and conscience" ("Life," 374, 375). It is that active voicelessness that plays itself out in the events of the Clitherow trial. According to Mush, Clitherow "mildly" refuses to be tried for her offense; she "gently" refuses to acknowledge a trial before any eyes other than God's own and so takes up the platform of silence in her defense. Exonerating her "tender" refusal to speak to Elizabethan authorities, Mush insists that she was fearful of putting friends or relatives in jeopardy of their souls for having to testify against her. Other sources promise that her refusal to plead kept other priests and recusants from being incriminated, and in a much more material sense, kept her husband from forfeiting any of his father-in-law's gifts of property.[65] Ironically, Clitherow's reticence to speak before her accusers illustrates a topos of ideal female behavior during Elizabeth I's middle years. "If it would not serve, then, without all contention, [she would] keep silence," Mush explains.

Mush necessarily faces more obstacles in recounting the events of Clitherow's martyrdom than did Bale with his martyr's history. For one thing, Mush's more precarious casting of the model woman as "obedience personified" is in striking contrast to the more aggressive resolve she must possess as a sentenced martyr awaiting her death for failure to conform. Clitherow's confrontations with her accusers must therefore trace a delicate line between conviction and humility, between resolute performance and quiet docility. Mush accommodates the split somewhat awkwardly, presenting opposing sentiments simultaneously in sometimes jarring discontinuity. Recalling the particulars of an arraignment that he would have been unable to attend, Mush writes "then Judge Clinch stood up, and said: 'Margaret Clitherow, how say you? [are you] guilty of this indictment or no?' . . . [Margaret Clitherow] said mildly with a bold and smiling countenance: 'I know no offense whereof I should confess myself guilty'" ("Life," 413). "Mild" speech and "bold" countenance are the closest Mush seems to come to resolving the iconographic paradox inherent within the "Life."[66]

Mush's framing suggests both the tightening of patriarchal reins that was to occur in England throughout the Reformation and Counter-Reformation and the refiguring of female subjecthood that was its end result. Through a proliferation in governmental policies and practices on religious and domestic prerogative and an expanding sense of what and who may determine those policies (numerous informal agencies join the state in negotiating an increasing number of potential oppositions), Clitherow as an Elizabethan subject faces a relationship to self and state markedly different from that of her Henrician predecessor, Askew. That relationship calls for different strategies and alternative forays at gender- and state-definition. Accordingly, what constitutes appropriate "woman-hood" becomes more fully legislated and more carefully practiced in 1580s recusant circles; it becomes more fully defined, but so too the proliferation in sites of definition provides additional avenues for justi-fication and defiance.

In the "Life," Mush employs an ideological privileging of the flesh to foreground Clitherow's status as religious icon. He calls on the Catholic primacy of performance to resituate the mundanity of Clitherow's middling-rank religious practices as potentially sanctifying. As a do-mestic illustration of "good household works," she becomes a site from which Mush can, as he might with any other Catholic "relic," enlist prayer or demand inspiration. And it is to her active silence rather than her knowledgeable words that we perhaps ought to look to situate her limited control over identity and gender definition. In performance, Clitherow can exaggerate the legitimate and unlettered realms of mid-dling-rank household chores to define and defy her adversaries.

Mush's and Clitherow's Catholic foregrounding of good works ought not to diminish for us the increasing authority of the written word to shape popular opinion and direct public policy in the sixteenth century. By its very nature – its insistence on educational expertise – that word was gender-coded. It addressed particular historical concerns – concerns that refocused the responsibility of political government away from outward shows of force, toward increasing documentation, contractual law, and written evidence. That it was not as easily accessible to women, however, offers us an intriguing polarization in identity transformation during this period. It is women who most frequently embrace different ideological standards in shaping their lives. Not simply one half of a shared and gender-neutral articulation, women often initiate illicit or marginal definition precisely because theirs is the more compromised status, depending for its legitimacy on the situational standing of a gendered identity in other than gendered terms.

Rewriting the story

"The Life of Margaret Clitherow" offers evidence of Mush's narrative perspective, not Clitherow's. The woman who died in 1586 left no textual evidence or written documentation behind. The sum total of our information about her is available through Mush and through scattered mention of her in other contemporaneous discussions. But the bias of the printed record ought not to deny access altogether. There is too much at stake historically to disregard the suppressed voices of early modern women and too little remaining narrative to depend absolutely on these voices for recovery work. If we were to refuse the compromised narratives, the stories that have been filtered through masculinist history, we would, I think, do serious injustice to what is, even after a generation or so of careful scholarship, a fledgeling historiography.[67] We would lose stories like Clitherow's simply because women did not sit in judgment, write policy, or hold religious office in late sixteenth-century England. If we were to abandon Clitherow's confrontations with English authorities because she does not speak them for herself, we would forgo as well those narratives that attend to the intersection between a woman's construction of a self and the state policies and procedures that attempt to deny her that scope.

Even if there were an adequate number of extant female voices, they would never provide a complete picture;[68] they would never in isolation show us the totality of women's lives because women have never lived their lives in isolation. Their identities have always been circumscribed, by policies, by practices, many of them authored by men. Looking at Margaret Clitherow through the eyes of her confessor can remind us of the pressures that Clitherow faced in negotiating female identity. It can remind us of all of the shapings that took place beyond the level of awareness, beyond the strategic or cognitive. It can also remind us that men, in varying positions of power and authority, can and did determine both Clitherow's "Life" and Clitherow's death.

Recreating a voice where voice has been erased is a risky endeavor. For all intents and purposes, I can only speculate – imaginatively construct a discourse to account for Clitherow's absent voice. While that act is itself highly suspect (more reflective of the reconstructor than the reconstructed), I do think that there is a need for such undertakings. Stephanie Jed offers one of the more persuasive examples of such imaginative rewritings in her article, "The Tenth Muse: Gender, Rationality and the Marketing of Knowledge." Jed provides us with a fabricated, late seventeenth-century, "natural" history from the "New World" that delineates the supposed qualities one might find in a "Tenth Muse." In what is clearly a constructed narrative, Jed's hypothetical author calls to our attention two particular examples of "Tenth Musedom": Anne Bradstreet and Sor Juana Inés de la Cruz. Jed's manipulation of the historical record in the creation of this fictive account reveals, in a way not previously available, the connections between colonial economies, constructions of knowledge, and the cultural brokering of women poets like Bradstreet and Sor Juana. Indeed it is largely through her imaginative recreation of events and perspectives that such discussions are able to take place at all.

Jed also shows us that fictive intervention need not occur in a vacuum. There are ways that we can situate created moments, ways we can contextualize and qualify in order to minimize the dangers. Paying attention to the issues and incentives that directed Clitherow's engagements by juxtaposing them with those of other similarly vested and criminally prosecuted women can provide one such context. Written accounts like Askew's can serve as historical frames for analysis; they can offer models through which we can consider similar negotiations and posit shared desires.[69] Parallels do exist between the events and issues that Askew and Clitherow address – parallels in the ways that both encounter authority and respond to shifting social requirements and obligations, and parallels in the ways that each refuses to give in. While we must assume those correlatives advisedly, with an ever-present awareness of our own stakes in making connections and of the inevitable compromises that are their necessary result, we must continue making them.

Separated by forty years, the *Examinations* and the "Life," nevertheless, mirror one another in their claims to a spiritual truth. The breaking down of religious hegemonies and the uncertain swings between ascendant and descendant authorities insist upon that similarity despite insurmountable difference. The shared freedoms/constraints imposed on each taboo religious position via the state, in turn, allow these women to navigate subject positions in like ways. The flexibility that Askew found in biblical exegesis, inserting her self, albeit marginally, into a discursive debate that remained open as long as there were separate religious platforms available, must have had echoes in Clitherow's recusant articulations as well. Where Askew sought access through the written word, however, Clitherow looked to avenues more accommodating to middling-rank recusant women. In 1546 and 1586 the conflation of Catholic and Protestant religious articulation allowed both women to articulate positions which embraced neither extreme – positions that destabilized and restabilized the roles of mother, wife, and religious subject, that shifted again the configuration of legitimate subject identity for English women.

Given those fissures and their consequences for marginalized religious focus, I want to consider Clitherow, like Askew, as in some sense functionally resistant – an active historical agent in the disruption as well as the production of institutionally sanctioned authority. As a result of a combination of alternatives and a multitude of potential choices among them, Clitherow is successful in constructing an "identity" for herself which "resists" and "re-creates" gender expectations and the institutionally mandated, religious subjectivity allotted her.[70] Where Askew's *rhetorical* positionings offered a variety of articulations, enabling her to write a legitimate personal history, defend a construction of self as celebrated martyr, and negotiate an acceptable position outside marriage and despite the restrictions imposed on her as a woman, Clitherow's *performed* negotiations among the various forbidden rituals and sacraments of a now-taboo Catholicism may prove no less flexible, no less empowering.[71] Askew's written responses evinced a recognition of and a resistance to the more confining structures of religion and gender – a realization that the ambiguity of her multiple status might somehow resolve or neutralize limitations imposed on her in other ways. So too, it seems to me that Clitherow's performed responses might prove equally validating.

In Mush's account, Clitherow's negotiation is always unidirectional. Acknowledging and promoting her obligations as woman, wife, and mother, Mush nevertheless insists that her final allegiances are to God. This need not, however, have been absolutely the case. Where Mush has Clitherow promise on her conversion to Catholicism that "[she was] fully resolv[ed] rather to forsake husband, life, and all, than to return again to her damnable state" ("Life," 369), her actions in this regard could certainly have been more ambivalently motivated. Mush's assertion –

that Clitherow will forsake husband for religion – has direct implications for her in terms of marital dissatisfaction and potential freedom from its narrowed strictures.

As I explained earlier, Mush's articulation of this either/or scenario on issues of family is unstable; it is, in and of itself, far more anxious than Bale's. The announced obligations and requirements of the married state have intensified in the years prior to Clitherow's martyrdom. Given that greater intensity, the institution of marriage becomes in Mush's account an especially charged site of persecution and social mobility for Elizabethan women,[72] a site where adherence to competing demands from a now marginalized church might prove particularly advantageous. Clitherow's question: "may I not . . . receive priests and serve God . . . without my husband's consent?" reveals the results of that slippage ("Life," 381). In the "Life," Clitherow is informed by her confessor that "it is [to her] husband's most safety not to know these things" ("Life," 381). The legitimating of a set of behaviors separate from and unknown to her spouse changes the dynamics of Clitherow's married existence, even if it does not upend it entirely. It is perhaps to her husband's "most safety not to know these things," but it is certainly to Clitherow's advantage as well, in the additional freedoms that such secrets promise. Mush writes of Clitherow's response to the priest's command, directing the celebratory nature of her reaction onto things Catholic. Hearing the priest's answer, "she, stricken with great joy, said: 'I thank you, Father. By God's grace all priests shall be more welcome to me than ever they were'" ("Life," 382). In Mush's account, Clitherow, *obediently* embracing the priest's directives, is "stricken with great joy" at their prospect; not simply perhaps because they allow her access to Catholic worship, but also because they promise her greater mobility within her marriage in justifying her right to keep secrets from her husband.

Clitherow's dependence on the church to justify negotiation within the family is fitting, given the ideological emphases that she might be facing in 1586. As a middling-rank woman defined primarily in terms of her husband's status within the community and her own within his house, Clitherow can frame her actions in accordance with the contradictory requirements of the Catholic Church. Where Askew turned away from church to seek personal definition through the secular – "I have never been so sure of myself than at this moment," she insisted – Clitherow, confined, perhaps, to a by now institutionalized and privatized secularity, as wife, mother, and homemaker, relies, in this instance, on the spiritual to "resist."

Foregrounding obedience to (oppositional) religious requirements, Mush's account reveals a legitimate means to avoid gender constraints, but the opposite might just as well be true. The actualities of Clitherow's trial and execution seem to bear this out, even if only temporarily. Before Clitherow is to be executed, she gives her accusers cause to reconsider. They discover the possibility of her pregnancy. In 1586, English law requires a staying of the sentence until after delivery.[73] As a potentially pregnant woman, Clitherow may be temporarily absolved from penalties relating to her religion. Like Askew, she can turn to a second definition of self – a second subject position – to avoid persecution in the first. Like Askew, she can abandon religious requirement to embrace a definition of self that is reliant on other factors, this time on biology. Here Clitherow's *physical* status as fertile woman allows for the possibility of additional considerations outside the confines of spiritual insubordination. Clitherow's obligation to carry children to term briefly overrides her responsibility to either church or state. In this case, however, the conviction is not stayed. Unwilling to substantiate her pregnancy – to promise it concretely – Clitherow gives up her prerogative as female subject.

While there is physical evidence of a reversal of negotiations between sexual status and religious affiliation in something as materially manifest as a pregnancy, the cross-over need not be so final or so bodily implicated. In a hypothetical inversion of Clitherow's earlier question regarding her husband and her obligations to the church, gender requirements may win out as well.[74] As it stands, Clitherow's query, "may I not receive priests . . . without my husband's consent?" is presented in Mush's account as a rhetorical question. It is an already-done, an already-assumed: "may I not" do what I already intend to do? What if Clitherow's question were reversed, however? What if she were to ask instead, "Must I receive priests if my husband disallows me to do so?" Refusal to accommodate an unpleasant or impoverished priest, failure to abide by Catholic obligations which may jeopardize her position within the recusant community, each of these denials can as easily be deflected with a protestation of a second set of competing requirements – requirements that depend upon Clitherow's status as woman and as wife.

Where Askew's interpretive freedom is the direct result of her ability to read texts as she chooses, Clitherow's may, in fact, come from the various ways that her behavior may be construed. Choosing to leave the impact of her various actions multivalent, without final explanation, Clitherow could, hypothetically, legitimate her mobility within them. Prior to her execution, Clitherow spent several periods of time in prison separated from her family and from the responsibilities attendant to her role therein.[75] According to Mush, those prison experiences are some of her happiest: in prison she is freed from the usual requirements of her station and is able to devote her energies to the Lord without interruption. Obviously Mush's account puts forward a polemic "reading" of prison life and of Clitherow's response to it. His need to make her fit into the saintly mold insists that, like Bale, he keep interpretive variation to a minimum. Her prison experiences mean one thing and one thing only. When Mush writes that "[Clitherow] accounted [the prison] a most happy and profitable school, where the servants of God (as delivered from all worldly cares and business) might learn most commodiously every Christian virtue" ("Life," 370), his assertion undoubtedly presents Clitherow as a model of Catholic prison behavior and attitude.

The requirements of prison life for those who could pay to keep a servant and be maintained comfortably, however, may have offered additional satisfactions for a woman of Clitherow's standing. Although prison life was undoubtedly restrictive and the conditions within it frequently appalling (many recusants and priests died in gaol before trial), it may have had its advantages as well. Mush tells us of one of Clitherow's lamentations about prison and her desire to return to it: "Would to God, if I might stand with the duty to my husband and my house, that I were in prison again, where I might (being delivered from the disquietness and cares of the world) attend wholly to the service of my God . . . I fear God saw something in me for which I was unworthy to continue among them" ("Life," 371). Again the potentiality of multiple requirements in Mush's presentation suggests the possibility of transferal and active choice. In prison, Clitherow is "delivered" from a "duty . . . to husband and . . . house." According to Mush, she even speculates on her unworthiness for so privileged a position.

Mush's text reads Clitherow's responses as inspired by her Catholic faith and her willingness to serve God, but her prison term itself may offer escape from a strident emphasis on family obligation. In addition it may promise Clitherow new standing within a "community" of the religious – standing that is not contingent on her father, her husband, or her abilities to keep a clean house. As a recusant woman, resisting English Church and English laws, Clitherow justifies her behavior by calling on Catholic obligation, but in doing so she conceivably earns the recognition of her peers and avoids restrictions that confine her authority to the family. Prison offers her additional access as well. Mush tells us that it is there that Clitherow learns "to read English and written hand" ("Life," 375), an exercise we may assume unnecessary for a butcher's wife. In prison, Clitherow is offered an empowering experience – learning to read – that is unavailable to her outside its confines.[76]

At another point in the text Mush directs our attention to Clitherow's "pilgrimages" – to journeys she takes outside the confines of household to visit holy places or to meditate on the Lord's gifts to her. Mush initially tells us, "after the priests had first suffered martyrdom at Knavesmire . . . and by their holy blood and death had sanctified the reproachful gallows, she greatly desired often to visit that place, for she called it her pilgrimage."[77] Labeled "pilgrimages," Clitherow's journeys fall under legitimate Catholic observance. They are, in and of themselves, a sign of her religious fervor, an example of obedient and praiseworthy "extra effort." They also, however, promise movement beyond the confines of the house, outside the domestic restrictions of "family."

Clitherow's pilgrimages take her "half a mile from the city . . . accompanied with two or three virtuous women" ("Life," 395). Mush writes, "this being the common place for execution for all sorts of malefactors, distant half a mile from the city of York, [it] made the passage sometimes more difficult to her, because she might not adventure thither but by night because of spies, and only at such time as her husband was from home" ("Life," 395). Under cover of night, without her husband's consent, and accompanied by women friends, Clitherow legitimates, through Catholic belief, her expeditions and the literal mobility they offer her; like Askew, she justifies her articulation and extends it to include satisfactions that are outside the religious parameters that enable her to resist in the first place. Not surprisingly, in this instance, the English reformed church that she is rejecting aligns itself with traditional gender restrictions. Clitherow must travel at night "because of spies" – because of people who will reveal her as both illegal Catholic worshipper and as "masterless" wife.

In Mush's account, the descriptions of Clitherow's travels are laden with references to her desire in these actions, to her satisfaction in being allowed them. At one point Mush writes nervously of the over-extension of such desire. Clitherow "wants" too much and accordingly is restricted in her journeys by Catholic as well as Protestant demand. Mush justifies the prohibition with a disclaimer, but his reticence to permit her travels also alludes to a recuperation of her actions to the religious obligations they are *supposed* to be fulfilling. He writes, "by reason of this wicked time, her ghostly Father thought [it] not good to permit her so often to go as she desired" ("Life," 395). Reminding us of Clitherow's spiritual obedience to the will of her confessors and the hierarchy of church that that office represents, Mush graphically monitors her free access to these journeyings, denying, perhaps, the additional satisfactions that may be served in fulfilling her obligations to Catholicism. In this univocal reading of her situation, Mush parallels Bale's own interpretive hierarchy, silencing his martyr as effectively as did his counterpart.

The secrecy of Clitherow's travels adds to their appeal, by allowing transgressive, yet personally justified, behavior. She can break rules –

defy restrictions – in following orders. Given the legitimacy of such hypothetical agency, what might prompt Clitherow's potentially subversive (negotiable) desires to assert themselves most markedly in moments of contradiction? What is it about the prohibitive that invites attempted negotiation and agency? Obviously, Clitherow is offered remuneration in the tangible sense that I've already described. Despite the risk involved in her forays, she is allowed additional scope (freedom to travel without her husband, freedom to converse with other men within the confines of her husband's household, etc.), but, given the acknowledged benefits, why are the moments of extension so risky?

In 1586, Clitherow's articulation of self is, I think, directly linked to the unavailability of the object, to the restrictions imposed upon it, and to the risks it generates. In 1586, the element that prohibitive behavior foregrounds most dramatically is the primacy of the singular subject – a notion of identity as unique, peculiar to individuals. Clitherow desires access to travel *because* it is denied. Her desire satisfies what is by now an ideologically sanctioned construction of self as individual and privatized – a construction that realizes its identity only in separation and contradiction from "others." (In this case "other" represents all of the women of Clitherow's social rank and background who, as obedient wives and conforming Christians, are denied such scope.) Mush frames Clitherow's life as singular and unique. Apparently there were a surprising number of recusant butchers' wives in York who shared with Clitherow in defending Catholic ritual and maintaining the sacraments in their families, women Clitherow would have known and worshipped with on a daily basis.[78] Yet given Mush's sense of private space, in terms of both audience and domesticity, Clitherow is never considered within this active religious community. She becomes a singular, isolated example, a paragon of private worship.[79]

Accordingly, Mush develops the notion of Clitherow's pilgrimages in terms of the "private" – in terms of her "singular" relationship with her confessor. Translating his earlier accounts of her visits to the gallows to encompass all excursions that defy her marital obligations, Mush explains,

when she was invited with her neighbours to some marriage or banquet in the country, she would devise twenty means to serve God that day more than any other at home; for she would take horse with the rest, and after she had ridden a mile out of the city, one should be there ready provided to go in her stead, and all that day she would remain in some place nigh hard, where she might quietly serve God, and learn of her ghostly Father some part of her Christian duty as her heart most desired, and at night return home again with the rest as though she had been feasting all the day long. ("Life," 397)

Again we can construct a hypothetical scenario that offers Clitherow interpretive variability in her actions. Arranging an elaborate cover to account for her absence, Clitherow negotiates between both Catholic and Protestant constructions of her disappearance, both religious and gendered considerations of her behavior. Her desire to avoid the banquet ("she would devise twenty means" to miss it), and her strategies in accomplishing her will ("one should be there ready . . . to go in her stead"), not only release her from social obligation, but promise her undisturbed time alone with her ghostly father. Free of husband's eye and, we may assume, free as well from other Catholic penitents who could interrupt that time with other needs and obligations, Clitherow's "private" communions with her confessor *outside* the restrictions of formalized church or family setting promise her additional space.

Clitherow's secret seclusion need not be solely the result of either penitential devotion, as her Catholic hagiographer would have it, or, for that matter, a taboo sexual desire as her inquisitors would like us to believe in her trial proceedings.[80] It may instead offer her an opportunity to be listened to and indulged in, in an environment that rarely allows either to its middling-rank women. It may offer her "speech" in a culture that privileges female "silence."[81] Legitimating the intimacies of her life, validating the reality of arguments with neighbors and responses to husband and children, Clitherow's "private" conversations with the Catholic priests that she harbors offer her the benefit of traditional Catholic confession with fewer restrictions as to its results.

Within the amended forum of her undisturbed sessions with her spiritual advisor, Clitherow is, in fact, more empowered than a traditionally constituted Catholic communicant might be. Her confessor, despite the written authority that Mush creates for him, is, in his more perilous position as *ipso facto* traitor, dependent on his penitents and their good will. He requires their support in terms of food and shelter, as well as their active and vigorous protection to avoid discovery. Thrown into a position where the bulk of his daily encounters are with women like Clitherow – women who can "privately" conduct the Catholic Mass with less financial risk than their "publicly" conforming husbands – Mush must rely on and cater to his charges as well as direct them.

Thus, it comes as no surprise that Clitherow may find additional leverage even within her confessional relations with her spiritual Father, both at home and abroad. These negotiations, in fact, satisfy to such a degree that in another account she "procure[s] some neighbours to feign the travail of some woman, that she might under that colour have access and abide with her ghostly Father the longer" ("Life," 397). Here the connection between gender and religion is even more pronounced.

Clitherow's communications with her spiritual adviser take the place of her responsibility at childbed, while her obligation as midwife allows legitimate movement "outside" the confines of the house, within the community.

Not only do Clitherow's interpretive acts offer her free space as unrestrained pilgrim, but they also offer her leeway as religious penitent who is authorized to converse with her spiritual Father. Given the divisive conditions of Catholic obedience in 1586, even Clitherow's most stridently *Catholic* behaviors are open to additional negotiation and response. When Mush writes, "how joyful I have seen her when she had two or three Fathers at once. How would she laugh for inward joy to have God served in her house divers times in one day . . . [thinking] how she deceived the heretics" ("Life," 389), his narrative may funnel into a Catholic polemic that seeks to present its case convincingly, but it may also foreground Clitherow's additional desires and their fulfillment. "Deceiving the heretics" – successfully performing outside their ken – points again to the importance of secrecy and risk in generating Clitherow's agency in the first place. Withholding information from husband, neighbors, and authorities, Clitherow can define herself as "self" and construct a fictive subjectivity that is momentarily separate.

The ideological primacy of voicelessness in 1586, of decorous silence for women, has interesting implications when juxtaposed to other contradictory requirements within late Elizabethan culture. Clitherow's secrecy – her refusal to volunteer information that may jeopardize her physical mobility – justifies itself through silence; the less said, the better kept the secret. Indeed, Clitherow's silence outside the confessional extends her freedoms within it, by ensuring that that Catholic activity remains unspoken but never unperformed. Given the deference expected of wives, mothers, and daughters within the home, Clitherow's extension of that requirement into another arena, the civil courts – literalized in her public refusal to be tried – suggests additional possibilities and complications.[82]

In Mush's account, Clitherow's accusers, aware of the potential public uproar that a refusal to plead will bring, want her obedience, not her silence. "Yesternight we passed you over without judgment, which we might have then pronounced against you if we would: we did it not, hoping you would be something more conformable and put yourself to the country for otherwise you must needs have the law" ("Life," 415). During the course of her trial, Clitherow is asked thirteen times to reconsider her decision. In several of these instances, her accusers promise that she cannot be found guilty on the slender evidence of one child.[83] At one point, "the judge, yet desirous to shift the thorn out of his own conscience into the whole country, and falsely thinking that if the jury found her guilty his hand should be clear from her blood, said again, 'Good woman, I pray you put yourself to the country'" ("Life," 416).

In recounting the judge's plea, Mush situates responsibility for the execution "privately," within individual conscience. The judge is, according to Mush, "desirous to shift the thorn out of his own conscience into the whole country," something Mush clearly rejects as impossible. In addition, although Mush insists that Clitherow will be found guilty regardless of any promises to the contrary, his account reveals a rather more anxious and uncertain court response to Clitherow's stubborn refusals: "all the people about her condemned her of great obstinacy and folly, that she would not yield; and on every hand persuaded her to refer her trial to the country, which could not find her guilty . . . upon such slender evidence" ("Life," 416). Whether or not Clitherow's options are as obvious as Mush seems to assume, her refusal to speak openly no doubt disrupted the court and antagonized her opponents. In a gendered public display of the female requirement to be silent, Clitherow found a forum for disagreement that had both backers and sympathizers, a forum that could redirect the court's responsibility for her punishment onto individual conscience and private guilt.

While neither Clitherow nor her supporters were finally able or willing to deflect the legal repercussions of her defiance (her martyrdom, no doubt, was advantageous to the Catholic cause), the actions leading up to and including that defiance were not without effect or audience. They may have had a direct impact on the way that other married women of Clitherow's status and belief took up religious positions. In recorded form, they may have broadened the spectrum of authority that middling-rank Catholic mothers were able to claim in questions of conscience, childhood education, the spiritual regulation of servants, and the presentation of the Mass. They may even have played a key role in the domestic shaping of Counter-Reformation English Catholicism. Indeed, the family-centered, seigneurial form of Catholic worship (literally "ecclesiae domesticae")[84] that was to predominate in the early seventeenth century, while it was generated by a wide range of political, religious, and economic factors including the nature of Catholic persecution, the scope of governmental surveillance, and the status of priests as missionaries, may have derived as well from a gender-specific elaboration of the spiritual as domestic and the domestic as spiritual, and both as well-kept household secrets. Yes, the hagiographical account of Margaret Clitherow as perfect Catholic Elizabethan wife and mother no doubt served the English mission well from the standpoint of inscribed saintly deeds and appropriate spiritual conduct, but the avenues of cultural and religious transformation affected by those maneuvers and that text were in all likelihood far broader-ranging.

The Louvain psalter

Documenting history inevitably produces fictions – a certainty I am likely to forget moments after I have acknowledged my limited access, the tenuousness of my connections, the inherent narrativity of any frame that I impose on my material. Announcing accepted markers of evidence and proof, of historical fact – letters, wills, statutes, and court records – I proceed undaunted and unfazed. Take, for instance, this chapter. The possibilities and positions suggested within Mush's "Life of Margaret Clitherow," limited as they are by the framings that he has chosen, do provide space for discussion, discussion solidly and absolutely bounded by this moment and its theoretical concerns and preconditions, by my desire to locate and describe history in terms of agency and choice. That I am politically unwilling to forgo such figurings ought to go without saying, but then how to authorize, how then to document and render more "factual" my material speculations? In answer I return once again to the fiction of fact and the fact of fiction, and the story-telling – my story-telling – continues . . .

In 1586 Clitherow, butcher's wife, would-be saint, dutiful Elizabethan mother, was criminally prosecuted for her failure to speak. Her Counter-Reformation Catholicism did nothing to protect her from legal retribution. If anything, the English mission encouraged such martyrdoms. Pressed to death for her failure to respond to civil authorities, Clitherow faced a particularly gruesome and protracted end. According to the account provided by Mush, the whole ordeal took an unconscionable six hours to perform ("Life," 432). We are told that Clitherow was survived by at least three children – three children who in all likelihood experienced her trial and punishment in the most intimate and palpable of terms. Two of them ended their lives outside England on the continent in Catholic religious communities, despite legal prohibitions to the contrary.[85] One, Clitherow's eldest child Henry, had been sent to France prior to his mother's death. He entered the Capuchin Order in 1592, eventually transferring to the Dominicans.[86] Another, Clitherow's daughter Anne, entered St. Ursula's at Louvain in Brabant and professed as an Augustinian Canoness Regular of the Lateran in 1598. There she spent the rest of her days experiencing, in all of its not so glorious reality, the kind of religious life of which her mother had apparently dreamed. History and coincidence have a way of coming together. Imagine . . . in 1995, while doing research on English women's conventual lives at

St. Augustine's Priory at Newton Abott, in Devon, I was fortunate enough to come upon traces of Clitherow's life.[87] Looking through a collection of prayer books from St. Ursula's that had been relocated to the library of the convent, I discovered what at first appeared to be a fairly nondescript early seventeenth-century Psalter.[88] The last portion of the book had sustained moderate water damage and was sealed shut. I was able, after some careful prodding, to separate several of its pages. There, folded neatly between the last two leaves of the book, was a letter. This letter, apparently written from prison two years prior to Clitherow's execution, seemed to be in her own hand.

Bearing a late sixteenth-century watermark (a vase), the paper on which the letter has been written is of moderate quality and weight. It is in surprisingly good condition despite some tearing along fold lines. Water damage has made several words within the text difficult to read. These have been indicated in brackets. The lettering in this text is irregular and uneven, suggesting either an inexperienced or a hurried writer. In addition, aside from errors of spelling even by sixteenth-century standards, grammatical and syntax irregularities point to a writer with limited educational training or resources. While I have left the text of the original intact, I have, for the sake of clarity, introduced additional punctuation. This letter reads as follows:

12 March 1584

My derest doghtyr Ann,

Have M. holpe yew wyth thys yf ye have troubyll.

Yr mothyr rose at fyrst lyte last mournyng aftyr a nyght yn full darknysse wyth no moone an no fewl and no thynge to shew us lyte save the mercye of the Lorde God. Yn hys wysdome he toke Abell Cardyng aftre supper of the sycness. Abel wast not ryte of hys hede. Blynde to alle, he called nat for God but begge us to restore hym. I noe not wat to thynke but sat besyde hym throwe oute. Fathyr Rawlyns found me thus at brek of day holdynge my rosarye to hys colde lyppes. May the Lorde have mercy on hys sole. I noe thys mysfortune that I am yn maks a gret warch to ye.[89] I praye that thy worldlye burdyn I hath lefte ys nat to gret, for yt ys on yr favoure an thy favour of the Lord that I must relye. Geve leve to tell freelye what hath bene done in my housholde whylst I yam here. Have yew byn watchfull of Jayne? I worrye she wyl [neglyk the broode] untyl middedaye and lose thyr producyon. Wat worldlye prys hath myne mysfortun brogt yew to? Thy bedde cloathes that wast broght ys fyne. Those I had got was quyte soyled as thys place ys thrung with smoak an sycnesse.[90] The olde now lye a toppe those yer synt [to brayke the colde] as agyn thys fortnyght yor father sent nat enogh to pay for fewl. I care nat for myselfe, [but Thomas Palmers wyfe ys] needy with the syknesse and unmyndfull of the grace geven unto her to dye here yn thys place. Father Rawlyns sayd I was to be praysed for my goode charyte wyth her. I tolde hym yf yt plese Godde to tak me heare I wyll not feare the colde swet but wyll taketh them as throwes yn chyldbedde by whych our sowle ys broght out of a korrup bodye ynto felycyte. Wat thynke yew of thys? I had my rosarye an kys yt yn hys syte. Manye wytnesse thys an spok on my gode heelth yn thys place of sycnes. Also Myssus Barton saw all and begge me to pray for her. I tolde her that they who are yn the myddest of reproches and fals acusacyons beforre the trybunall oght to thynke themselfs blessyd for beyng tryd by thy tormynts of hys [pacyon.] Our delyverye to thy lyte ys thus assuryd an tryumfynt. I preye gyve ye thys promys: I am fyrm resolved befor Jesu Chryste to perform thy fathers wyl, lyve yn hys feare, dye yn hys favoure, and remayn yn hys glorye for ever and ever.

> Yor lovyng mothre,
> Margret Clytheroe

Recognizing patterns in the way that various affiliations – family, religious belief, community, status, place, legislative focus – direct and constrain subject negotiation can tell us much about our own cultural maneuvering. As one of my colleagues rather humorously pointed out, subjectivity is never simply formed on the fly. Rather, it is a matter of seizing possibilities offered by concrete situations and acting upon them. Identifying and, on occasion, reimagining the strategies that early modern women like Clitherow employed to maneuver within and among various groupings can further clarify what is at stake in oppositional politics and what *may be* at work in cultural process. Historical recovery offers a particularly compelling frame for such study as it is only in retrospect that we can attend to changes and mark connections. Process – recovered, recreated, and retold – can render our analyses of social configuration dynamic. When we consider the relational and situational, the processual and the temporally attentive, notions of agency take on a material viability not otherwise possible. Remember, however, causality only occurs after the *fact*. Story-telling professes and presumes its own proofs.[91] Margaret Clitherow's letter *is* my letter, just as my history will always be the narrative that speaks hers.[92] Authorized and authenticated by its place within academic discourse, by the notes, by the details, by the sense that without it something significant will have been lost, the *fact* of Margaret Clitherow's legacy is telling. For it is in exploring her past that we begin the process of understanding our own inevitable and always implicated articulations. It is in creating her history that we can try as well to imagine alternatives.

On the title page of *Ester hath hang'd Haman*, Ester Sowernam's 1617 response[1] to Joseph Swetnam's *Araignment of Lewde, idle, froward and unconstant women* (1615),[2] Sowernam offers up the following detail. In naming herself, she promises that she is "neither Maide, Wife nor Widdowe, yet really all, and therefore experienced to defend all." Although the immediate motivation for Sowernam's lines is no doubt to counter Swetnam's cursory dismissal of women who are neither maids, wives, nor widows (he calls them "unmarried wantons"), the neither/nor positioning that Sowernam chooses is both unsettling and enigmatic. Numerous writers have taken up her puzzling claim. Linda Woodbridge wonders whether the assertion suggests male authorship[3] or perhaps a "protest against categorizing women by marital status and sexual experience." Ann Jones, in turn, sees Sowernam's contention as a defense strategy, legitimating her right to speak.[4] Certainly the ambiguity of Sowernam's naming is challenging. What exactly is she trying to tell us? That she is not a she? That she is opposed to categorical definition? That she is justified in speaking? While the above readings seem both valid and useful, we might add another interpretive possibility to this already vexed proposition by considering Sowernam's assertion literally, as an ironic acknowledgment of the actual material circumstances of an as yet nebulous marriage contract. Sowernam's ambiguous claim that she is "neither Maide, Wife nor Widdowe, yet really all, and therefore experienced to defend all" may foreground its own uncertainty, I suggest, precisely because it lacks the appropriate legal documentation.

There is an extensive textual tradition within which the words "neither maid, wife, nor widow" are repeatedly voiced. In seventeenth-century England, the expression is a commonplace, in most circles politely deprecatory – a roundabout way of calling a woman a whore. The epithet appears in various guises and genres during the period, from conduct books to comedies.[5] Probably the most familiar text to evoke and interrogate these labels, at least within twentieth-century literary scholarship, is William Shakespeare's *Measure for Measure*. In the play,

Duke Vincentio ostensibly questions the jilted Mariana to uncover her identity. In his queries he positions her outside the categories of widow, wife, or maid but does not immediately assume her whoredom. The duke's ambivalence softens but will not suspend judgment on women like Mariana who have been forced outside acceptable boundaries of female definition. While Shakespeare's handling of the commonplace is interesting in that it revises the epithet (albeit marginally), it is not until 1617 when Sowernam publishes her tract that the equation is fully interrogated, explored in her claim that women are "all" and "neither" simultaneously.

Sowernam's lexical recasting (allowing both avowal and denial) turns Shakespeare's apparent uneasiness into an autobiographical double boast, something she can claim as her own on the title page of her tract. Her textual maneuvering – foregrounding and neutralizing the expression – may, as Woodbridge suggests, offer a critique of the ways in which current categorical divisions intersect, but it is the slippage between wife and maid, between widow and wife, that her text seems to question, not the categories themselves. Insisting upon legal form and court procedure to authorize and legitimate her discussion, Sowernam seems to position the gender debate squarely within the English law courts. As a result of this rhetorical grounding, we may begin to see in her initial assertion a more specific and gendered anxiety being addressed – an anxiety about the business of middling-rank marriage for women and the honoring of the marriage contract.

In this chapter I want to look at the connections in Sowernam's text between an emerging understanding of marriage as a *legal* (largely "middle-class")[6] *institution* and the *financial* and *moral* imperatives that bolster its construction as a function of the state. Sowernam's text turns marriage into a system of fair market exchange – on the one hand, demanding financial obligation from men (itself charted in market terms), and on the other, promising in return the construction of an internalized code of conduct for women. Sowernam's text replicates middling-rank mercantile practices of barter and invokes a pseudo-legal discourse to legitimate them. Drawing parallels between contract law and marriage practice, Sowernam's account negotiates contemporary anxieties about marriage as a reorganization of mercantile property and foreshadows a later concretization of those anxieties in amended civil legislation. At the same time, in its attention to the multiple dimensions of middling-rank marriage for women, *Ester hath hang'd Haman* persuasively announces a cultural rewriting of conscience as chaste, feminized, and dowried – a marketable moral commodity. For Sowernam and other seventeenth-century women of the middling ranks, purity is a small price to pay for the ethical, legal, and financial status that it will eventually provide.

While Sowernam's tract loosely parallels other early Stuart texts in its recognition of marriage as a key site of cultural instability,[7] it reinterprets those predominantly male-authored accounts with an eye toward securing boundaries, upholding contracts, and protecting women's legal rights. It also prefigures later explorations in its explicit gendering of moral regulation as a means to and extension of those ends. Two male-authored play-texts – the first, Shakespeare's *Measure For Measure*, published before Sowernam's pamphlet in 1604, and the second, the anonymously written *Swetnam the Woman-Hater*, published after it in 1620[8] – share *Ester hath hang'd Haman*'s obsession with marriage, and share as well its concerted focus on "family values" though each approaches these questions from its own historically discrete and gender-specific position.

In *Ester hath hang'd Haman*, Sowernam rewrites Shakespeare's ambivalence in questions of female chastity, securing for women a real and saleable "value" in pre-nuptial negotiations. At the same time, she anticipates the author of the later play in positioning that chastity as status-specific – a code of conduct that separates women of the middling-ranks from their economic and social "inferiors" and frames their middling rank moral ethos as normative.[9] Following her lead, the anonymous author of *Swetnam the Woman-Hater* positions good women – chaste women – as speakers of conscience, but he does so with an eye to established hierarchies. In that play, women's moral purview, though acknowledged, is both circumscribed and lampooned. Unfit for the roles allotted them, women must defer to the state for instruction and success.

The differences in publication date between *Measure for Measure*, *Ester hath hang'd Haman*, and *Swetnam the Woman-Hater* are evocative, especially in what they suggest about the making of state subjects and the establishment of domestic and legal spheres as regulators of public behavior and personal conduct. While *Measure for Measure* culturally imagines morality as a spiritual issue, leaving conscience to confessors, Sowernam's *Ester* and *Swetnam the Woman-Hater* both gender that domain. In these later productions, confessors and conscience are sexualized. Women stand guard over men's minds, and men enact laws to keep women and religious voice in tow. In all three accounts the institution of marriage takes center stage as the domestic site of social control. In satisfying their contractual obligations, husbands and wives morally, legally, and financially attend to the one element of obedience that the state cannot adequately monitor – private conscience.[10]

Maids, wives, and widows

I want to return for a moment to Sowernam's introduction – to her assertion that she is "neither Maide, Wife nor Widdowe, yet really all, and therefore experienced to defend all." First, I want to pose a hypothetical scenario that may account for the multiple subject positions that Sowernam both denies and embraces in her self-naming. I want to suggest via that assertion the potential ambiguity of much early seventeenth-century marriage negotiation, especially for women of the middling ranks who stood to lose reputation *and* livelihood in an ill-defined or un-negotiated marriage contract. Suppose for a moment that Sowernam and an unidentified partner exchange marriage vows privately and without witnesses.[11] In accordance with English convention and Roman canon law, they offer up spousals,[12] pledging their love eternal, but do so without banns and without ritual. They honor the vow and consummation occurs. In 1617, as far as English law is concerned (which is not very far), Sowernam's marriage is not only legitimate, but also for all intents and purposes absolute and irrevocable. Let me also imagine that Sowernam's "friends,"[13] in upholding her side of the marriage bargain, bequeath to Sowernam and her partner a cash settlement of £150 – a substantial dowry that transfers, upon consummation, to Sowernam's husband, to do with as he pleases.[14] What if Sowernam's partner, however, is less than honorable in upholding the contract; what if he abandons her and keeps the money?

Given the scenario that I have just outlined, Sowernam's promise that she is "neither Maide, Wife nor Widdowe" makes considerably more sense. As a sexually initiated woman, Sowernam can no longer embrace that definition of self that is embodied in the term "Maide." At the same time, the honorific "Wife" is equally inappropriate. If she is not seen in the eyes of the community as a married woman (and the secrecy of their vows makes such ambiguity possible), the only identity that she can legitimately claim is Swetnam's dismissive "unmarried wanton." The last of Sowernam's rather restricted options – widowhood – is not available either. Having never been recognized as a legitimate wife, she can be no "widow." Yet Sowernam simultaneously affirms that she is all of the above "and therefore experienced to defend all." Indeed, the specific material circumstances that I have suggested enable the paradox. Sowernam might be a "maide," having never entered a publicly acknowledged marriage. She might also be a "wife," having pledged her troth and offered her body, and finally she might be a "widow," having been forsaken by a husband, who, according to convention, might now be considered dead (Powell, *Domestic Relations*, 63ff.).

In words scripted thirteen years earlier in a play performed before King James I on December 26, 1604, "caled 'Mesur for Mesur,'"[15] Shakespeare voices Sowernam's appositive as a series of questions by Duke Vincentio to Mariana, Angelo's betrothed. The duke's identification of Mariana's status, or rather her lack of one, comes to define her position outside standard categorizations for English women. "What, are you married?" he asks her:

M: No, my Lord.
D: Are you a maid?
M: No, my Lord.
D: A widow, then?
M: Neither, my Lord.
D: Why you are nothing then; neither maid, widow,
    nor wife! (5.1.172–79)

In this passage, the duke's culturally familiar erasure of Mariana's status – "you are nothing then" – is immediately emended in Lucio's unsolicited and overtly definitional reading. "My Lord," Lucio interjects, "she may be a punk; for many of them are neither maid, widow nor wife" (5.1.180–81). To Lucio, Mariana is simply a "punk," a whore, an "unmarried wanton." Here too, as in the scenario that I have imagined for Sowernam, her ambivalent status rests on a broken contract. According to the duke, Mariana "should this Angelo have married, was affianced by her oath, and the nuptial appointed," when, sometime between promise and ceremony, her marriage portion was lost at sea. Extracting himself from a no longer advantageous marriage, Angelo denies his oath by accusing Mariana of dishonor. With reputation and dowry gone, the majority of her conversations spoken off-stage and out of audience earshot, Mariana is without cultural or dramatic definition. In Shakespeare's imagining, she is neither maid, wife, nor widow; she is "nothing then."

Measure for Measure, like Ester hath hang'd Haman, underscores the precarious nature of female status outside the marriage contract. It reveals an anxiety about contemporary codes of sexual conduct and moral regulation and questions how offenders should be handled within the legal system. It does not, however, construct its argument either to vindicate women or to defend them against a common male antagonist (Joseph Swetnam). Rather, in a far more ambivalent, and I believe masculine-coded, maneuver,[16] Shakespeare's play presents women as part of the problem. The duke's conscious refusal to acknowledge Mariana a punk – "silence that fellow!" he demands on hearing Lucio's spurious aside – may recognize Lucio's charge as inappropriate, but it nevertheless will not validate Mariana's status. Lacking a "true" contract, she will always be "nothing," regardless of "virtue" and in spite of chaste seclusion. It is this ambivalence that I think so distinguishes Shakespeare's play from Sowernam's later exploration. Sowernam's desire to restore credibility to women – to disallow that nebulous positioning – necessitates the kinds of maneuvering that will occur in her account. It is that unusual positioning, announced in the most marginal of venues – a single-issue printing of a female-authored text – that will operate so adroitly in satisfying the state's needs to control its people.

The Querelle des femmes

Sowernam's text is a defense of women, part of a continuing English debate on gender questions.[17] Like the majority of controversy writings before it, *Ester hath hang'd Haman* follows certain expected traditions and refers to common elements of argument in women's defense. Linda Woodbridge offers perhaps the most thorough description of what constitutes gender polemic as a genre.[18] In her book *Women and the English Renaissance: Literature and the Nature of Womankind, 1540–1620*, Woodbridge identifies these key stylistic traits of the genre: a genuine sense of debate with an opponent either imagined or personified; a thesis about women that involves the use of logic and rhetoric for evidence; the appearance of *exempla*, drawn from both history and literature; and, finally, a format that imitates a classical oration or dialogue.[19]

Sowernam's tract makes use of many of these strategies. She looks to biblical, classical, and historical *exempla* to prove women's worth. She overturns cultural stereotypes associating women with sharp tongues and lascivious morals, with ostentatious clothing and empty heads. She also chooses to focus specifically on women's status in relation to marriage. This "take" on women is, in fact, one of the few available to her. In *The Lawes Resolutions of Womens Rights*, the anonymous author reminds us that, from an English legal perspective, all women "are understood either married or to bee married" – either maids, wives, or widows (6).

What is unusual, then, is what Sowernam chooses to address within that categorization and how she frames her analysis. By centering her discussion first on the marriage ceremony, with its uncertain legal status, and then on the obligations and responsibilities required of middling-rank marriage partners, and by voicing both within a pseudo-legal trial setting, Sowernam underscores a status-based anxiety about current marriage policy. She suggests the importance of economic safeguards for women in the form of real legislation and criminal prosecution against those who fail to honor the contract.

English marriage law

From a legal standpoint, defining categories of female and male responsibility lagged far behind the moral imperatives advocated by these authors, particularly within the realm of English marriage law. In the first two decades of the seventeenth century, England's marriage policy was a hodgepodge of conflicting and imprecise Roman canon law and ecclesiastical court precedent. The English break with the Holy Roman Church in 1534 came too soon for the Council of Trent's 1563 decree – that all marriages not contracted in the presence of a priest and witnesses were rendered illegitimate – to have any effect.[20] While there had been some attempt at the end of Henry VIII's reign to impose stricter and more exact specifications on English marriage policy – defining spousals and issuing banns – vague wording and constant repeals rendered most marriage regulations ineffectual,[21] and the real problem of contractual legitimacy was largely ignored.

What constituted the marriage contract itself during this period was far from clear. No two documents agreed on what rendered a contract legitimate, when that legitimacy occurred, or from whom it derived its authority. From a legal standpoint, the criteria that kept a contract from becoming valid varied even within the same text. Where the failure to meet certain qualifications allowed for the separation of married partners but kept the contract between them inviolate (forbidden seasons, prohibition by church, precontract), other restrictions literally rendered the contract invalid (existing marriage, adultery, consanguinity). Occasionally the same sets of restrictions (vows of chastity, incest, murder) appeared within both categories to the confusion of all concerned.[22] In addition to the qualifications that prospective marriage partners had to meet, both parties had also to be freely consenting. A forced marriage was both illegal and unenforceable, but proof of consent was often difficult to secure in any legally verifiable manner.[23]

The process of securing and legitimating the marriage contract was vague as well. Because English law accepted a number of different oath exchanges as legal and binding – including among them a church ceremony, a civil service and a simple and potentially private exchange of vows[24] – the possibility of marriage fraud or at the very least contract dispute multiplied. In cases where vows were exchanged privately or in defiance of parental support, proof of broken contract depended not on physical evidence (though pregnancy often made some charges more visible than others) but rather on a mutual acknowledgment of words uttered in secret, behind closed doors. In one sense, the absence of proof in cases like these rendered marriage crime untraceable, unknowable, and unenforceable; it also fixed contractual litigation squarely within the province of conscience and morality.

Problems also surfaced in questions over who had the authority to resolve complaints and confer legitimacy – representatives of the church or the state. While the shift from ecclesial to secular *court* jurisdiction occurred in the middle years of the sixteenth century when marriage disputes began to be tried "after-the-fact" as "breach of promise,"[25] it was not until substantially later (1652) that civil magistrates acquired the same sort of jurisdiction in officiating over "before-the-fact" marriage proceedings.[26] This shift reordered the legal definition of marriage from sacrament to contract, from spiritual union to civil arrangement. By 1645, when parliament passed a general ordinance reminding the English people that "the Presbytery . . . shall not have cognizance of anything wherein any matter of Payment, Contract, or Demand is concerned, or any matter of Conveyance, Title, Interest, or Property,"[27] marriage policy was well on its way to becoming a civil affair. The inability of state and church to provide a single verifiable ceremony further amplified the possibility of contract dispute in marriage questions. Despite the technical battles going on throughout the English legal community over the status of marriage law, it was only in rare cases that violations and complaints were taken to court, even to nullify an unconsummated or legally invalid marriage.[28] There were, however, hundreds of dissolutions at the point of contract-making – in the hazy middle ground between professed oath and physical consummation – between private declaration and public acknowledgment.[29]

Faulty contracts

Three separate cases of ambiguous contract (Angelo/Mariana, Claudio/ Juliet, Lucio/Kate Keepdown) occur in *Measure for Measure*, and each claims a different relationship to legitimacy.[30] Angelo breaks contract with Mariana by charging her with less than honorable conduct. Because she has purportedly committed adultery, their contract is no longer binding. Angelo represents his obligations to Mariana as invalid, but in the duke's eyes their marriage is legal. "Fear you not at all," Vincentio promises Mariana,

> He is your husband on a pre-contract:
> To bring you thus together, 'tis no sin,
> Sith that the justice of your title to him
> Doth flourish the deceit.   (4.1.71–75)

Claudio and Juliet's arrangement, on the other hand, bears a marked resemblance to the hypothetical encounter with which I began. Because Claudio and Juliet exchange vows in secret, without "outward order," their troth-plight is unverifiable. Claudio, like the duke, insists that his exchange of vows with Juliet embodies true contract:

> she is fast my wife
> Save that we do the denunciation lack
> Of outward order. This we came not to,
> Only for propagation of a dower
> Remaining in the coffer of her friends.   (1.2.142–46)

In these two versions, Shakespeare constructs the marriage scenario as valid: "He is your husband," the duke insists; "She is . . . my wife," Claudio promises. Only Lucio's encounter with Mistress Kate Keepdown is patently unlawful. We are told by Mistress Overdone that Lucio promised Kate marriage, but the context of their exchange remains unclear and discredited. In the eyes of the state (Duke Vincentio), Lucio is a father but not yet a husband:

> If any woman wronged by this lewd fellow –
> As I have heard him swear himself there's one
> Whom he begot with child – let her appear,
> And he shall marry her.   (5.1.504–07)[31]

In this play, broken promises, a lack of outward order and an uncertain dower provide the material for failed marital negotiation and lead to social upheaval and moral license.

Like *Measure for Measure*, *Swetnam the Woman-Hater* deals with the legal handling of sexual infractions: the king's daughter Leonida has passed an unsupervised and illicit length of time with her princely lover Lisandro. Caught together by the king's ill-scheming advisor, Nicanor, both are legally charged with sexual incontinence. Because the sentence imposed on them demands death for the "guiltiest" partner in this sexual crime, a trial is held to determine who is to blame, men or women.[32] At the first hearing, the men win. Lisandro is to be banished and Leonida beheaded. Justice is served, however, when the king's long-lost son, Lorenzo, intervenes on behalf of his sister. Witnessing the tyranny of his father's decree, the prince pastorally circumvents its execution in the guise of a benevolent "stranger."[33] Assuming the role of an Amazon, he (as she) first defends his sister's marriage to Lisandro in court against the notorious Misogynos (she is nevertheless charged), and argues on behalf of women in general. This attempt failing, the prince/Amazon feigns his sister's death and advises the queen how to manage her husband, eventually choreographing a masque to catch his father's conscience and reveal Nicanor's crimes.

Recentering the problem of faulty contract onto interfering parents and forced marriage, *Swetnam the Woman-Hater* presents the lovers' imposed separation as a fight between fathers. Indeed, Leonida's father tells us that if the king of Naples (Lisandro's father) were to know of his son's suit, he would himself come to see it dissolved. In order to keep the lovers apart, the king Atticus foolishly places his daughter in the hands of his advisor, Nicanor, for safe keeping, and Nicanor, hoping to secure the crown for himself, attempts to coerce the princess into marrying him against her will. Because the lovers share common social and economic positions as well as an absence of other possible legal impediments and because they also freely consent to marry, the play recognizes Atticus's parental refusal to condone the marriage as tyrannous and Nicanor's coercion as criminal. To deny the lovers the right to marry is, in this play, without legitimate foundation.

Swetnam the Woman-Hater's sympathies concerning forced marriage illustrate another potential arena for abuse and fraud in marital negotiations. At the same time, they underscore the problem of ambiguous contract without a formalized oath-exchange or the state authority to back it up. At the play's end the lovers are finally united in a legally verifiable and publicly acknowledged marriage – a marriage at which the the king (not the church) officiates. Even here the lovers are loath to accept the king's word without *explicit contract*. Although Atticus offers the lovers marriage informally, by a joining of hands, it is not enough. Prince Lorenzo voices their anxiety: "You are a king; yet they are loth / To take your word without an othe."[34] The lovers' uncertainty necessitates a more formal and irrevocable marriage ceremony, one replete with witnesses and royal "othe."[35] "As we are King of Sicil; 'tis confirm'd / Firm, to be revoked never, / Untill death their lives dissever (5.3.171–73), the king vows, and Lorenzo verifies the fact of that promise with additional proof. He adds, "Here are witnesses – I now to testifie this royall match" (5.3.175).

Ester hath hang'd Haman attests to its own sense of broken contract, but Sowernam's defense illustrates an awareness of contract litigation by posing its opposite – an example of contractual success. Underscoring the idea of a legally stable contract agreement, she focuses first on the exchange of marriage vows. She looks to the marriage service itself, to Genesis and the moment of the first union. She writes,

when woman was created, God brought her unto Adam, and then did solemnize that most auspicious Marriage betwixt them, with the great Majestie, and magnificence that heaven, or earth might afford. God was the father, which gave so rich a jewell: God was the Priest which tied so inseparable a knot, [and] God was the Steward which provided all the pleasures. (7)

Recognizing the primacy of the ceremony in legitimating and formalizing the marriage bond, Sowernam both affirms its importance as a public event and underscores its indissolubility. That she calls out three distinct authorities – father, priest, and steward[36] – to solemnize the union and ensure its cultural credibility, suggests an understanding of the uncertainty involved in current marriage practice and how it becomes legitimated. As I mentioned earlier, the seventeenth-century marriage debate focuses on divisions between religious and civil authority, on the relative status of prelacy and magistrate and on where to draw those lines (a fight which came to its most obvious head in the years preceding the English Civil War). Taking into account any and all eventualities, Sowernam promises witnesses from *each* of these offices in the form of family, church, *and* state (father, priest, *and* steward). She also insists that the wedding ceremony be attended with "great Majestie" and "Magnificence." Sowernam's retelling of the Genesis account secures what amounts to an official and publicly acknowledged recognition of the marriage union for all interested parties.[37] Her narrative offers the kind of parental, civil, *and* ecclesial legitimacy that will stand up in courts of Chancery in questions of property and rights of inheritance, and in archdiaconal courts in charges of fornication, slander, or worse.[38]

Sowernam's insistence upon this first marriage ceremony (between Adam and Eve) as a public event, despite the absence of witnesses other than God, seems to address the logistics of the marriage service in mercantile terms. In one of her dedications, Sowernam identifies her male readers specifically by employ. She titles them "the best disposed and worthy apprentises of London." The demographic composition of London apprenticeship generally included young men in the early stages of their careers – careers as mercers, drapers, grocers, carpenters, tailors, weavers, etc.[39] These apprentices, some of whom were second and third sons of families with prior landed status, represented one of the most mobile and marriageable groups of the "middling ranks."[40] For these London tradesmen and craftsmen-to-be, however, weddings occurred late. Apprentices generally had to wait until they were established in careers and could afford to support a household. With seven- to eight-year indentures beginning in their early teens, most apprentices were in their late twenties by the time they achieved journeyman status.[41] In addition, trade marriages were often less publicized, the ceremony surrounding them far more subdued.[42] Indeed, pre-nuptial negotiations were frequently arranged rather quickly, especially if family ties had been geographically severed by relocation during an apprenticeship or if finances were tied up in fledgeling business ventures.[43] Rewriting an essentially private and religious creation story (the Genesis account) into a publicly recognized wedding service, Sowernam reminds her mercantile readers – whose eventual marriage dealings may be equally late, private, or hasty – to honor the contract no matter the circumstance as God the Father, God the Church, and God the State will always be watching.

In addition to promoting marriage as a public event, Sowernam continually reiterates its irrevocability. Of Adam and Eve she writes,

The woman was married to Adam, as with a most sure and inseparable bond . . .
For this cause, saith Adam . . . shall a man . . . cleave onely to his Wife. This word cleave is uttered in the Hebrew with a more significant emphasie, then any other Language may expresse; such a cleaving and joyning together . . . admitteth no separation. It may be necessarily observed, that that gift of the woman was . . . made inseparable by giving and taking the Ring of Love, which should be endlesse. (7)

Mentioning variations of the word "inseparable" three times and "cleaving" three, Sowernam reminds her readers that contracts, once made, ought not to be broken. Indeed, numerous other related terms come up in this brief account: "joyning," "endlesse," "bond," "sure," and "onely." For Sowernam, then, it is not the loosening of affective ties that is paramount (as it will be for later male writers, like Milton,[44] with vastly different agendas) but rather the promise that vows once made will not be unmade. Sowernam wants to ensure that once the marriage contract has been negotiated, it will carry with it both legal and financial security for women.[45]

In the early years of the seventeenth century, English women had no real property rights or legal claim to restitution in the event of ambiguous or faulty marriage negotiations. Accordingly, Sowernam defends what little legitimate authority women may possess within a heavily male-favored marriage market. Refusing both the non-identity allotted to women in *Measure for Measure* and the blame-placing that occurs in *Swetnam the Woman-Hater*, Sowernam insists that vows be honored. By necessity her assertion of legitimate contract becomes more exaggerated than it does in either of the plays. By law, husband and wife become one person, and that personhood resides in men. Husbands acquire absolute control of their wives' personal property, which they can sell at will. A husband's debts become a prior charge on a wife's marriage dowry. Her legal right to hold and dispose of her own property, then, is limited to what she can specifically claim in a marriage contract.[46] Accordingly, if that contract remains nebulous – of marginal legal value – she has no real recourse for restitution.[47] Her economic rights are further compromised in that it is women of the middling ranks in particular who are being systematically removed from the workplace, formally denied guild privileges, and relegated to a legally vacant domestic sphere.[48]

A question of value

For Sowernam, questions of female prerogative ought to be both legally and ethically grounded. That is to say they should rely on a system of mutual and complementary obligations, obligations outlining appropriate behavior and responsibility for both women and men.[49] "There can be no love betwixt man and wife, but where there is a respective estimate the one towards the other," Sowernam tells London apprentices, underscoring the contractual nature of marriage and the ideological underpinnings of what translates as love. Coding the exchange between husband and wife as "a respective estimate," Sowernam chooses property terms of value and worth to articulate that bond.

Sowernam's text understands relationships between men and women as financially motivated. In order to fulfill their part of the bargain, husbands must offer their wives economic security in the event of widowhood or catastrophe. Sowernam's narrative is suspicious of those men who flaunt their wealth in elaborate court attire, as the money they spend on clothing will be unavailable for the domestic necessities and continued support required in married life. She writes:

we see divers [suitors] weare apparell and colours made of a Lordship, lined with Farmes and Granges, embrodered with all the plate, gold, and wealth, their Friends and Fathers left them . . . will or dare a woman trust to their love for one moneth, who will turn her of the next . . . They rather suspect his worth, then wish his love, who most exceed in braverie. (38–39)

The material specificity of Sowernam's accusations suggests an all-too-familiar understanding of misdirected funds and a recognition of "wealth" and "worth" as an inheritance to be maintained and enriched. She sees both property ("Farmes and Granges") and possessions ("plate, gold, and wealth") subject to the vagaries of fickle husbands-to-be.

Sowernam's text addresses the consequences for wedded wives of men's failure to meet their financial obligations. According to her account, women are adequately compensated for their "services" only outside marriage. She writes, "if a woman or maide will yeeld unto lewdnesse, what shall they want? But if they would live in honestie, what helpe shall they have?" (45). This emphasis is repeated several times throughout the text. "How much will they make of the lewd?" she asks, "base account of the honest? How many pounds will they spend in bawdie houses? but when will they bestowe a penny upon an honest maid or woman, except it be to corrupt them?" (45–46). Sowernam's account demarcates the lewd from the honest, the pounds from the pennies, in order to situate and quantify exchange *within* the married household.

Foregrounding the primacy of the contract, Sowernam believes that men's financial obligations toward women should occur within marriage where they can be exchanged for appropriate goods and services: chastity, silence, and obedience. In order to ensure adequate compensation, Sowernam willingly employs women in the few roles still available to them, all in exchange for real income. Women are to be "helpers, comforters, Joyes, and delights," she insists, "and in true use and government they ever have beene and ever will be" (10). None of the roles that Sowernam's account attributes to women are new. What is new is the way that they have been remanded into service, the way that they have been figured as contractual and utilitarian. As an example of "true use," women's roles replace, or at the very least augment, their marriage dowries. Helping, comforting, and delighting men fulfill one half of an identifiable set of mutual oaths and obligations that all married partners must honor.

To Sowernam, "vowes, oathes, and protestations" ought to be subject to the weight of English law and upheld accordingly. It is husbands, however, whom she sees as most derelict in their duties. Again and again, she reiterates the importance of men honoring their obligations. She insists that if they wish to alleviate the cause of aggravation and discontent in women, then it is their responsibility to amend their behavior. "Forbeare thy drinking, thy luxurious riot, thy gaming, and spending, and thou shalt have thy wife give thee as little cause at home, as thou givest her great cause of disquiet abroad" (44). If men will simply fulfill their part of the bargain, then women will "behave." Throughout her account Sowernam reiterates the uncertain legal status of current marriage promises, writing, "what care [men] . . . if they make, a thousand oathes, and commit tenne thousand perjuries, so they may deceive a woman" (23). Later, she wonders,

what vowes, oathes, and protestations doe [men] spend, to make [women] dishonest? . . . Some will pretend marriage, another offer continuall maintenance, but when they have obtained their purpose, what shall a woman finde . . . she hath made herself the unhappie subject to a lustfull bodie; and the shamefull stall of a lascivious tongue. Men may with foule shame charge women with this sinne which they had never committed if shee had not trusted, nor had ever trusted if she had not beene deceived with vowes, oathes, and protestations. (45)

That Sowernam continually reiterates the failure of current "vowes, oathes, and protestations" to be honored locates the problem of contract breaking in the courts and on paper. Lacking verifiable evidence of contract in the form of written affidavits and a formalized court procedure to process them, seventeenth-century women will continue to be deceived.[50] Sowernam's perception of men as the root of this failed obligation plays out in every aspect of her account. She sees men as responsible for all of women's supposed failings, from teaching them to scold to soliciting them to lewdness.

The barre of fame and report

Sowernam justifies her right to rebuttal "at the barre of fame and report," defending women from the social ramifications of Swetnam's slanderous remarks. She adopts a rhetoric evocative of legal discourse. In fact, the whole of her account is a model of logical exposition.[51] She defends her points with direct proof and examines counter arguments with a lawyer's tools, calling on authority, experience, and custom to provide evidence in her favor. Perhaps the most rhetorically persuasive aspect of Sowernam's presentation is its literal trial setting.[52] She locates the bulk of her defense within the courtroom and before two female judges, Reason and Experience. Couched in a pseudo-legal rhetoric, her attack arraigns, indicts, and finally sentences Swetnam for his crimes against women. She begins a lengthy summation with the following: "Joseph Swetnam, thou art endited by the name of Joseph Swetnam of Bedlemmore, in the Countie of Onopolie: For that thou the twentieth day of December, in the yeare &c. Diddest most wickedly, blasphemously, falsly, and scandalously publish a lewd Pamphlet" (29).

Because Swetnam refuses to plead, Sowernam is asked by judge and jury (Swetnam's jury, in this case, consists of his five senses and the seven deadly sins) to speak out on behalf of women: "But that the world might be satisfied in respect of the wrongs done unto us, and to maintaine our honourable reputation, it was concluded, that my selfe should deliver before the Judges, to all the assembly, speaches to these effects following" (31). While Sowernam carefully distinguishes between her response and the punitive action of "Stafford law" (a venue she would have trouble usurping as a woman),[53] her writing nevertheless relies heavily on legal precedent for authority. This emphasis underscores the absence in 1617 of any concrete legislation focusing on marriage rights and obligations. Recognizing the failure of current marriage policy to safeguard economic investment, Sowernam imaginatively directs potential reforms into legal channels. Her access to legal discourse as strategy suggests an increasing cultural willingness to look to civil government for answers even in issues that were once strictly the domain of the church. In Catholic England, marriage was a sacrament; but even after the Reformation it continued to carry with it an imagined sacramental status in the eyes of laity and clergy alike.[54]

In her unique handling of the court scenario, Sowernam neatly splits the impetus for her defense between two separate poles of authority, both safely within acceptable limits for women. As a legal document arraigning Swetnam before various aspects of his own conscience, her account follows court procedure but keeps its subject comfortably within the private realm. Not only does it address issues of slander and marital abuse, generally the domain of Chancery (the only court where women might seek legal redress), but it also restricts that defense to the internal workings of Swetnam's own mind, to his "secret thoughts," already associated with women in their interiority. In addition, by continually emphasizing the primacy of the law as absolute, Sowernam effectively shifts the burden of marriage reform into civil hands, the hands of parliamentary fathers, husbands, and sons who are most able to do something about it.

The intersection of a legal and a moral code of conduct, one determined in court, the other in conscience, addresses two separate aspects of the marriage contract simultaneously. First, in pretending legal action and legal retribution against miscreant husbands, Sowernam's format anticipates real legislation concerning the marriage contract. It looks to England's first bureaucratic attempts to fix marriage procedure, determine marital responsibility, and expedite the transfer of property between married parties. In 1652, Cromwell's Marriage Act brought specific legal weight to bear on marital status and obligation. This more formalized definition of the marriage service placed full legal authority over the business of marriage in magisterial hands. It mandated formal licensing and required that a minimum of two witnesses be present during the exchange of vows.[55]

Sowernam's twofold focus on court and conscience also looks inward, however. By consolidating the legal and moral right to judge, Sowernam asks that people begin monitoring the marriage contract from within. She institutes a code of appropriate conduct that equates morality with the law and places the first squarely in the hands of women. This refiguring not only offers support in the absence of legislation (demanding that individuals attend to their own obligations even if the law does not specifically demand it of them), but it also promises women a bargaining chip in the marriage contract. Clearly, husbands are supposed to bring with them financial security in the form of sufficient food, clothing, and shelter "so long as ye both shall live," but wives also must carry out certain specified obligations. As moral guardians of appropriate marital behavior, women fulfill prerequisites of their own, supplying husbands with sound moral advice and ensuring them credibility within the community. It is no coincidence that Sowernam argues her case not in a traditional court of law but rather at "the barre of fame and report" with its obvious allusion to public opinion and moral credibility.

In order to accommodate the idea of fair mercantile exchange within the marriage contract, Sowernam constantly reminds her readers that husbands already receive adequate remuneration for their support. By positing women as real property in both body and reputation, she evens up the ante, insisting that "young men . . . [are never] called honest men, till they be married: for that is the portion which they get by their wives when they are married, they are forthwith placed in the ranke of honest men . . . And the reason presently added, for hee hath a wife; she is the sure signe and seale of honestie" (23). In Sowernam's configuration a wife's dowry (her portion) is the chaste reputation that she brings to her husband, the economic equivalence of her "fame and [good] report." As a wife she becomes the "sure signe and seale of [her husband's] honestie." This positioning once again underscores women's roles as moral guardians; they determine reputation within the community. It also insists, however, that women be complicit in a developing marriage ideology that actively denies them agency outside the moral sphere and continues to insist on their status as property.[56]

Chastity in the plays

Just this kind of ideology informs both plays. In *Measure for Measure*, to be assured of a lasting and economically secure situation, women must maintain a chaste reputation. It is, after all, the chaste Isabella who eventually secures the most "officially" advantageous marriage offer at the play's end. Ostensibly she will wed the duke, acquire his title and privilege, and offer up her "virgin knot" to conceive sons, one of whom will inherit the family title. Like Sowernam's faithful wives, Isabella will be compensated for her efforts in the satisfaction of a binding contract. That a chaste reputation appeals can be seen not only in the Duke's promises of marriage to Isabella at the play's close, but also in Angelo's unrestrained desire for her, in his translation from "a man of stricture and firm abstinence" to a man of "sharp appetite" (1.3.12; 2.4.260). In Shakespeare's representation, it is Isabella's unyielding honor that Angelo wants to violate. He laments,

> O cunning enemy, that, to catch a saint,
> With saints dost bait thy hook! Most dangerous
> Is that temptation that doth goad us on
> To sin in loving virtue. Never could the strumpet
> With all her double vigour, art and nature,
> Once stir my temper: but this virtuous maid
> Subdues me quite.   (2.2.180–86)

While Angelo's solution is wildly inappropriate (marriage is not even a consideration here), his attraction nevertheless serves to underscore the value that virtue will bestow on women who maintain it.[57] "Virtuous maid[s]" subdue where "strumpet[s]" never shall.

Sowernam's account sees virtue in market terms – as something men desire. Her defense, like *Measure for Measure*, also recognizes that consumers may be motivated by less than honorable impulses in securing the product. Justifying women's beauty (and equating beauty with chastity), Sowernam's defense first codes chaste appearance as a gift and then establishes its worth as both immeasurable and benign. She writes:

And for the woman, who having a Jewell given her from so deare a friend, is she not to be commended rather that in the estimate which she sheweth, she will as carefully and as curiously as she may set out what she hath received from Almighty God, then to be censured that she doth it to allure wanton and lascivious lookes? The difference is in the minds . . . things indifferent, whose qualities have their name from the uses, are commonly so censured, and so used, as the minde is inclined which doth passe his verdict. (37)

Sowernam's description constructs female appearance as a gift "received from Almighty God." The shift here, from selling to giving, maintains the language of exchange by pointing to precious and marketable objects – "Jewell[s]," "estimate[s]," and "gift[s]" – yet it removes honest women from the public taint of the market. Prostitutes sell their wares, purchased with paint and perfume; chaste women only display theirs, "given . . . [in good faith] from so deare a friend." At the same time women's chaste demeanor becomes a "thing indifferent," its potential for abuse dependent on an outside observer who is solely responsible for his own "wanton and lascivious lookes." Paralleling *Measure for Measure* in this focus as well, *Ester hath hang'd Haman* imagines culpability in masculine terms. Women do not corrupt men. Like Angelo's "carrion," men corrupt themselves.[58] In both accounts however, attributing vice to men means denying volition in women. Like so much property, chaste women become "things indifferent," put to "use" only in the way that men choose to respond to them.

What distinguishes each account, then, what separates Sowernam's female-coded rendering from the play that precedes it, is their different perceptions of chastity's "use." In *Measure for Measure*, Isabella's "too cold" chastity is marked with ambivalence because it usurps its prerogative by refusing to succumb to male authority. Shakespeare questions the "value" of chastity by juxtaposing its loss to a loss of life (a man's life). Isabella's words – "then, Isabella, live chaste, and brother, die: / More than our brother is our chastity" (2.4.183–84) – have elicited as much recent commentary as the rest of the play, both condemning and vindicating her eventual and highly circumscribed "choice."[59] Fore-grounding Isabella's supposed freedom to decide Claudio's fate, *Measure for Measure* erases the real dynamics of power behind that choice. Isabella's decision (chastity over life) masks the inescapable brutality of her real alternatives (rape or murder); and it does so by casting her chastity as a killing virtue. Regardless of how we frame our eventual readings of the play, her "choice," then, has been scripted to unsettle.

In *Measure for Measure*, Isabella's chastity is threatening because it is outside the parameters of marriage and heterosexual relations. By positing it in the context of Catholic convents (by James I's reign, considered "foreign" to much of the English population), Shakespeare creates in chastity an ambivalence that Sowernam (for the sake of the women she defends) must necessarily refuse. In *Measure for Measure*, it is imperative that Isabella's chastity be remanded into service, put to use within a legitimate marriage scenario, before it can be embraced. In order to counter the anxiety that absolute female virtue generates, Isabella's refusal to recognize and embrace male bodies must be remedied in married consummation. The duke's hasty and disjointed insistence on their eventual union, a union that will occur after the play's end, offstage, reveals the extent of this play's unease with resolutely chaste women and the necessity of returning them to male control: "But fitter time for that," the duke awkwardly admits, inserting his wedding proposal between two criminal sentencings (5.1.491). Where *Ester hath hang'd Haman* scripts chastity as the embodiment of female perfection, *Measure for Measure* pushes and prods it into safe haven. As long as Isabella remains chaste *for the Duke*, her virgin knot available to him alone, then all is well. The promise of marriage, even if only in the wings, serves to mask those aspects of an inviolate female body that male-centered texts like Shakespeare's see as threateningly outside masculine control.

In Sowernam's contrasting version of events, concepts of chastity are unquestioned and empowering for women. Like *Measure for Measure*, her tract points to virtue as the most lucrative of dowries for a bride. It is a "sure signe and seale" of men's honesty; but Sowernam has altered the frame here. She has shifted the argument to illustrate to male readers the "value" of chaste women, and she has refashioned the definition of virtue itself, making it both benign and attainable. First, she wants to underscore chastity's significance for husbands-to-be. Where in Shakespeare's drama Isabella's virtue makes *her* a suitable bride for a duke, elevating her status and prerogative accordingly (when the duke offers her marriage he claims to do it "for [her] lovely sake" not his own),[60] in Sowernam's account virtue becomes a commodity that men must purchase in order to succeed in their business dealings.

Sowernam writes to London apprentices, in her preface: "what is excellently best [the just reputation of a woman], that I commend to you: doe you finde the gold, I doe here deliver you the Jewell, a rich stocke to begin the world withall, if you be good husbands to use it for your best advantage." Here Sowernam depicts a woman's "just reputation" as a "Jewell" delivered to the highest bidder, "a rich stocke [that will enable good men] to begin the world withall." In Sowernam's scenario, female reputation is something that future husbands may "use" to their "best advantage." Sowernam's reversal of virtue's "value" (from an example and warning for females, to an incentive for males) elevates and secures the status of chaste women. In the marriage market, she ensures women sales, and demands a fair price for their efforts. By refocusing the argument, Sowernam refuses to construct female power as either problematic or outside societal control. Chastity need never be contained, possessed, or made merciful as it is inherently obedient and acceptable behavior for women. It simply requires good men to recognize its "value" and "use" it accordingly.

Chastity, once neutralized (safely within the marriage market), will serve the same function in *Measure for Measure* as it does in *Ester hath hang'd Haman*. It will promote masculine reputation and honesty. For Duke Vincentio the problem of public opinion is real; it affects his ability to govern. Not only have his laws been called into question or at the very least ignored, but at a personal level his reputation is in jeopardy. Lucio's continual jibes about the duke's sexual proclivities serve to underscore the potentially rumor-laden circumstances of bachelorhood, and the public and private consequences of that unmarried status, particularly within positions of authority. Lucio insists that before the duke "would have hanged a man for the getting a hundred bastards, he would have paid for the nursing a thousand." "[The duke] had some feeling of the sport," Lucio continues, "he knew the service; and that instructed him / to mercy" (3.2.115–17). Lucio's assertion, discrediting the duke's good name in exaggerating his sexual incontinence (Vincentio is the father of a thousand bastards), also undermines the legitimacy of the duke's laws (he will not hang his subjects for a crime that he has himself committed). The idea is reinforced in the duke's early speech to Escalus, where he sees his "strict statutes and most biting laws" as "more mock'd than fear'd" by the majority of the people whom he governs (1.3.19 and 27). The chaste Isabella will offer the duke, in his capacity both as a husband and as a ruler, a "riche stocke to begin the world," as soon, of course, as she "deliver[s] . . . the Jewell."

Reputation reveals a parallel set of concerns in *Swetnam the Woman-Hater*. In the 1620 play, the anonymous author insists that we see

Leonida as a virgin. She is chaste *despite* her unaccounted hours with Lisandro. From a dramatic standpoint, this positioning shifts Leonida's defiance of royal patriarchal authority from fornication to insubordination and realigns the problem of disobedience accordingly. Leonida visits Lisandro in opposition to the king's orders but does not "give him her body." *Swetnam the Woman-Hater* de-emphasizes the loss of marriage value that Leonida may face as a "deflowered" woman to promote instead the inadequacy of royal judgment. Like *Ester hath hang'd Haman* and *Measure for Measure*, it assumes and incorporates chaste women into its logic. It also classifies them. The princess's actions are vindicated; Lisandro defends her chastity in court. When, during his trial, he is asked to identify who is the guiltiest party, he insists, "I broke the Law, / And I must suffer for't: Then doe not wrong / Her spotless Chastitie" (3.1.93–95). The judges question the statement's veracity causing Lisandro to elaborate:

> If any here conceive her otherwise,
> That very thought will damne him:
> She's as chaste
> As ere your Mothers in their cradles were,
> for any act committed.   (3.1.96–100)

Calling on mothers as examples of chastity accomplishes two things in this play. First, the association between Leonida and her accusers' mothers places their own reputation (and legitimacy) on the line. The temporal disjunction between parent and child, however, is interesting for a second and more compelling reason. By alluding to mothers, women who have physically conceived children, and recasting them as children themselves (still in the cradle), Lisandro connects ideas of chastity to inheritance and generation (making it both "normal" and "processual"). He destabilizes chastity as a biological determiner of female worth. Chaste children are mothers now and so too will Leonida eventually lose one kind of chastity to gain a different but no less esteemed title as chaste wife and mother. On one level, this configuration simply reiterates *Ester hath hang'd Haman*'s earlier coding. Both texts assume chastity to be available *within* marriage as well as outside it – both see chastity as an aspect of acceptable and familiar female behavior (nor is this treatment unusual).[61] For *Swetnam the Woman-Hater*, however, an adequate marriage portion is not at issue. It is Leonida's status – her birth – that ensures her chastity, not the other way around. Where *Measure for Measure* poses chaste women as outside patriarchal control and *Ester hath hang'd Haman* celebrates their value on the seventeenth-century marriage market in increased saleability, *Swetnam the Woman-Hater* introduces Leonida's chastity only to verify her good breeding. Of course the king's daughter is chaste; she is a princess, after all.

Swetnam the Woman-Hater's presentation of chastity illuminates the injustice of the king's supposedly just laws, but, more specifically, it redirects the problem of chaste reputation into status terms.[62] The most unusual and/or telling analyses of chastity in the 1620 play focus on Leonida's serving woman, Loretta and her husband-to-be, Scanfardo (Nicanor's servant). Loretta's own questionable relation to chastity is initially revealed in her decision to expose Leonida's tryst with Lisandro. Loretta's inability to keep her mistress's secret (she tells Scanfardo of the lovers' meeting, and he passes the information along to Nicanor) illustrates the problem of chastity as it is announced in this text. Ostensibly, Loretta's lack of discretion is motivated by her own uncontrolled desire for Scanfardo – her willingness to please him as a lover. That a "loose tongue" is associated with an inability to resist sexual advances underscores the danger of unchaste sexuality at a linguistic level. Libidinous bodies translate to libidinous speech, and both become equated with rumor-mongering, mercenary politics, and criminal behavior. Scanfardo makes the intercourse/discourse connection explicit when he admits, "What will not women blab to those they love" (2.2.156).

Scanfardo and Loretta legitimate their sexual and political incontinence via status. Scanfardo blames the royal lovers for setting a bad example. Their sexual misconduct condones his own. Attempting to win Loretta to his bed before their wedding night, Scanfardo reminds her that the princess has done the same: "weele ev'n doe," he insists,

> As our betters have done before us,
> The example is easily followed,
> Having so good a Schoole-mistris.
> Shall we to bed?   (2.2.138–42)

Loretta too recognizes sexual precedent in royal behavior. Having sent the two lovers off to their private rendezvous, she thinks of love herself:

> now could I wish my Sweet-heart
> Heere too, I feele such a tickling . . . if he were here now, I would
> Never cast such an unwilling deniall upon him
> As I have done, having so good a president as I have.   (2.2.105–9)

These two assertions, spoken within moments of each other, suggest the problem of illicit sexual behavior to the smooth running of the state and to the control of its low-status population. When those with authority sin, the rest are sure to follow.

Positioning chastity as a maintainer of economic distinctions adds yet another layer of social responsibility to the middling-rank moral ethos. Its presence ensures a stable class dynamics. In order to support already established status distinctions and to reinforce obedient behavior from below, women and men of the middling ranks need to marry, monitoring their behavior appropriately. If they do not, their lessers, represented in this text by the likes of Scanfardo, not only will be sexually incontinent themselves but also will spread misinformation and disrupt social hierarchies, using the economic repercussions of both to their own advantage.[63]

In *Swetnam the Woman-Hater*, only men benefit from illicit sexual arrangements. Theatergoers are reminded that women (of any status) are "nothing" once they lose their reputation. While Loretta's information to Scanfardo temporarily buys his love (hearing of Lisandro's success incites Scanfardo's own desire) and literally lines his pockets with gold (he repeats her words to Nicanor in anticipation of actual payment), Loretta's purchase is fleeting: it eventually undermines her marriage plans, destroying her value. Scanfardo explains, "I'm very loth to leave my sport to night [with Loretta], / And yet more loth to lose that rich reward / My Lord will give for this discoverie" (2.2.157–59). The "reward" that Scanfardo will earn for his information literally replaces the sexual act in this equation. Loretta's lost chastity then is not just one of "maidenhead" but of lost value both in her mistress's eye ("Oh this *Loretta*, false, inhumane wretch!" [2.3.34]) and in her lover's ("Venerie is sweet. / But he that has good store of gold and wealth, / May have it at command, and not by stealth" [2.2.161–63]).

All three authors share common concerns about chaste reputation and its value on the marriage market, but each directs that authority to suit different ends. Where Sowernam privileges chastity as women's greatest asset (particularly women of the middling ranks who may come into marriage with a less than adequate portion), both Shakespeare and *Swetnam the Woman-Hater*'s author see chastity as a state problem – the one in making sure that chastity relents, the other in seeing that it does not. Where Shakespeare reveals chastity as potentially disruptive and outside masculine control (empowering chaste women if only by negation), the anonymous writer of *Swetnam the Woman-Hater* reduces women's chaste authority both culturally and dramatically. Instead, *Swetnam the Woman-Hater* refashions reputation as a status problem. For *Swetnam*'s playwright, lost reputation means bad business. In a culture that is losing many of its traditional markers of difference, a culture attempting to make those distinctions that remain between social groupings more profound and harder to negotiate, sexual misconduct is necessarily threatening. Sexual incontinence erases boundaries and empowers the "wrong sorts of people."[64]

What gets lost in the tradeoff

Although all three accounts recognize chastity as important in marriage negotiation, neither of the male-authored texts requires it to quite the same degree as *Ester hath hang'd Haman*. That Sowernam must, of necessity, posit chaste reputation as integral to female behavior is both disturbing and inevitable. In order to secure equal obligation from men, Sowernam must be complicit in constructing and defending an image of middling-rank femininity that erases female bodies, anticipates their failure to live up to expectation, and in literal terms is necessarily short-lived (after all chastity need only be violated once). What this means is that female-centered texts like Sowernam's must promote a more encompassing notion of chaste living, one that accommodates women who are no longer virgins – that is, women who have become wives. In *Ester hath hang'd Haman* chastity comes to embody myriad domestic requirements, requirements which confine women within the household, monitor their behavior both inside and outside that sphere, and restrict their interactions.

As moral exemplars of proper behavior and conduct, Sowernam's women must be above reproach. She warns, "for corruption, *boni pessima*, the best thing corrupted proveth the worst, as for example, the most glorious creature in heaven is by his fall the most damned devill in hell . . . so the like in women, in their most excellent puritie of nature, what creature more gratious! but in their fall from God, and all goodnesse, what creature more mischievous" (25). Because Sowernam must account for those rare instances where women misuse their moral authority, she inadvertently ends up justifying a double standard. Women and men do not err equally. Failing to uphold the contract, women are to be condemned especially, likened to "the most damned devill in hell." This double standard is further complicated by other gender distinctions that operate in tandem with it (e.g., a denial of a female erotics to ensure male sexual responsibility and a restriction of female mobility to promote male obligation within the household). In an attempt to make men legally and morally responsible for their relationships with women, both within the constraints of the recently formalized marriage contract and outside its domain as potential suitors, Sowernam denies women any erotic experience whatsoever. For Sowernam, the only legitimate allusions that can be made in regard to the female body are necessarily externalized, outside women's experience in the way that they are seen and evaluated.

Responding directly to charges of an insatiable female desire, Sowernam writes, "and this shall appeare in the imputation which our adversarie chargeth upon our sexe, to be lascivious, wanton and lustfull: He sayth, *Women tempt, alure, and provoke men.* How rare a thing is it for women to prostitute and offer themselves? how common a practise is it for men to seeke out and solicite women to lewdnesse?" (45). In her redefinition of sexual encounters, Sowernam juxtaposes two options: women seduce men or men seduce women. In both scenarios the outcome is negatively framed. Women can either "prostitute" themselves (rare) or men can "solicite" them to "lewdnesse" (common). Regardless, women are always "subject to a lustfull bodie." Attempting to differ-entiate between what is said and what is done, between social fiction and social fact, Sowernam assumes an inherent guilt; somebody or something must be to blame, and she requires that someone to be a man. Recognizing chaste reputation as integral to women's being and essential to the refigured marriage contract, she is unable to construct a positive female erotics unless it is externalized – translated into chaste beauty and perceived from the outside by men who will either account it part of the marriage portion or mis-"use" it in "wanton and lascivious lookes." This understanding necessarily encodes woman as victim or paragon, without agency, without sexuality, and without pleasure.

The domestic confessional

The erasure of female sexuality figures into women's newer roles as guardians of reputation, and it is this latter obligation that will serve the state so adroitly in extra-legal ways. In *Ester hath hang'd Haman*, women of the middling ranks, ostensibly free from the desire to "sin," become domestic confessors. They monitor *and legislate* the moral domain – the domain of "secret thoughts" and private conscience. In fact, in keeping with countless other works of the early seventeenth century, all three texts focus on issues of conscience catching; each attempts to resolve discrepancies between thought and action, between conscience and conduct. Sowernam's tract invokes notions of a gendered domesticity – a domesticity that relegates wives to the private domain, to the education and rearing of their children, and to the maintenance of the interior spaces of the household. In *Ester hath hang'd Haman*, women's "natural" abilities as keepers of conscience are made manifest.[65]

Insisting that women are worthy overseers of their husbands' inner thoughts, Sowernam allows seventeenth-century wives to overturn certain conventionalized hierarchies of patriarchal power and control. She offers women an authority that had generally been accorded to the church. In Catholic England, priests, as deputies of the Lord, heard confessions and absolved penitents. During much of the sixteenth century, that office was effectively vacant, though the Church of England and its unacknowledged alternatives still attempted to govern conscience and maintain a more generalized disciplinary control over English subjects, with varying degrees of success.[66] Because of that absence, Sowernam's promise that women are eminently qualified to secure reputation, more eminently qualified than either men or the church, is necessarily empowering.[67]

As the physical embodiment of her husband's "chaste" reputation, a seventeenth-century wife ensures, in her cultural presence at her husband's side, that he is to be respected within the community. Though an "ideal" wife is almost by definition imagined in domestic terms,[68] her chaste behavior, nevertheless, offers her husband a type of *public* legitimacy. In his marriage to a good wife, he qualifies for full citizenship within the community. He becomes a good patriarch, a good neighbor, a good Christian, and a good businessman. In Sowernam's account, then, a chaste wife is the sign of her husband's public success. The process of moral legitimation is more complicated than this, however. Sowernam's construction distinguishes between the representational office that women take on (chaste wife as *example* of status) and the active role that they possess in directing moral behavior and conduct (chaste wife as *agent* in securing and maintaining status). In Sowernam's frame, women not only function as external signifiers of masculine integrity but also as interpreters and regulators of men's minds. They can ensure that what is seen from the outside (reputation) is literally synonymous with what cannot be seen (the basis for that reputation). Sowernam empowers women to act and to judge, all within the internal workings of the mind – within the conscience. She argues that women, chaste women, can discern that which is hidden from view, and she presents this configuration as advantageous – advantageous not only to husbands who can make the most of their newly secure married status but also to an English state that is plagued by a growing inability to control its citizens and determine their behavior.

To some extent, the nature of controversy writing allows for the certainty of Sowernam's absolutes. That she can equate "seeming" with "being" and insist that Swetnam's "conscience" will eventually catch him goes with the territory. As an example in argument and logical exposition, her defense necessarily erases the subtleties and contradictions inherent in an uncertain stance or an ambivalent conscience.[69] What

Sowernam's tract does, however, is to take advantage of that generic certainty to promote a particular form of authority for women in the marriage market. What the male-authored plays conversely do is to suggest, dramatically this time, the anxiety that early modern audiences must have felt over an inability to square action with intent and outward form with inner substance. That all three texts grapple with moral authority is hardly unique or gendered. It is in their choice of solution that gender necessarily figures so prominently.

At an allegorical level, Sowernam continually feminizes her discussions of culpability and intent. She frames her legal discussion of Swetnam's offense within the conscience, recruiting two "judgesses," Reason and Experience, to determine his guilt. Sowernam's allegorical judges, no doubt legitimated via their Latinate roots *ratio* and *experientia* and via their conventional usage during the period, are clearly and intentionally gendered. Sowernam addresses them specifically with feminine pronouns and identifies their title in gendered terms (they are "judgesses" not "judges," "shes" not "hes"). It is their function *within* the trial setting, however, that illustrates Sowernam's gender coding so emphatically. Reason and Experience do not merely stand in for a metonymic connection between women and conscience. Their task within Sowernam's court is literally to "judge" the workings of a man's mind. Sowernam writes,

As for *Experience*, she is known of her selfe to be admirable excellent in her course, she knoweth how to use every man in her practise; she will whip the foole to learne him more wit; she will punish the knave to practise more honesty; she will curbe in the prodigall, and teach him to be warie; she will trip up the heeles of such as are rash and giddy, and bid them hereafter looke before they leape. To be short, there is not in all the world, for all estates, degrees, qualities and conditions of men, so singular a Mistresse, or so fit to be a judgesse as she, onely one property she hath above all the rest, no man commeth before her but she maketh him ashamed, and shee will call and prove almost every man a foole, especially such who are wise in their owne conceits. (28)

Sowernam's use of Experience in this passage serves two critical functions. On the one hand Experience figures broadly within this text as a foundation for Sowernam's arguments. "Experience" is one of the few forums available to Sowernam as a woman attempting to counter years of received knowledge about women's roles and qualities. On the other, she positions this feminized attribute as all-seeing, all-knowing, *and* all-interrogating of men's minds, and it is this last strategy that is so telling and directive in terms of moral reform. Not only can Experience recognize and identify inappropriate thinking, but she also can take legitimate and effective action to remedy it: "One property she hath above the rest," she can make men "ashamed." Sowernam writes that Experience will "use every man in her practise." She will "whip," "punish," "curbe in," and "trip up" men in order to teach them proper behavior and acceptable moral codes. The physical and disciplinary methods of Sowernam's "judgesse" not only echo legitimate punitive authority within the criminal courts – they too "whip," "punish," and "curbe in" – but they also suggest the essentially active nature of female control. Experience will not simply teach men by example, she will "use" them "in her practise." No one is "so fit . . . a judgesse as she."

A good wife, then, does not simply offer her husband a reputation by her own deportment. She is also meant to be an active force in ordering her husband's behavior. Advising fathers to marry off wild sons, Sowernam promises, "if [you] have a sonne given to spending and companie-keeping, who is of a wild and riotous disposition . . . help your sonne to a good wife, marry him, *marry him*, that is the onely way to bring him to good order, to tame him, to bring him to be an honest [man]" (23). Here Sowernam's emphasis is not on securing reputations – on attending to perceptions – but rather on keeping inappropriate behaviors in check. Sowernam insists that women can "bring [their husbands] to good order." Good women will "tame" the men they marry. In Sowernam's configuration, then, wives are not simply the "signe and seale" of their husband's reputation and the guardians of their own chastity; they are also literal agents monitoring men's actions and emending them accordingly.

Within the logic of her argument, Sowernam makes a connection between causal certainty and women's ability to discern. Countering Swetnam's charge that women cannot tell a truth, much less identify one, Sowernam insists instead that is women who consistently make accurate and useful distinctions in judgment. "Women can make difference betwixt colours and conditions," she writes, "betwixt a faire shew, and a foule substance" (38). The knowledge that Sowernam accords to women becomes yet another telling point in securing an advantageous marriage contract. With an inherent ability to recognize a*nd correct* "foule substance[s]," women ensure their husbands both a good name and a good conscience, and they reinforce state needs as well. Satisfactory completion of their part in the marriage bargain attends to that aspect of civil obedience that is outside the state's domain. While legal retribution may address certain identifiable crimes (theft and murder, among them),[70] it will not accommodate a rebellious or insubordinate mind. Treasonous ideas are far more difficult to legislate against than the acts they may or may not initiate.

In defending women against Swetnam's many charges, Sowernam simultaneously creates, or at the very least augments, a marriage contract that demands mutual obligation from married partners and locates that obligation spatially in separate realms of private and public, conscience and conduct. In order to counter Swetnam's arguments, she constructs discrete configurations of male and female responsibility. While her defense attends emphatically to what men ought to be doing in this regard (caring for wives and families, earning adequate livings, responding to community concerns), it nevertheless identifies and prioritizes women's roles as well. As chaste keepers of both the physical interior of the home and the moral interior of their husbands' minds, Sowernam's seventeenth-century wives honor the contract and reinforce the civil status quo.

Conscience catching in the plays

The problem of moral reform is one *Measure for Measure* shares with *Ester hath hang'd Haman*. This 1604 text, however, is neither so gender-explicit nor so absolute in its handling of these questions. Despite generally putting things to rights from a magisterial perspective (the duke at least *addresses* all of the major crimes perpetrated in this play), *Measure for Measure* still leaves numerous loose ends – unrepentant criminals and treasonous thoughts among them. In punishing offenders, the duke's laws successfully attend to bodies. Prisoners will be executed for their offenses or given executive reprieve. It is the issue of penitence – the prisoner's recognition of an interior guilt – that is so difficult to secure.[71]

Bernardine is a case in point. The duke's first question about Bernardine's status focuses not on his physical punishment, but rather on his frame of mind. The duke asks, "hath [Bernardine] borne himself penitently in prison? How seems he to be touched?" (4.2.138–39). It is the disguised duke's office as friar to attend to the spiritual well-being of his charges – to prepare them to "meet their maker" and to secure their souls for the hereafter; but this anxiety is shared by the state as well. In fact, in *Measure for Measure* both offices serve one and the same function. They both desire to unite conscience with conduct, and thought with action. That Bernardine is not ready to die, that he refuses to admit to his crime and willingly embrace the sentence he has been accorded, is clearly seen as a problem in this play. Despite countless real threats of execution, Bernardine remains unrepentant. The provost explains, "we have very oft awaked him as if to carry him to execution . . . [but] it hath not moved him at all" (4.2.148–51).

Bernardine's two public declamations both soundly refuse to acknowledge the legitimacy of his punishment. "I have been drinking all night," he says, "I am not fitted for't" (4.3.42–43). Moments later he follows up this assertion with a second: "I will have more time to prepare me, or they shall beat out my brains with billets. I will not consent to die this day, that's certain" (4.3.54–55). Bernardine's refusal to submit secures him a temporary reprieve. The duke approves his stay of execution because Bernardine is "a creature unprepar'd, unmeet for death; / And to transport him in the mind he is / Were damnable" (4.3.66–68). While the duke's concern here is ostensibly for Bernardine's soul, what is perhaps truly "damnable" to the state is its inability to control men's minds. Without sufficient resources or procedures to monitor his citizens' behavior after the fact (once crimes have been committed), the duke requires that obedience be internalized. Bernardine's denial of the sentence passed against him – his refusal to accept his execution as deserved and to recognize in his acts a wrong that ought to be punished (his crime is never specified) – underscores the dilemma that the duke and his deputies face in trying the citizens of Vienna.

Perhaps the most emphatic declaration of this unfortunate split is uttered by Isabella in the play's closing scene. On her knees before the duke, Isabella begs for Angelo's life and at the same time articulates the real limits of the duke's legal authority to monitor behavior (ironic because, in attempting to convince Vincentio of the justice in what she says, Isabella reveals to him instead the inadequacy of his own power to control his people). She argues:

> For Angelo,
> His act did not o'ertake his bad intent,
> And must be buried but as an intent
> That perish'd by the way. Thoughts are no subjects;
> Intents, but merely thoughts.   (5.1.448–52)

Denying the right of the state to ascribe subject status to Angelo's "thoughts" – "Thoughts are no subjects," she insists – Isabella once and for all separates conscience from conduct and locates legitimate punishment and control only after the fact. Her division leaves questions of conscience (treasonous or not) a protected domain, the property of the populace, not its governors.

Measure for Measure does not accept Sowernam's gendered solution to this problem of conscience. Isabella's only part in securing Angelo's confession rests in her function as a vehicle for the duke. Instead, *Measure for Measure* relies on the duke's double role as civil *and* spiritual father to ensure appropriate penitence from the guilty. That the duke chooses the habit of a friar is no accident. In an ideal ordered state, the function of law is to minister to both conscience and conduct, to make subjects obedient in both mind and body. Shakespeare's consolidation of roles graphically suggests civil authority's ostensible power to accomplish both tasks simultaneously. As a friar who will hear confessions and learn minds, Vincentio can legitimately attend to conscience. It is his office to do so. As Duke of Vienna, he can, in turn, enact laws that demand outward compliance from his subjects and offer bodily punishment to offenders. While neither role is entirely effective in *Measure for Measure*, the conjunction of both offers some degree of success.[72]

Measure for Measure, though it continually calls into question the state's ability to square conscience with conduct and seeming with being, nevertheless attempts to empower the state with the authority to recuperate secret thoughts and mold them into acceptable forms. The duke's last words concerning Bernardine suggest that he has not yet given up his attempt to unite outward punishment with inward remorse. Dispatching the provost to other work, the duke commands: "see [that] this be done, / . . . / whiles I / Persuade this rude wretch willingly to die" (4.3.78–80).

The duke expects full confessions from each of the prisoners in his charge – no one will be forgiven without an avowal of guilty conscience. Juliet, Angelo, and Claudio must each accept their punishment and admit their guilt. Interrogating Juliet in regard to her already visible crime, the Duke wants to make sure than she is penitent in mind as well as body. "I'll teach you how you shall arraign your conscience," he tells her, "And try your penitence, if it be sound, / Or hollowly put on" (2.3.21–23). Here, the Duke needs to know if Juliet's outward contrition is "sound" (matched by an inner sorrow). Trying to identify her position with certainty, the Duke distinguishes outward "seeming" from inward "being" as a shame generated in fear rather than in joy (a repentance that is not heartfelt). He is worried:

> lest [she does] repent,
> As that the sin hath brought [her] to this shame,
> Which sorrow is always toward ourselves, not heaven,
> Showing we would not spare heaven as we love it
> But as we stand in fear.   (2.3.30–34)

When Juliet admits to a guilty conscience – "repent[s] . . . as it is an evil, / And take[s] the shame with the joy" (2.3.35–36) – Duke Vincentio is satisfied.

Claudio's numerous backslidings suggest the elusive nature of securing conscience to a single and physically demonstrable end as well. That Claudio vacillates between accepting his punishment as legitimate and ascribing to it an authority that is both arbitrary and self-serving, illustrates a potential weak link in criminal prosecution and moral reform. Initially Claudio recognizes his actions as wrong. He admits to Lucio, "our natures do pursue, / Like rats that ravin down their proper bane, / A thirsty evil; and when we drink, we die" (1.2.120–22). Later, however, he reevaluates that initial assertion of guilt to question Angelo's role as lawmaker. Claudio's eventual recasting of events suggests that Angelo's too severe strictures stem not from some ideologically pure concept of "justice," but rather from a personal "tyranny" that could be legitimately overthrown or at the very least openly questioned. According to Claudio, Angelo "puts the drowsy and neglected act / Freshly on [Claudio] . . . for a name" (1.2.159–60). Evoking public law to secure private reputation discredits both the lawmaker and the law itself. That Claudio can argue, even if only temporarily, from a position that perceives his sentencing as unjust reveals the limitations of state power in regulating behavior. Despite this backsliding, Claudio's final avowal that he is resigned to dying suggests that he is finally all of one purpose – that his penitence "is sound" – and the duke corroborates that testimony: "[Claudio] professes to have received no sinister measure from his judge, but most willingly humbles himself to the determination of justice . . . and now is he resolved to die" (3.2.228–33).

Angelo's eventual contrition echoes what must have been the party line on state criminal control. Yet it is his crime over all of the rest that iterates the real problem of judgment and control. In a very tangible sense, Angelo's corrupt authority is not only the most abusive of and threatening to state-ordered notions of control and obedience, but it is also the most overtly deceptive and duplicitous of the offenses committed in this play. Angelo's denial of guilt, almost to the play's close, reminds viewers that without a furtive and all-seeing duke, conscience need have no connection with conduct, that outward conformity accounts for very little in judgments that lay claim to moral certainty. Angelo covers his crime well and intends to keep doing so as long as he is able. Once caught,[73] however, Angelo completely acquiesces, insisting that the separation between intent and act is and always has been fictive, will always be remedied by an all-seeing and all-knowing state authority. "Oh my dread Lord," he promises,

> I should be guiltier than my guiltiness
> To think I can be undiscernible,
> When I perceive your Grace, like power divine,
> Hath looked upon my passes . . .
> But let my trial be mine own confession.
> Immediate sentence then and sequent death
> Is all the grace I beg.   (5.1.365–70)

Positing civil authority – embodied in the duke – as a "power divine," Angelo claims that his guilt will always be "discernible," that policy will account for criminal intent as well as criminal act. In his apology, he literally equates confession with trial and penitence with punishment, insisting that each is subject to continual scrutiny.

Despite vastly different configurations of legitimate moral regulation, one coded in terms of the church, the other in terms of female authority within the household, both *Measure for Measure* and *Ester hath hang'd Haman* recognize the proper domain of the moral to be located within. It is to be a private affair, unveiled only behind closed doors. As spiritual counselor, Duke Vincentio negotiates the same interior realm as that allotted to women. His is a "secret harbour" (1.3.4). It is no accident that Lucio refers to him as the "old fantastical duke of dark corners" (4.3.156). Indeed, the duke's "dark corners" invoke the solitude of the private confessional (itself a fairly recent feature of early modern culture).[74] Discovering "what may man within him hide" is a secret endeavor, unconducive to public scrutiny.[75] Donning a habit and learning the office enable the very public duke (who has "ever lov'd the life removed") to "visit both prince and people" in concealment (1.3.8, 45). Accordingly, Shakespeare aligns public and private, not in gendered terms, as both seem to be figured in Sowernam's tract, but rather in a culturally more familiar and perhaps residual binarism that sets the spiritual in opposition to the secular and assumes both to be masculine.[76]

Measure for Measure calls forth the same troubling questions that *Ester hath hang'd Haman* addresses. While the play refuses to secure subject regulation in any final or satisfying manner (this, in marked contrast to the adamant certainty of *Ester hath hang'd Haman*'s moral universe), like Sowernam's defense it clearly recognizes regulatory practices as central and attempts to negotiate some sort of transcendent position from which to claim authority. In 1603, *Measure for Measure* looks to a residual Catholicism,[77] evoked in the duke's role as confessor, to augment a state authority that is, at best, only marginally effective. Thirteen years later, *Ester hath hang'd Haman* emphatically recasts that authority within a new province. In middling-rank marriage, wives will intervene on behalf of the state to keep English husbands and sons morally in line.

Swetnam the Woman-Hater, published perhaps in anticipation of a new monarchy under James's son Charles, also genders the relationship between conscience and conduct, this time by belittling both. One of the most significant narrative upheavals to occur within the 1620 play comes in its gendered and generational reformulation of pastoral disguise: *Swetnam the Woman-Hater* disturbs the church/state connection of

Measure for Measure's friar/duke, by shifting the dynamics of state power in marriage questions from spiritual/secular to female/male, and placing legitimate royal authority in the hands of the king's prodigal son. In the later play, Duke Vincentio's disguised friar becomes Prince Lorenzo's disguised Amazon and the criteria that distinguish legal from moral domain change accordingly. Like *Measure for Measure*, *Swetnam the Woman-Hater* is far less certain of the lasting legal efficacy of its resolutions than is Sowernam's tract. Repentance is both hasty and contrived for the play's two main antagonists. Misogynos, though he is criminally convicted within the women's court, refuses to acknowledge guilt, railing at his captors as they sentence him. It is not until the play's end that he finally relents. Even then he admits to his guilt only in epilogue, offering us a traditional apology that claims little else but theatrical forgiveness. Nicanor's duplicities are similarly unresolved. While he admits his guilt and accepts state punishment for his misdeeds, that conversion too is abrupt and cursory. Conscience squares with conduct only briefly in the presentation of a formalized masque. Its allegorical recreation of the moral sphere (including within it a feminized version of Repentance) reminds Nicanor of the criminality of his actions and the culpability of his thoughts.

Even the lovers refuse to recognize the sentence imposed upon them by the state as either legitimate or deserved, and their refusals to confess reiterate the state's inability to square conscience with conduct. Once caught, both lovers take on an assumed guilt in an effort to save each other, but their penance is practical rather than heartfelt: the law insists that there be a principal offender – a *"Primus Motor* that beg[an] the cause" (3.1.39) – but neither party will allow that assertion any stability. Leonida insists, "Then since the guilt alone remaines in Mee, / Let me be judg'd, and set *Lisandro* free" (3.1.85–86). Lisandro counters, "I broke the Law, / And I must suffer for't" (3.1.93–94). Both admit to breaking the law and willingly embrace punishment as just retribution. In arguing their complicity both simultaneously proclaim innocence (she is innocent, I am not; he's not guilty, the fault is mine). The overall effect is to underscore the inappropriate nature of the king's sentence against them. Indeed, in a recitation of the princess's last words, the king's faithful counselor, Iago, reiterates the separation between the punishment she receives and the penance she fails to embrace. He tells the king, "the last words she spoke, said, I rejoyce / That I am free'd of Fathers tyrannie" (5.1.51–52).

Leonida's failure to mold conscience to crime unsettles the king. Her confident refusal – identifying Atticus as her father not her king – reveals the limits of his authority (he can punish her actions but not her thoughts). His response to her dying words, nevertheless, assumes the connection between conscience and conduct. "Forbeare to utter more," Atticus insists to Iago.

> We are not pleas'd
> With these unpleasing accents: Leave the world
> So cheerfully, and speake of tyrannie:
> She was not guiltie sure. We'le heare no more.   (5.1.53–56)

That the king believes in Leonida's innocence *because* she refused to accept her death as a just punishment – "She was not guiltie sure" – suggests that the state (naïvely perhaps) equates guilt with criminality and accepts both as the proper domain of the law courts.

Leonida's response to Nicanor's offer of marriage also suggests that her thoughts will remain unsubjected despite whatever real pressures Nicanor may exert to regulate them. When asked by Nicanor how Leonida responded to his suit, Loretta tells him, "at length; having recal'd her spirits / She broke forth into these words . . . / Tho' my body be confin'd his prisoner, / Yet my mind is free" (2.1.93–98).[78] Nicanor may control Leonida's actions, but he will never secure her mind. In the next scene he declares, "Now, the Princesse, / Although I have her Person, yet her Heart / I find estrang'd from mee, and all my love / Is quitted with contempt" (2.1.152–55). Opposing body and mind, person and heart, within the context of a forced marriage poses their antithesis as something to be celebrated not reviled. Within the logic of *Swetnam the Woman-Hater*, an unsubjected mind is a mind yet free from tyranny.

Where *Measure for Measure* sees duplicity as a problem, *Swetnam the Woman-Hater* uses it to advantage. The 1620 play underscores the separation between conscience and conduct as an opportunity to criticize an aging king and lampoon the gender debate.[79] Where *Measure for Measure* juxtaposes the duke's civil authority with his spiritual role as confessor, *Swetnam the Woman-Hater*, like *Ester hath hang'd Haman*, genders the whole question of internal surveillance by turning friar into Amazon, bachelor duke into married king, and volunteered spiritual confession into forced feminine advice. In order to better "observe the times and humors of the court" (1.3.103), Prince Lorenzo disguises himself as a woman.[80] In his role as Amazon, the prince defends female prerogative on-stage and off. In two court trials, neither entirely successful, the prince/Amazon serves as an advocate for women. Despite and perhaps because of the failure of either law court to judge appropriately, the disguised prince must catch the conscience of the misled king and his ill-scheming advisor, Nicanor, by extra-legal means. It is in this behind-the-scenes maneuvering that the connection between gender and morality is most blatantly exposed. While Nicanor devises the idea of a masque to pull King Atticus out of his depression (the performance reveals to both men the error of their ways and demands their eventual contrition), it is the prince as Amazon who choreographs that courtly entertainment, discovers the plot to discredit the lovers, and secures the lives of Leonida and Lisandro until the case can be proved to their advantage.

Prince Lorenzo, like *Measure for Measure*'s Duke Vincentio, carries out the various negotiations required in this play covertly; and much of his arranging occurs off stage, out of earshot. After the king passes sentence on his daughter, Lorenzo secures her life by demanding that her beheading occur in private (in the silent masque of her execution he himself carries the ax). Lorenzo asks that she not "basely / Be hurried forth amongst uncivill men; / But that [the] Queene, and [he], and some few others . . . / May see her execution" (3.3.284–88). That privatizing of a supposedly public execution enables the prince to perform some additional maskings of his own (none of which the play recounts), maskings that are here hidden and feminized. It is Lorenzo's gender-bending that allows him access to the queen, and it is their private confederacy that most emphatically equates conscience with women.

In *Swetnam the Woman-Hater*, Queen Aurelia insists that the state's punishment of the lovers is tyrannous. Both she and the king's counselor Iago advise the king to mend his ways. In addition, both serve as a type of externalized conscience, continually reminding the king of his faulty decision. "Will you . . . / Be so unjust, severe, nay tyrannous" (3.3.271–72), Aurelia asks immediately after the sentencing. The king's counselor, Iago, repeats her words almost verbatim moments later. Hearing of the trial's result, he calls Leonida's punishment "a sentence most unjust, and tyrannous" (4.1.23). Iago's words of warning, while ostensibly those of a king's advisor, have been feminized in *Swetnam the Woman-Hater*. Atticus recognizes Iago's abilities as "womanish." "Old Iago is a froward Lord," the king complains,

> Honest, but lenative, one-swaid too much
> With pittie against Justice, that's not good:
> Indeed it is not in a Counsellor.
> And he has too much of woman, otherwise
> He might be Ruler of a Monarchie,
> For policie and wisdome.   (5.3.40–46)

Tne king's understanding of Iago as "too much of woman" again points to moral regulation as a feminized territory. Like Aurelia, Iago will "nip [the king] to the verie soule" (5.3.55).

The judgments offered by Aurelia and Iago are reiterated throughout the remainder of the action. At one point Aurelia even directs her criticisms into a more generalized attack on royal prerogative and an argument for legitimate rebellion by the citizens of Sicily. "What say the people?" she asks, "doe they not exclaime, / And curse the servile yoke, in which th'are bound / Under so mercilesse a Governour?" (4.5.87–89). It is Aurelia's and Iago's actions not their sentiment that position them as surrogate conscience to the king. The active role they take on reinforces the literal agency required of women in correcting conscience. Both performers physically follow Atticus around the stage, reminding him of his offense. Iago, warned that his incessant words displease the king, responds,

> no matter, I'm glad I touch'd his conscience
> To the quick. Did you not see
> How my relation chang'd his countenance,
> As if my words ingendered in his brest
> Some new-bred passions?   (5.1.83–87)

The queen, in turn, after charging Atticus with a litany of invectives, promises to him, "Goe where thou wilt, still I will follow thee, / And with my sad laments still beat thy eares, / Till all the world of thy injustice heares" (5.1.108–10). *Swetnam the Woman-Hater*, like *Ester hath hang'd Haman*, posits women as guardians of men's thoughts. In Aurelia's promise to "follow" the king "where [he] wilt" with her "sad laments," she figuratively stands in for royal conscience.

Although both Iago and Aurelia offer advice and articulate conscience in *Swetnam the Woman-Hater*, neither does so appropriately or successfully. Without intercession from the "new" state (the prince not his father), both the king and Nicanor would remain unrepentant. Like *Measure for Measure*, *Swetnam the Woman-Hater* locates at least part of the ability to regulate and control with the state (albeit in the guise of a woman). Atalanta (the disguised prince) readily accepts the queen's request for an advocate to "defend the innocency of women" and secure Leonida's reprieve. (If she succeeds, Leonida's punishment will be banishment not death.) In Atalanta's opening words to the court, she promises that the cause that she handles is so just that "were corruption seated / upon [their] hearts . . . [she] would not feare, / But that [her] pregnant Reasons soone shou'd purge, / And clense [their] secret bosomes from untruth" (3.3.60–64). Claiming her "cause" capable of uncovering "untruth[s]" – "of clens[ing] . . . secret bosomes" – Atalanta once again locates moral regulation in women's hands. Even her "Reasons" are gendered – "pregnant" and waiting to conceive. As an advocate, the disguised Atalanta accepts that task as her own. As Amazon, she will cleanse the court of its "untruth[s]." As prince, she will enforce her purgatives with royal authority.

The performance of the masque at the play's end is the literal means by which both Atticus and Nicanor are made to repent.[81] Here too that performance has been feminized.[82] The various roles of the maskers reiterate the connection between gender and conscience-keeping. Repentance is a woman, and she secures Nicanor's guilt via that sexual marker. In his confession, he must literally *woo and win her*. "But let Repentance stay," he insists. "On my knees, / She must be followed, call'd and su'd unto, / And by continuall Prayers, woo'd, and wonne, / Which I will never cease . . . / I doe repent me" (5.3.103–8). Nicanor's suit is *spiritualized* in its allusion to "Prayers," but it is more emphatically *sexualized* in that he posits Repentance as a lover to be wooed and won. Repentance will "uncover" hidden intent and make it visible. Nicanor admits, "Now all will be reveal'd, I never dream't / Upon Repentance, I: but now I see, / Truth will discover all men's Trecherie" (5.3.114–16).

Where *Measure for Measure* translates the disjunction between conscience and conduct into two realms, spiritual and secular, both open to state intervention in the literal persona of the duke/friar, *Ester hath hang'd Haman* and *Swetnam the Woman-Hater* rewrite that separation in gendered terms, terms that operate on at least one level in contradiction to received notions of mind and body. This maneuver suggests a growing need to resituate moral authority in a more tenable and less precarious location than religious discourse. While *Swetnam the Woman-Hater* and *Ester hath hang'd Haman* agree in the main as to the gendering of authority in two separate spheres of influence, private and public, interior and exterior, the reframings of that authority are, nevertheless, in marked contrast to one another.

Where *Ester hath hang'd Haman* frames its options in absolute and laudatory terms, *Swetnam the Woman-Hater* is far more ambivalent. Sowernam authorizes and applauds women who will discover the truth of men's minds, seeing in that ability a valuable component of the marriage portion. *Swetnam the Woman-Hater*, though purportedly a play in women's defense, continually problematizes that celebratory status by falling back on negative stereotyping for comic effect. Aurelia's lamentations to the king border on the extreme and threaten to transgress the boundaries of acceptable behavior for women. Where the logic of the play demands "soft suggestions," Aurelia instead hurls insults – insults that openly usurp the king's prerogative. "Where is *Aurelia*? Where's *Iago* gone?" Atticus charges.

To studie new Invectives? If agen
They dare but utter the least syllable,
Or smallest title of inveteracie,
They shall not breathe a minute. Must a Prince
Be check't, and schooled, pursued and scolded at
For executing Justice?   (5.3.8–14)

Coding the queen's and Iago's insults as both scolding and chronic (inveterate), Atticus reminds theater-goers of the very accusations against women that the play pretends to undermine.[83]

All three of the above works take on questions of moral and legal legislation. *Measure for Measure* codes the separation between realms in terms of the duke/friar's spiritual *and* secular authorities. The friar consoles the mind, the duke attends to the body. In contrast, *Swetnam the Woman-Hater* realigns authorities and offices. When the duke/friar becomes the prince/Amazon, religious contrition is translated into sexual guilt. As an elite representative of government, Duke Vincentio's confessor/king retains absolute authority over the proceedings in Vienna. Though he may be pastorally absent from the court with his office temporarily filled by a deputy, real authority is still his to take up and throw off when desired. The same is not true in the 1620 text of *Swetnam the Woman-Hater*. Although real authority still rests with the king's son, in this later play the gender split – female/male – locates at least part of the power to monitor and regulate in popular terms, within private homes in relations between husbands and wives. Indeed the prince's as-yet-unauthorized status as *future* ruler – he is not yet king – further delineates a shift in the locus of power from elite to popular understanding. This does not mean that the idea of monarchical authority is being called into question in the later play;[84] rather it suggests that other lesser authorities have been called in to ease the burden of the state. What *Swetnam the Woman-Hater* documents is a type of incipient bureaucratizing of institutional control at various other levels of government (including the domestic).

Trajectories

In *Ester hath hang'd Haman*, Ester Sowernam's rhetorical maneuvers underscore a gap in "middle-class" marriage policy. Simultaneously embracing and denying the only categories of womanhood available to her, Sowernam does not redress a *faulty or ill-conceived categorization* of women, but rather, in response to an ever-expanding and financially powerful London mercantile economy, she attempts to ensure that the boundaries between categories are drawn with greater precision and more uniformity. On the title page of her defense she defines herself as "neither Maide, Wife nor Widdowe, yet really all, and therefore experienced to defend all." In doing so, she asks only that those categories remain discrete: once a wife always a wife. She outlines a marriage service that is both public and irrevocable and demands of its participants separate yet shared obligations. At the same time she frames a sizeable portion of her argument as a court trial before "the barre of fame and report." Each of these maneuvers suggests a desire to locate gender reform in the material circumstances of the middling ranks, a willingness to take on the marriage market and negotiate its uncertain terrain.

Sowernam's careful attention to categories and to securing status within them insists that she negotiate the contract and offer adequate compensation. Middling-rank women must marry, and in order to marry well they must be sufficiently provided for. In early seventeenth-century England, courts are not threatening sexual offenders with death.[85] Instead, uncertain marriage laws are still ensuring that a percentage of the population is born out of wedlock,[86] and that women who fail to secure a legitimate contract (many of them from the middling ranks) can be left with child and without adequate means to support themselves.[87] Accordingly, I want to stress in Sowernam's textual differences from her male counterparts not only the generic or historic variations resulting from different media or intervening years, but also the gender-specific circumstances of her writing.

Recentering the problem of the English marriage contract to focus on questions directly relevant to women's financial well-being, Sowernam recasts Shakespeare's earlier handling of marriage policy and moral regulation in new light. Where Shakespeare sees in chastity the potential for anarchy and leaves confessions to confessors, *Swetnam*'s author and Sowernam both assume chaste behavior for women, differing only in how they choose to empower that moral guardianship via the middling ranks. Like *Swetnam the Woman-Hater*, *Ester hath hang'd Haman* places the "business" of regulating men's minds in women's hands – it genders secret thoughts, feminizing conscience to accommodate contract. Where Sowernam celebrates women's newly authorized status, however, recognizing regulation as a legitimate and potentially powerful forum for female authority, the author of the 1620 play both lampoons and limits that function. It is up to the state – to the monarch's prodigal son (Charles I perhaps?)[88] – to see that women carry out their obligations appropriately and with decorum. Women may advise as long as the real business of control (legislative authority) remains with the state.

Measure for Measure and *Swetnam the Woman-Hater*, the first predating Sowernam's account, the second hard on its heels, serve as tidy reminders of both the cultural possibilities for subject articulation and state making that authors like Sowernam can initiate and the trajectory that such rewritings might eventually take within already-inscribed patriarchal terms. Yes, the moral reforms that Sowernam's tract advances will continue to reside within the English home – they have become a woman's domestic responsibility, her part of the marriage bargain. As chaste wives, seventeenth-century English women will be asked not only to embody chaste conscience in and of themselves but also to remind husbands and children of the sanctity of that moral domain in their private and public concerns. I want to stress again, however, that the limits of women's moral authority are to be felt palpably and profoundly. In refiguring the cultural terrain, the wanton has become the nag; and good women, chaste women – indeed, "middle-class" women – acquire the moral high ground only to lose definition in countless other facets of their lives.

4   Gender formation in English apocalyptic writing

> Thus Reader in a word to thee, what the unsealed words of this Prophesie imports; We even in the same Estate with them . . . Here impeached of the sin against the Holy Ghost, guilty of the blood of these his sacred Ambassadors . . . wonders of the highest kinde at their word, waters turn'd into blood, War forshewed, Heaven shut, and the like, smite the Earth with plagues as often as they speak the word, yet these rash wretches . . . clad in sack cloth . . . triumphing over their corps slain by the Beast coming out of the smoking pit or Abyss . . . making War with them, with his furious Train, armed at all points this British Beast.[1]

In the 1640s the prophet Lady Eleanor Davies warned her readers of imminent doom, of the coming of the apocalypse or endtimes. Like many writers during this period, Davies constructed a millennial accounting of the British nation.[2] She posited individual sin within an already established Calvinist frame, anticipated an immediate and specific end to the world as we know it, and demanded death for her adversaries. As individual sinners, Davies's readers were "impeached of the sin against the Holy Ghost" and "guilty [if only by association] of the blood of . . . his sacred Ambassadors." Her endtimes warning was equally explicit. The "unsealed words" of Davies's prophecy called directly on images from Revelation – plagues, waters turned to blood, and the presence of the Beast – in their promise of social upheaval. Davies's proselytizing promised both a literal and figurative war on the unrepentant. In a punitive rhetoric that acted on fears present in her readership, Davies mapped a predetermined future from a previously sinful past and positioned herself as an all-powerful narrator beside a cowed and guilty audience.

Holy hatred – Davies's marked aggression toward a perceived enemy and her insistence in making her audience share in that aggression – is a trait common to most 1640s accounts of the apocalypse. To a certain extent, evangelical fervor ensured this level of intimidation. Reaching out to any and all comers, this later Davies text, and others like it, promised universal hell-fire and damnation – a moral catechism on correct behavior and the repercussions of failing to abide by its tenets. It is the dual focus on personal guilt, emphasized in a seventeenth-century recovery of Calvinist theology,[3] and penitential reform, embodied in its all-too-literal apocalyptic ramifications during the civil-war years, that necessitates a response. Readers, steeped in the sins and transgressions of their times, must amend their behavior before it is too late. They must account for their own actions, and they must also ensure that Britain does the same.

The rhetoric of holy hatred clearly plays into and is generated from negotiations between individuals and state authorities. Davies's emphatic warnings appear at a moment when the state is in the process of being transformed, when modern notions of the subject–individual are in their nascency, and when puritanism is helping to model a growing British population into more easily governable state subjects. Apocalyptic writing of the 1640s marks that emergence by eliciting specific behavior from its readers and illustrating legitimate forms of that behavior in the way that its authors are able to position themselves and their audience. In this chapter, I want to explore the connection between a rhetoric of holy hatred and the simultaneous rewriting of national and individual consciousness that it parallels. Although historians have long acknowledged the years prior to the English Civil War as transformative in terms of state and subject formation,[4] none has approached that shift as it is constructed and/or reflected in apocalyptic writing, and none has done so with any consideration of how notions of gender determine state/subject relationships in the very process of promoting them.[5]

Articulating an obedient and productive state subject, most seventeenth-century apocalyptic writing posits that subject as male. Preachers like Edmund Calamy, William Sedgwick, and Henry Burton define subjectivity in terms of themselves. These writers assume a same-gender connection with their readers and build upon that connection in the way that they construct their subject. Davies's writing is far more constrained given the markedly different role it plays within the newly emerging British state. Her texts match those of her contemporaries in hatred and aggression, but they do so only at the expense of what her contemporaries might have conceived of as an appropriate subjectivity. Davies's unusual rhetorical style marks her gendered relation to the state (her place as its subject); but it also calls out to her readers the problem of female subjectivity as it is constructed within a by now predominantly masculinized domain of religio-political polemic. Judged in terms that they did not fulfill and neglected in those that they successfully carried out, Davies's writings have been relegated to the margins: to the margins of history and of sanity.

Apocalypse and the call to arms

Millennial writing proved a particularly useful and surprisingly militant forum for airing political and religious grievances in the years leading up to the English Civil War. In a very real sense, apocalyptic writing invoked a dynamics of subject articulation and social change in the way that it negotiated space between opposing forces. For example, in the prophecy cited above, apocalyptic rhetoric poses insurmountable polarities, binary divisions that are irreconcilable but easily chartable. In her assertions of England's final days with their repeated threats of hell fire, Davies separates the "saved" and the "damned," "us" and "them," and "right" and "wrong," into clearly demarcated oppositions.

Paul Christianson explains how these binaries work in relation to militancy and political action:

with its polarized view of the universe, its stress upon an imminent catastrophic end to the normal world, and its propensity toward prophecy, apocalyptic thought operated as a powerful rational and emotional weapon in ideological dispute. The combination of retribution for enemies with the creation of a new order of righteousness provided an inspirational mixture with explosive potential. People who view the church and society in which they live in black and white terms, who convince themselves that their cause will triumph despite seeming odds against it, and who detect signs that the victory of the ages draws near, make formidable friends or foes, hopeless compromisers or moderates. (*Reformers and Babylon*, 7–8)

As a spur to action in times of extreme duress, apocalyptic or millennial writing can be quite effective. In the binarism of its vision, it ensures a narrowed and directive course of action with no room for speculation or uncertainty for either its audience or its authors. While the absolute nature of this framing no doubt proved beneficial to established writers, the moral certainty of the millennium could cater as well to writers who lacked traditional forms of authorization for their writing.[6] In a treatise dedicated to her daughter, Davies can insist without apology that her prophecy is "not with Froath filled up, or Interlarded with differing Opinions of others, such old pieces having No affinity *and* agreement *with* this BRITISH *garments* or displayed COATE *by blessed Prophets pend.*"[7] For Davies, the apocalyptic righteousness of her own directives is enough; her prophecies need not be defended or contradicted "with differing Opinions of others"; and her certainty is endemic to the genre.

Even authors who lay claim to a far less immediate relationship to God (Davies declares her prophetic skills equal to those of both Daniel and John) can still insist on an absolute authority not available outside of religious writing. Because millennial writing focuses outward, on the social implication of its vision for readers, it seems to offer its authors almost total impunity. Speaking the endtimes, apocalyptic writers rarely insert themselves into their discourse and never question the validity of their own claims. A contemporary of Davies, John Selden, reiterates the righteousness of religious truth as a spur to military action: "If men would say they took up arms for anything but religion, they might be beaten out of it by reason; out of that they never can, for they will not believe you whatever you say."[8]

Millennial writings need not be so much a call to arms as a form of legitimation after the fact. The use of prophecies – particularly traditional prophecies that lay claim to antiquity for their authority – can serve as "validating charters" for actions already completed, actions including the overthrow of monarchies or the rejection of the church.[9] Prophecies testify to the righteousness of potentially disruptive or subversive social behavior by covering it with the mantle of the past or the future. Of course there is a flip side to this dynamism as well. The utopian aspect of apocalyptic and millennial writings often makes the options they present untenable.[10] In the extremity of a millennial stance, the stakes are either all or nothing, liberation or bondage. Accommodation of any variety is unacceptable. Nor are such confrontational stances all that easy to sustain given the tremendous energy that they require.

Obviously there is no way to gauge the actual success or failure of apocalyptic propaganda in generating and justifying the English Civil War, no way its repercussions can be mapped across something as complicated and historically ambiguous as subject articulation or state making.[11] Certainly millennial writings were used by many of the reformers during the 1640s as a platform to air social discontent or to legitimate transgressive behavior after the fact. The puritan gentry must have had relatively easy access to such polemic, especially when censorship restrictions broke down during the war years. To what extent these texts served as a direct, or even indirect, call to arms can at most, however, be a matter of conjecture. Suffice it to say that Sir Francis Bacon thought them quite incendiary. In an essay entitled "Of Prophecies," he wrote that "they ought all to be despised . . . though when I say despised, I mean it as for belief; for otherwise, the spreading or publishing of them is in no sort to be despised, for they have done much mischief."[12]

Theorizing mid-century state formation

Millennial writing, then, proved astonishingly flexible in validating, if not specifically motivating, revolution in mid seventeenth-century England.[13]

It also possessed far more specific cultural directives in the way that it fed into a rhetoric of state- and subject-formation. Holy hatred, evoked in the always-present threat of global destruction and the concomitant knowledge of punitive measures to come, assumed, created, and augmented perceptions of personal guilt that, in turn, went far in constructing and policing an obedient national (state-centered) subject. Recognizing a rise in the supervisory capacities of government in the early seventeenth century, Philip Corrigan and Derek Sayer trace the development of different registers of state control as England's economic base changed. Of particular significance to this discussion is their focus on the increasing density of a governing *polis* – a burgeoning bureaucracy – to enforce personal order and ensure discipline. "It is not so much the fine detail of enforcement of this or that statute or proclamation that matters," they write, "as the steady, exemplary and accumulative weight of growing state regulation" (*The Great Arch*, 70). Using the broad range of practices and procedures implemented during the late Tudor and early Stuart periods as a sort of palimpsest for behavioral redefinition,[14] we can begin to connect material changes in state formation with people's changing sense of themselves and their civic responsibilities.

The transition from state as monarchy to state as republic occurring in the 1640s provides a particularly vivid example of this kind of mutual redefinition. As I see it, the concept of the regulatory itself changes in status and direction immediately before and during the Interregnum by permanently restructuring the individual's sense of what and who constitutes government. State subjects, instead of seeing themselves as beholden to a ruling body outside and above, embodied in the king, symbolically *become* the state (via parliament),[15] obliged to defend it as they would defend themselves.[16] This not only aligns them more directly with an idea of national identity, but it also establishes an alternative sense of self as active individual agent. By 1642, Henry Parker can, in fact, rhetorically equate parliament *with the state* and hence demand of it action against the king: "if the Parliament be not vertually the whole kingdome it self . . . as well in matters of state as matters of lawe, if it be not the great councell of the Kingdome, as well as of the King . . . let the brand of Treason sticke upon it." Parker's equation, impossible ten years before, is now explicit: parliament is "vertually the whole kingdome it self."[17] This shift ensures, at least rhetorically, a potent new form of regulation and control by insisting that subjects begin to monitor both the state and themselves as its singular representatives.[18]

The Civil War brought with it two contradictory impulses – one to think in terms of a nation and the other to recognize individual status within that totality. Beginning with what he calls "dividing practices,"

Michel Foucault loosely charts this regulatory split as it appears in its later (eighteenth-century) concretized form within the state.[19] Dividing practices, he explains, divide the subject internally, and they insist on *personal* regulation; people internalize power economies that exist outside them, submitting to private reflections of conscience or self-knowledge – reflections that direct and monitor behavior. In this operation, subjects are made to perceive of themselves as individuals – individuals who must not only admit to the particularities of their subjectivity, but who must also internally regulate those same impulses through personal guilt, compliance with perceived authority, etc.

While England's early Catholicism no doubt played a historic role in ensuring an eventual forum for this self-regulation via the confessional, the first decades of the seventeenth century marked the advent of a more secularized version of this strategy of legitimation in "the political dethronement of God."[20] What happened was "less the demise of religion as a 'moral technology' than a shift in its forms . . . [a shift] from the visible coercion of Church courts and public penance to internalized disciplines of conscience and sect; a shift thoroughly consonant with a wider enbourgeoisement of social relations and identities."[21] Responding to a growing population, the secular state could take advantage of this shift by reorganizing the way that it ordered and defined appropriate behavior. Given that social regulation was no longer sufficient – that Charles I's monarchy was no longer satisfactorily administering justice or accounting for the bulk of the populace outside its control – the rewriting of the spiritual insisted that individuals look out for themselves, subsidizing current forms of regulation and discipline with a more encompassing moral imperative.

"Most of the time, the state is envisioned as a kind of political power which ignores individuals," Foucault writes, "looking only at the interests of the totality . . . But I'd like to underline the fact that the state's power (and that's one of the reasons for its strength) is both . . . individualizing and . . . totalizing" ("The Subject and Power," 231). For Foucault, the state's success in maintaining a status quo environment, and the appropriate economies to ensure it comes in its joint ability to focus the development of powers around these two separate poles: "one, globalizing and quantitative, concerning the population; the other, analytical, concerning the individual" (215). Foucault's somewhat simplistic bifurcation of state authority into two seemingly opposed strategies, the one self-directed, the other nation-directed, has interesting implications for our understanding of millennial writing, particularly given apocalysm's own tendency to polarize and divide. In apocalyptic discourse, Foucault's separation is literalized in a strategic call to arms.

At one and the same time that seventeenth-century preachers were demanding that people look inward for direction, to the particular and the individual, they were also calling for uniformity and sameness in church doctrine, for a broad and national outlook.

Anna Trapnel, reiterating God's message to English sinners, emphasizes the singular and private. "I will not judge what you doe, when you meet, and speak and pray together," she explains, dismissing communal, congregational repentance, "but I will follow you into your secret places, your Houses, your callings . . . those that breath after thee Lord, they are searching after their secret sins . . . they cannot prosper that cover their secret sins, there is such a covering of secret sins."[22] In contrast, others like Edward Boughen, writing in support of a united church, insist that "the first means to set us all at one is that we preach the same doctrine; the second that we all practice the same Discipline; the third, that we all be of the same opinion . . . it is not enough therefore for some of us to preach the same doctrine, all, all of us must preach the same thing."[23] Boughen sees spiritual uniformity as crucial to church policy in that *all* parishioners will be given the *same* advice and made to feel the *same* obligation. Here he advocates sameness, not difference, common cause not individual identity.

Ranter Abiezar Coppe articulates both poles of this cultural duality simultaneously when in 1649 he describes his own vision of the apocalypse: "immediately [I saw] an innumerable company of hearts filling up each corner of the room where I was. And me thoughts there was variety and distinction, as if there had been severall hearts, and yet most strangely and unexpressibly complicated or folded up in unity. I clearly saw distinction, diversity, variety, and as clearly saw all swallowed up into unity."[24] Coppe's juxtaposition is significant in the way that it accommodates and arranges both tendencies, in the way that it privileges one term over the other. In order for these two seemingly contradictory impulses to coexist, Coppe as English subject must create a value system that will determine their relative importance; he must find a way of connecting and ordering both spheres. That "diversity" for Coppe is ultimately "swallowed up into unity" is hardly arbitrary. The one must precede the other to ensure its appearance. In fact, it is this hierarchical movement (from individual to totality) that seventeenth-century apocalyptic discourse manages to chart so graphically.

Unfortunately, while the teleology that I have just described supposedly accounts for both feminine and masculine constructions of apocalyptic subjectivity, in the way that each responds to and internalizes the power economies around it, it necessarily neglects the gender-specific nature of these negotiations. By mid century, women's and men's written access to regulation differs as a result of separate obligations – obligations that vary according to available resources and distinct cultural demands. A possible consequence of this unequal positioning is that female subjectivity does not always or perhaps ever fit the patriarchal norms of state and subject regulation as they are generally conceived within civil-war polemic. It is already disruptive, even in the way that it articulates *legitimate* behavior for women. In Davies's apocalyptic writings, contradictory female subject and state regulation is literalized in an unavoidable doubling of expectations and requirements; her writings construct a subject status that can never be fulfilled.[25] While Davies is only one of a number of women writers of the apocalypse, her writings are nevertheless evocative of the kinds of complications that occur when policy and policing are determined outside women's material experiences.

Apocalyptic writing and its place in the state

The apocalyptic texts written in the years prior to and during the English Civil War are symptomatic of the struggle toward a new western subjectivity. They reveal a fascination with both exactitude and broad general outlines: exact dates (1644), exact people (Archbishop Laud = the Beast, the pope, the Antichrist), exact sins (failure to keep the Sabbath), and general ills (famine, fire, plague), general enemies (liars, drunkards, sinners), general chaos (political, religious, familial). What is even more illuminating, however, is how the interplay between specific and general within these accounts consistently aligns and hierarchizes that duality. British apocalyptic texts invariably posit a catastrophic world end with England as its epicenter. They do so by equating the personal with the universal, the individual with the national, in a unidirectional arrangement. Protestantism, particularly mid-century puritan versions of it with their emphases on holy hatred, places men and women as the sole proprietors of the religious salvation of their country. Only *personal* recognition of guilt and a willingness to surrender oneself to God's commands characterize the elect and assure eventual *national* redemption.

The English apocalyptic writing that developed as a result of continental reforms was, in many ways, markedly different from its predecessors.[26] Specifically, it was far more teleological and end-focused in its understandings. Early English reformers like John Bale

endowed the British protestant version [of the apocalypse] with its particular historical cast. For the first time, the history of the Christian Church and society were employed systematically to elucidate the prophecies of St. John and unlock the mysteries of Revelation. Bale's interpretation seems to have acted as a paradigm. He framed his insight into the nature of reality into a coherent system or framework of thought with its own inner logic and vocabulary . . . Bale took the nebulous implicit historical thrust of apocalyptic thought and made it explicit.[27]

Pre-Reformation apocalypse tended to approach religious history as a series of isolated events and players, removed in time and space from their readers.[28] In juxtaposition to this more or less random accounting, the linear specificity of English apocalyptic writing insisted upon the direct application of an amorphous religious chronology to a relatively consistent set of historical events, people, and institutions; it created a single-line cause/effect narrative for the state and for its religious calling.

We can see this teleology in sixteenth- and seventeenth-century notions of providence. Where earlier natural catastrophes, in the form of fire and famine, were dealt with in a piecemeal fashion, through such acts as the intercession of saints, the wearing of amulets, and donations to the church, and where the success or failure of these strategies was, in some sense, tied to parallel ideas of chance or luck – the efficacy of external magical powers, good priests, properly executed rituals, etc. – post-Reformation perceptions of such disasters were far more circumscribed. Keith Thomas writes that:

the correct reaction on the part of a [post-Reformation] believer stricken by ill fortune was therefore to search himself in order to discover the moral defect which had led the Almighty to try him . . .
It was also customary for national disasters to be regarded as God's response to the sins of the people. The Homilies taught that penury, dearth, and famine were caused by God's anger at vice . . . The Bible showed that plagues and misfortunes were usually a punishment for some notorious sin, and that divine vengeance was as likely in this world as the next. (*Religion and the Decline of Magic*, 83)

Given the parameters of this less flexible frame in apocalyptic and millennial writing, the national trauma that England was experiencing – in wars, high taxes, an unsympathetic episcopacy, changes in work structure and conditions, lack of parliamentary voice, and the destruction and abuse of property – was not only evidence of a cataclysmic and imminent end, but also proof positive of the individual transgressions of the British people and their king. In 1642, Calamy's general warnings stem from specific and identifiable sources – the great men who make up Parliament:

Great men are the Looking-glasse of the Countrey where they live . . . if they be wicked, the whole Countrey is much the worser by them. . . .
As this Reformation must be personall, so also it must be nationall . . . A

particular man by turning into God, may turn away a particular judgement. But when the sins of a Nation are generall, and the judgements upon a Nation generall, the turning must be generall.[29]

For Calamy, an internalized notion of the subject-self becomes linked with its national, state-centered parallel. In English apocalyptic writing, the individual experience of guilt – the personal threat of hell fire and damnation – becomes synonymous with national crisis at both a spiritual *and* a secular level. The narrative voice in these texts reveals for its readers a sense of self as an active and volitional part of history and as an integral part of a uniquely national concern. Davies's general warnings of the endtimes also stem from specific and highly personal sources. She writes,

> Drunkard also, Here's to You,
> beware the Trumpets Call:
> For from *Pride* yours, and surfeiting,
> proceeds our Troubles all.
> Praying down with your *Twelve-tyde-Shews*,
> Stage-Playes and foolery then,
> Left in a Moment chang'd as He,
> Turn'd into Divils from MEN.[30]

The equation couldn't be more emphatic: "For from *Pride* yours, and surfeiting, / proceeds our Troubles all."

The causal connection between individual and state effectively broadens, at least rhetorically, pre-Reformation personal stakes from emphases that center on family, or at most community, to a recognition of a more totalizing and consuming obligation to a nation or national cause.[31] "Personal sins are made national when they are not punished by authority, and national sins are made personal when they are not laid to heart by the subject," Thomas Case insists, calling out the individual only to give it social ramifications.[32] Techniques of holy hatred, used liberally in the years surrounding the English Civil War, bring to the fore "the government of individualization"[33] – that aspect of control which constrains individuals to act in certain socially acceptable ways. In a culture where the religious and the political, the spiritual and the secular, are inexorably moving apart yet still traverse the same fields of discourse,[34] the apocalyptic tradition both promotes those connections in the consolidation of a new hierarchy and reveals points of contest within it in the conviction and execution of England's king.

A "universal" apocalyptic discourse?

Most of Davies's apocalyptic contemporaries were men. Addressing the personal transgressions of their audience (evidenced in specific cases of blasphemy, drunkenness, etc.), these writers invariably pull individual sin into the social realm, insisting on its repercussions at a national level. William Bridge illustrates that connection in a sermon delivered to the House of Commons: "take an evil, and though it were never so private before, yet if it pass here it will take a higher degree and commence national wickedness . . . This is a fearful evil, and very dreadful, that a personal sin should become national."[35] Recognizing the social implications of sin means demanding a kind of congregational accountability for others as well as the self. "You must do all this obeisance not only in your persons," Calamy insists:

but you and your house, you and your tenant, you and all that depends on you. For every master . . . stands accountable to God for his family as well as himself . . . The same God that requires us to serve him as *private persons* requires us to serve him in our *public relations*, and though thou beest never so careful of thy duty as a private person, yet thou mayest go to hell for neglecting thy duty as a master, as a magistrate, as a Parliament man.[36]

For Calamy, it is not enough to attend to personal sin; Calamy's readers must also recognize responsibility as "master[s]," "magistrate[s]," and "Parliament m[e]n." Indeed, the pursuit of the personal for its own sake, be it in ferreting out individual sins or demanding reward in their absence, is unacceptable – a "crying abomination." Calamy writes, "if there be any among you that drive your own designs, and seek your own ends more than the public good . . . These are crying abominations, and the Lord calls for . . . repentance this day."[37] Perhaps the most politically explosive voicing of this unidirectional imperative can be seen in the way that it is used to legitimate regicide. In "The Charge Against the King," it is Charles I's *personal* interests that so compromise his position as state regent. His accusers insist that

all which wicked designs, wars, and evil practices of him the said Charles Stuart, have been and are carried on for the advancement and upholding of a *personal interest* of will, power, and pretended prerogative to himself and his family, against the *public interest*, common right, liberty, justice, and peace of the people of this nation by and from whom he was entrusted as aforesaid.[38]

Again and again, the language of reformers and separatists reiterates the absolute and limited nature of options for the British and the militant certainty of any eventual outcome. In *Meroz cursed*, printed in 1642, Stephen Marshall legitimates merciless action to defeat the Antichrist and fulfill God's prophecy.[39] He writes, "if this worke be to revenge Gods Church against *Babylon* . . . [then] he is a *blessed man that takes and dashes the little ones against the stones*" (12). Marshall's imagery, culled from the Geneva Bible, demands that its readers respond militantly to God's requests, in the form of murder. Nor is Marshall's sense of things singular. Many others use apocalyptic writing to justify active vendetta or revenge. In *Jerichoes Down-Fall* (1643), Thomas Wilson contrasts the recent outbreaks of fighting in England with the Irish rebellions: "cruell *men have shed blood*, the blood of Saints, the blood of Prophets, and in justice *they must have blood to drink*: for they are worthy, *Rev* 16.5,6. Reward *Babylon* as she hath rewarded you, *double to her double*, in the cup she hath filled, *fill to her double*, 18.6."[40] Here bloodshed and violence become legitimate revenge and proper behavior for believing Christians.

In a 1642 invocation against the royalists to parliament, William Sedgwick uses the pronouns "you" and "he" interchangeably, augmenting the secular power of parliament over the king by conflating its action with God's own:

though it lye under mountaines of Kingdomes, you shall *thresh them* to dust: though it be buryed under Nations, and Empires, customes, antiquities, he will *drive the Nations asunder, scatter the everlasting hills*, nothing shall stand in his way; wherere he findes his glory, he will seize upon it; and if they yeeld not speedily, it will cost them deare.[41]

Again, the call for militant action (holy hatred) relies on eschatological visions for its fulfillment. Threshing one's enemies to dust becomes the political equivalent of complete surrender to God and unconditional acceptance of His commands.

In seventeenth-century apocalyptic writing, political practicalities and religious rhetoric are synonymous. To Calamy, recent Catholic military victory (in Germany, Bohemia, the Palatinate, and Ireland) illustrates the biblically announced ascendancy of the Antichrist. He warns, "Oh let us set God on work this day, to destroy the implacable enemies of his church; arise oh Lord, and scatter the Irish rebels! Arise oh Lord, and confound the Antichrist, and build the walls of Jerusalem."[42] Sedgwick is equally literal and apocalyptic in his parallels:

The shaking of the German Empire, that great bulwark of the beast, speaks the wrath of God bordering upon the men of sin. It is nearer than a border; God hath poured out some wrath upon the very throne of the beast. Prelacy is . . . conceived to be that throne, and we have seen it pulled down in Scotland . . . Yea, may not a strict observer see the beginnings of the dissolution and breakings in the kingdom of the beast itself.[43]

Finally, Thomas Case makes the connection between political rebellion and religious righteousness explicit and irrevocable, asking, "And what is the quarrel all this while [if it is] not religion and the truth of God?"[44]

In the above accounts the interplay between individual sinners and the nation they must defend is reinforced by a causal certainty. If you avoid sin and take direct action against those who will not do likewise, then the nation will be saved (if only in the 1,000-year reign of Christ that will follow the apocalypse). The directives for appropriate subject/state formation within apocalyptic rhetoric are hardly absolute, however, nor are the narrative positionings within them. Instead they are gender- and status-specific, marked by requirements that delineate men from women and status from status. The same imperatives that demand militant action in the gender-specific writings of Davies's contemporaries, the same imperatives that delineate a specific and unidirectional move from individual recognition to national response, change shape – are realigned and refocused – in Davies's accounts, requiring different negotiations and alternative calls to action.

Women and subjectivity: the case of Lady Eleanor Davies

During the course of her career, Davies wrote prolifically.[45] She personally published over sixty individual tracts, some as many as forty pages in length.[46] In her writings, she accurately prophesied the deaths of her first husband John Davies, Lord Buckingham, Archbishop Laud, and King Charles I.[47] Additionally, she advised Queen Henrietta Maria of her eventual fortune in childbed, as well as of the sex of the children that she would bear.[48] As a result of these direct prophecies, and for her more general warnings of apocalyptic revolution, Davies became something of a popular success.[49] Her career, however, was also marked with periods of incarceration and near oblivion. She spent two years, from 1633 to 1635, in the Gatehouse at Westminster for publishing texts illegally. For this she was fined £3,000, an exorbitant amount at that time which she apparently did not pay. A year later, proclaiming herself "Primate and Metropolitan" (Laud's titles), she entered Lichfield Cathedral, anointed the wall hangings around the altar with a mixture of tar and water, and seated herself upon the bishop's throne.[50] For these actions she was committed first to Bedlam, where she remained for sixteen months, and later to the Tower. Davies was imprisoned again briefly in 1646 and 1651, and committed by local constable to Wood Street Compter.[51] She died in 1652, almost penniless.[52] Located at St. Martin's Church, her epitaph reads: "Plurimus major quia humilior, in eximia forma sublime ingenium, in venusta comitate singularem modestiam . . . possedit."[53]

In her writings, Davies parallels the concerns of her contemporaries. She focuses on issues of political and religious concern; she molds recent and upcoming events into a millennial vision that foresees the end of the Antichrist's reign; and she promotes a new form of historical subjectivity. She also, like her fellow reformers, focuses on militant rhetoric, especially as the war years draw near. Still, Davies's status as a woman in a culture that expects markedly different behaviors from men and women, demands a different twist to her writings and to their authorial claims. Not only does her gender necessitate the religious tenor of her writings, but it also insists that she continually resuscitate an aristocratic privilege she had lost as a result of marriage. In claiming God's authority to legitimate her prophecies, Davies can selectively circumvent any secular authority that seeks to restrict her actions or diminish her status. In calling on pedigree, she can insist on the same privileging, this time by virtue of title. The fifth daughter of George Touchet, Baron Audeley and Earl of Castlehaven, Davies could lay claim by birth to one of the oldest peerages in England and Ireland. Yet Davies's first marriage in 1609 to the king's attorney in Ireland, the poet Sir John Davies (son of a tanner), must have weakened that standing considerably. Accordingly, it comes as no surprise that when Davies chose to remarry in 1626 she wed a man who professed to royal blood.[54]

In *From the lady Eleanor, her blessing to her beloved daughter*, Davies foregrounds both religious right and birthright by paralleling her own inherited aristocratic superiority with the spiritual primacy of a life of chastity: "for so births PREROGATIVE *surmounts or goes* before *that gain'd* by Marriage as *descent* and *blood*, a Character not to be blotted out, wherewith follows the state of VIRGINITY, the presidency theirs, *Not in subjection as others*."[55] At the same time the virgin state, held in "presidency," reaffirms God's legitimacy as the first husband, deemphasizing Davies's less prestigious worldly marital status and counteracting the many "subjections" she may have to face because of it. Despite their affinity with a puritan rhetoric advocating social restitution, Davies's writings, then, are necessarily elitist; they demand and construct for her an unbroken line of hereditary *and* spiritual privilege. As an aristocrat, Davies continually reminds her readers of that status and initially envisions herself as part of the king's inner court with access to royal conference. Her first tract, published in 1625, focuses on the more removed threat of Roman Catholicism and ends with blessings to both king and queen.[56] By 1633, however, her relation to royal favor had changed considerably. Formally denied access to the royal family and to court, Davies was, by this time, without jointure as well[57] and dependent on whatever funds her estranged second husband would allow.

The economic implications of this standing must have placed Davies in an unusual and precarious situation in relation to the court and to the peerage. So too, the disadvantage of her gender ensured her power-lessness. Accordingly, her authority, indeed any authority she was to claim, depended on her ability to convince others of her prophetic power – in this case a prophetic power that sprang not from the aristocracy, but from the growing puritan "middling ranks." The blending and disrupting of allegiances here begins to suggest the unavoidable complications that being a financially dependent woman must have created in motivating discourse even in a period where economic and religious concerns determine political affiliation to such a large extent. That Davies can depend on no single status to authorize her writings or define her identity intimates the kinds of contradictions that she must negotiate *within* her texts as well.

Here too, traditional and often conflicted roles realign apocalyptic adversaries. As a woman, Davies must include not only state concerns of all-powerful episcopacy, but also marital concerns; in denying her right to write, her husbands both become targets of no less importance to her than the Arminian opposition. Davies's gender ensures a unique confrontation with questions of seventeenth-century subjectivity. "Female" perspectives on the personal and the social, given their dislocation from subject as active and independent public agent,[58] translate apocalyptic warnings into different configurations with surprisingly disparate results. Accordingly, though Davies may ostensibly write her prophecies for an audience of men – in most cases, the same audience that her contemporaries address (members of parliament, the king, Fairfax, Cromwell, etc.) – she creates in her texts a notion of subjectivity that is gender-specific and that approaches issues of personal guilt and intimidation in ways that ensure not only eventual obedience to a newly configured English state (constructing docile subjects within it) but also uneasy acceptance of the patriarchal strictures that make up its operation for women writers/readers. Her prophecies also, as a result of their different emphases, follow a markedly different trajectory – more than 300 years of oblivion and dismissal. Given the predisposition of her audience, it is no surprise that Davies's potentially incendiary material only goes so far and with such limited effect. Her readership expected certain established forums for apocalyptic writing and responded to her writings predictably – via both state and individual forms of "masculine" subjectivity.

Gendering rhetorical strategy

Within the chronology of Davies's apocalyptic writings, she discusses current national and international concerns and situates them within the temporal history of the British monarchy. She acknowledges neighboring religious and political conflicts in France, Germany, Spain, and Bohemia.[59] She accounts for problems internal to England in the form of high taxes,[60] lack of parliamentary voice,[61] labor disputes, and destruction and abuse of private property.[62] She also recognizes the connection of each of these concerns to the English crown, intimately discussing its various governments from Henry VII through Charles I. All of these arguments indicate a willingness to engage in a history that extends beyond the confines of family or community, a history that is national in scope.

Davies's presentation of this history, however, serves rather different ends from that of her contemporaries. Generally, the national complaints she offers do not rally her readers to action. Where Edmund Calamy calls his audience to arms – "Oh Let us set God on work this day, to destroy the implacable enemies of his Church . . . and scatter the Irish rebels"[63] – Davies's exhortations do not. She berates her readers for their failure to acknowledge the sanctity of her prophecies; she warns them of the eventual apocalypse to come, yet she demands from them no bloodshed – no directives in the form of active rebellion or physical confrontation.

By focusing repeatedly on the vindication of her *own position* as prophet and visionary, Davies deflects the national aspects of apocalyptic or millennial writing into a reaffirmation of *her* personal authority. To avoid the repercussions of their aberrant ways, Davies's readers need only recognize her status as prophet and honor it. "Far be it from us to be like the deaf Adder," she writes, "That because once accursed for harkening when forbidden. Therefore it forbear . . . Preaching ye have always, and may hear them when ye please . . . But the little Book, The Spirit of Prophesie, Not always that."[64] Acknowledging the stopped ears of the English unrepentant, Davies demands not the overthrow of the king and his archbishop or a taking to the streets of his subjects, but the "signe . . . then on the posts of our doors," signaling acceptance of her prophecy (*The Star to the Wise*, 17). Her texts demand justification at a personal level, in the righteousness of her own assumption of authority, yet they ask for no militant response, at least not as it has been socially configured by her contemporaries. Denied an active role in politics, religion, and economy, Davies writes prophecies that offer her readers two choices – belief or disbelief in *her* texts – and no legitimate public forum for acting upon either. In affirming her status as individual, she simultaneously de-emphasizes the importance of a unified social response from her audience.

Where Davies's particular involvement in apocalyptic thought reveals a distinctly gendered handling of questions of action or its lack, it also seems to indicate a unique negotiation of processes of individuation for women within the modern state. While the texts of Davies's contemporaries tend to pull outward to a national subjectivity, directing personal guilt into socially conforming applications, Davies's own texts focus impetus on the personal, hence exaggerating the self-regulatory. Certainly this emphasis makes sense in a culture and economy that is simultaneously removing women from public contexts and strengthening notions of the home and family as the only legitimate female realms.[65] Accordingly, in Davies's writings, warnings of apocalyptic upheaval return again and again to the prophecies themselves.[66]

Given apocalyptic writing's general recognition of both national and individual concerns, Davies's presentations reverse conventional hierarchies. Continually alluding to her own prophecies – her books – as the figurative second coming of Christ, Davies situates herself *personally* as prophet, as symbolic virgin, and as British subject, within a social environment. She becomes a third-person participant in an apocalyptic vision that accounts for a whole nation: "In the first year of his Raign, when His first Parliament called at *Oxford.* Whether he now returned; a great voice from Heaven then, speaking to her, revealing in what yeer, or how long that time; she the Daughter of the *first* Peer or Baron."[67] Within this brief account, Davies's own religious experience retains primacy over the more socially conceived perceptions of the monarchy, Parliament, and "Universal Judgment." "A . . . voice from Heaven [spoke] to her," she admits, "she [being] the Daughter of the *first* Peer or Baron."

Continual references both to Davies's writings (how they are treated by husband, archbishop, and king) and to her tribulations (what she experienced in dealing with these various authorities) interrupt her more general warnings of national threat. In fact, she frequently replaces society with self. Describing her own incarceration, in a later publication, Davies parallels numerous fairly disparate social events with the more immediate experience of her sentencing:

And of like measure *October 23*, she committed close Prisoner, Excommunicated, Fined to his majesties use Three thousand pounds and to make a publique Recantation at *Pauls* Cross, as extant on Record, Twelve Hands signed by; also *Edge* Hill Fight, and the *Irish* Massacre 23 of October and Twelve of them at once Voted to Prison, for that Order of their nothing to stand of force ther done without them: His Majesty lastly Fined his three kingdoms to the use, & C. As for Pauls . . . where the time would fail how the first Blow at *Edge Hill* in *Oxfordshire*, the second *Newbery*, fought within a stones cast of her house at *Englefeld.* And thou *Bedlam* House, too little the Thousandth part to contain of then distracted since thence her coming.[68]

In Davies's complicated account, the £3,000 fine she owes, upon illegally printing her tracts, becomes both the king's fine to his three kingdoms, and the three skirmishes at Edgehill, Newbury, and (her own) in Bedlam prison. The twelve hands who sign her conviction (Laud included) dissolve perhaps into convicted rebels who are sent to prison after the Massacre. In any case, the Battle of Edgehill and the Irish Massacre become secondary to her own excommunication, echoing it in their temporal and linguistic proximity.

As a result of these rhetorical shifts, Davies's voice becomes inscribed within state-ordered considerations of control in a markedly different manner from the voices of her contemporaries.[69] Not only are her texts likely to become more easily disposable, subject to greater ridicule and indifference by virtue of their failure to fulfill certain accepted conventions, but her own status in relation to them is potentially suspect. As both author and object of her own discourse, both writing "I" and written "she," her stake in these texts increases. Her writing becomes more emphatic in what she must say about her role in these affairs and in the ways she is forced to situate herself within the text. The millennial accounts of her contemporaries generally omit both narrative positions. These men profess to be neither part of the events they describe nor of the texts they write. Edmund Calamy may demand that his readers stand up and be counted, but his own legitimacy as enforcer/proclaimer of that call need never be mentioned.

The effect of Davies's subject/object doubling emphasizes the role of the individual within larger contexts, but it also ensures a greater degree of personal invigilation – whether it be through an additional need for self-aggrandizement (I am a worthy prophet) or a more strident sense of personal guilt (if it were not for my/your evil, we would not be in this position). Accordingly, Davies, throughout her writings, locates specific enemies, individuals who are directly responsible for the endtimes. Sometimes these figures, like Archbishop Laud, are parallel targets to those of other reformers or separatists. Most apocalyptic writers insist, at least to some extent, on particular and highly visible opponents in their attacks – Laud, Charles I, the pope, the Anglican Church, etc.[70] Davies's confrontations and the prophecies she develops about them are more specific, however, in both their action and their outcome. Laud's position as the Beast centers not so much on his public failures, his insinuation with the king, his effect on church policy, but on his individual response to her writings and his specific treatment of them.[71]

According to Davies's account, Laud "ravished her childe," burning the pages of one of her prophecies with a candle: "Archbishop *Laud*, 19 of *Septemb.* translated, & C. reigning in his [Abbot's] stead, successor of him ... no sooner arrived then apprehended, of her childe ravished, a greater then the Parliament, *the Word of God*" (*The Everlasting Gospel*, 9–10). To Davies, the act of ravishment – a fittingly personal and gender-specific violation of her book – is "a greater [offense] then the [staying of] Parliament": *"the Word of God"* that Laud is burning, more significant than the political ramifications of Charles's neglected duties. In fact Laud's execution in 1644 literally replaces national apocalypse in her writings. The general approach of Doomsday turns in her accounts into a personally fulfilled vendetta. Laud's beheading not only serves as recompense for the burning of *her* texts but also as the fulfillment of her apocalyptic prophecies. She writes of Laud's execution:

Where after a Candle being sent for, about the third hour in the Afternoon, that with his own hand had burnt it, saying, *she hath taken good long time, till 44 for Dooms-day then; My Lords, I hope I have made you a smother of it*: in truth his own fatal hour, those years of *Nineteen and a half*, reaching to his Execution Moneth and Year, *Anno 44, January*, when parted head and body, like that aforesaid divided year, shewed afore sacrificed by his ungracious hand. (*The Everlasting Gospel*, 10)

The chronology of events – the rejection, then fulfillment, of her prophecy – serves as a model for most of her visions. Those men who cross her, disputing her authority or questioning the godliness of her messages, invariably pay the price in the meting out of her apocalyptic judgments.

Obviously the focus of intimidation in these texts is, at least partially, the result of gender-coding. Her contemporaries, many of them speaking within the safe confines of parliamentary sermon, are given greater credibility in their accounts. As it is unnecessary for them to call on direct authority from God for the right to speak, the assumption of prophetic voice is less open to ridicule and abuse. Accordingly, their delineations of the enemy become more generic. A coherence of status markers, religious affiliations, and group unity allow for a less specific, more socially fluid, concept of the opposition. Already subject to specific articulations of patriarchal authority, Davies must focus her attacks more narrowly, on specific points of masculine control. She cannot simply fall back on class or religion for support. Hence, though her considerations invariably rely on class dynamics (she writes only to those who share her elite background) and religious affiliation (she depends on a shared puritan platform),[72] her writings are further complicated by an effort to negotiate gender restrictions as well. Davies's enemies are not solely or simply institutional; they are not only of the church or of the state. Rather, they are adversaries who personally respond to her prophecies, negating her authority on the basis of gender.

In *The Lady Eleanor Her Appeal*, Davies's prophecies take on an immediate antagonist – her husband. Of his interference, she writes:

And since prophesies Thundring Reign began, what judgments since the year 1625 *July*, shal give you a list of some of them; beginning at home first, where this

Book of mine was sacrificed by my first Husbands hand, thrown into the fire, whose Doom I gave him in letters of his own Name (*John Davies*, Joves Hand) within three years to expect the mortal blow; so put on my mourning garment from that time.[73]

Using prophecy to defend her authority, Davies not only continues to defy her husband's orders – this text is, after all, a written defiance of that command – but legitimates her revenge as well; he will die for crossing her and verify her prophetic powers in the process. Davies repeatedly determines the enemy only *after* he questions her authority. In fact, her initial assumption of prophetic power is the direct result of just such an instance. Earlier in this same tract, Davies recalls the circumstances leading to her infusion with God's spirit. Harboring a mute boy, George Carr, at her home, Davies accounts for her first prophetic defiance of a patriarchal command, a command insisting that she turn the boy in as a vagrant. When "Justices of Peace and Church-men" question Carr's credentials, she retaliates in prophecy: "where the Chief Divines of the City present . . . as liberal of their slanderous tongues; [insist] that [the boy] no longer might be harbored in our house . . . setting all on fire . . . giving out he was a Vagrant, a Counterfeit, or a Witch. Immediately upon which the Spirit of Prophesie falling likewise upon me, then were all vext worse than ever" (7).

Davies's enemies here, all those who sought to take the boy from her house, ensure her eventual prophetic response, at least within the thematic confines of her writing. In her text, the recounting of their direct intervention in her affairs insists on an equally direct counterattack.

Her second husband is no more fortunate in his attempts to monitor her behavior. Davies writes that he too "escaped not scotfree: likewise burning my Book, another Manuscript."[74] Shortly thereafter he was

strooken bereft of his sense, instead of speech made a noise like a Brute creature, doubtlesse his heart changed into a Beasts too, for so would put his head into a dish of Broth, of Lettice or Herbs, and drink Oyl and Vinegar, and sometimes Beer all together, insatiable that way, knew no body but only my self through it was not my hap to be at *London* then, nor when my former husband as suddenly dyed.[75]

Davies validates the inevitability of Douglas's apparent stroke. She explains: "Some three months before in the presence of the Lady *Berkshire* & the Lady *Carlisle* . . . declared sentence upon him, *Not so happy to be as to dye, nay worse than death should befal him.*"[76]

Repeatedly, Davies's prophecies center on enemies who directly question her authority and who do so in a patriarchal capacity – as husband, as church father, as judge, as king. Davies tells of one "mocker," her second husband's uncle, Dean Young of Winchester, who, upon seeing

Douglas "bereft" of his senses, vowed that Davies "had turned him now into his long Coats indeed."[77] That jest, stereotyping Davies in terms of her roles as mother and wife and devaluing her prophetic authority, spurs yet another judgment of doom: "[at] which [the] foresaid Divine was drownd, soon after the Boat dast away, that then lose his jest, would sooner lose his friend."[78] No one and nothing are spared in her accounts. Houses where Davies's papers have been destroyed are burned to the ground;[79] printers who identify her to the authorities pay for their indiscretions in lost property and unexpected family mishaps.[80]

The nature of Davies's threats affects both her own relationship to her writing and to its reception. Emphasizing the self over the state not only opens up her writings to greater ridicule – they do not fulfill social obligations in a conventional and polemically unproblematic fashion – but also insists on an alternative creation of subjectivity. Exaggerating both praise, in an attempt to authorize a precariously gendered position, and intimidation, the only legitimate means of overcoming patriarchal command, Davies's texts may even appear contradictory. In any event, replacing reader responsibility with prophetic action, her writings become an end in themselves. They ask for interpretive confirmation to be effective. In her account, Davies insists that readers acknowledge her right to write; and she reinforces perceptions of self that are avowedly antagonistic to the state in the way that they valorize Davies herself. Given the established parameters of a supposedly "genderless" (i.e., masculinist) apocalyptic subjectivity, Davies's variations necessarily fall outside the norm.

Because of their failure to follow conventional patterns and expectations, Davies's writings have been dismissed by contemporaries as well as by more recent critics. Early in her career, she is mocked as a mad-woman, warned of the consequences of usurping a role that is not within woman's domain.[81] Among the *State Papers* for the year 1622 comes the first mention of Davies. A man named Brooke attacks her for verbally abusing his wife and child, declaring finally that she is "mad, ugly and blinded with the pride of birth" (Spencer, "The History of an Unfortunate Lady" 44). In 1633, Sir John Lambe, Dean of the Arches and member of the High Commission renames her with an epigram, "never soe mad a ladie."[82] Another account, published in 1641, this time referring generally to women who preach, is equally dismissive. "Thus I have declared some of the female academies," the anonymous writer admits, "but where their university is I cannot tell, but I suppose that Bedlam or Bridewell would be two convenient places for them."[83] The twentieth century has been no less quick to marginalize Davies's writings, insisting that they are the work of a madwoman. S. G. Wright's article,

"Dougle Fooleries," appearing in 1932, postulates that her narrative style displays "a definite mental weakness" (95). Theodore Spencer, writing in 1938, tempers the outright assumption of "mental deficiency" only to insinuate it throughout his account. In his conclusion, he offers one final dismissive comment, remarking that she is "mad, violent and proud, obsessed by religious delusions, intimately concerned with politics, [and] furiously anxious to justify [her]self in print" ("The History of an Unfortunate Lady," 59).

Within the last decade, feminists have attempted to rescue Davies from the finality of these earlier judgments. Beth Nelson considers that "she may have been mad, she may have been a true prophet; but she is certainly the first woman in England to appropriate the printing press for the public expression of her vision of herself in her world" ("Lady Elinor Davies," 403). Esther Cope wonders if she were truly mad, or "whether she was merely emotionally disturbed, and/or engaging in forms of opposition that [were] regarded as unacceptable."[84] Obviously, the question of madness itself, at least according to its current definitions, is an anachronistic one for Davies, if only because it fails to register the historical contexts out of which those initial charges came. Michael MacDonald reminds us that accepted definitions of madness in the seventeenth century were more overtly political and religious than they are now, less directly linked to notions of sickness and debility. It also seems to me, however, that to affix to Davies's texts any such arbitrary label is itself evidence of their successful erasure via the newly emerging (masculinist) subjectivity they attempt to defy. The irony of these accusations comes to the fore when we consider Davies's assertions in relation to those made by her contemporaries. That an indiscriminate "dashing of little ones against the stones" is somehow considered more "sane" than seeking redress for specific injustices underscores the problem of such labeling in masculinist terms.

Calling on a single and convenient blanket statement to explain away the complexities of Davies's style necessarily neglects the myriad influences directing her composing process. Even the more historically likely assaults on inadequate education seem highly inappropriate here. Though educational disadvantages may certainly have made Davies less familiar with accepted writerly conventions, her own readings, her obvious understanding of Latin,[85] and her extensive practice in composition (over the course of a lifetime of writing) offered more than satisfactory compensation in this regard. Neither ecstatic writing nor post-production negligence can account for the nature of her texts either. Fairly extensive emendations throughout her writings, presumably in her own hand, indicate that Davies had a sense of her work as a document to be read and understood, and a relationship to her writing outside of trance.[86]

Not only did Davies annotate her own works after publication, editing some words, underscoring others, and making more than occasional comments in the margins of her texts, but she also frequently alluded to the clarity of her own interpretations within them. Whether these assertions were the result of registered criticisms by her readers or an acknowledgment of the familiarity of her topic to anyone sharing her political and religious convictions, the emphasis is, nevertheless, a striking one. In fact, Davies continually refers to issues of clarity, insisting that if anything she is too plain in her texts. Given the immediacy of the issues that she is presenting and the imminence of an apocalyptic end to them, attempts at elaborate exploration seem so much wasted effort. In *Ezekiel, Cap. 2*, she asks, "And line upon line, even the Lords own words again and again expresly, what can be said more plain."[87] Later, in the same text, she insists that her own interpretations of the biblical verse are "plain enough to be understood."[88] Finally, in *Apocalyps, Chap. 11. Its accomplishment shewed from the lady Eleanor*, referring, I think, to Charles I, she promises that "any farther shewing, concerning the last time" will be "needless."[89]

The irony of Davies's claims comes to the fore for any modern reader. Without considerable background and unlimited patience, it is difficult to follow her texts, much less to understand them. Substitutions, naming one thing for another, interruptions, skipping from argument to argument, and omissions, leaving out words, actions, and context, complicate any initial confrontation with her texts. If, as her tracts assume, "farther shewing" is "needless," why then are her texts so dense? An explanation may be found in the following introduction. Davies writes, "As shewed in the Scriptures, There is nothing so secret, That shall not be discovered."[90] Emphasizing the act of interpretation itself, Davies's texts display a seemingly effortless virtuosity at making connections between people and events through language. In a culture already caught up in anagrams and biblical exegesis,[91] her extreme interest in puzzle solving may stem, in some measure, from a social and legal refusal to allow women equal access to interpretation.[92] It may, in fact, refocus the impetus of her apocalyptic warnings away from proscriptive advice and national concern toward personal vindication.

In many of her texts, Davies offers lists of anagrams or partial anagrams to justify and expand her interpretations. Calling herself "Eleanor Audeley" or "Reveale O Daniel," she names everyone else as well:

Belchazer, Be-Charles: Beware the *French*; the *house of medisis, to* wit: of him also take heed in the yeare 1642: R: *ESSEX, ESSE REX*, or *Devorex* his first yeare of Taking, & C. *Daniel*, the 5 Chap. *And* Darius *tooke the kingdome, being sixty-two yeares & C: which was divided between them two* Da *and* Cy: *Belchazer*, as much to say: with out Treasure or a Searcher & C.

THE *Caldeans*: The *Caledonians* or *Scots, LONDON, BABYLON, DUBYLON*.[93]

Anagrams insist that names and places are not what they initially seem, that immediate perceptions of things may not always be the correct perceptions. As a high-status prophet of no less import than the biblical Daniel, Davies is equally epigrammatic in her writing. Her readers must look beyond her gender or her diminished social standing to discover the truth of her prophecy and the purity of her birth.

In *To the most honorable the high court of Parliament assembled*, Davies links Charles I to the biblical Samson, using both anagram and derivation. "Now from Samson JAMES SON derived, and also Mother Rachels Name; hers added: drawn from Charles, to weare if for a Favor, as long as he lives here."[94] Word play and puzzle solving take various forms in these texts. In another text, Knightsbridge becomes associated with a plaster sent to the Knights and Burgesses in the House of Commons, while the plaster in turn, "made of the root of lesse [which, like the river, induces memory loss] and pure Oyl-olive," ironically "remembers" all those maimed in God's service.[95] Calling the ointment of the plaster "spittle," Davies constructs yet another play on words. Rewriting the "spittle" with the "bridge" that houses it, Davies alliterates, turning both to "the spirit and the bride."[96]

Numerology, too, plays an important part in situating Davies's prophecies. In *The Excommunication out of Paradice*, Davies verifies the Antichrist's imminent coming with a barrage of numbers and dates. Beginning with Britain, she moves first to Brutus, then to Julius Caesar, and finally to the month of July named for him. Laying all three aside temporarily, she takes up the Beast himself.

Pope Innocent . . . with Cross and Crucifix adored, like that of Gold, *whose height sixty cubits, and breadth six*, and thus running over the Number of his Name 666 namely, *Julius Cesar* and *August*, whose numeral letters *Vic Lvvvi* about the fortieth year of which Reign (*Augustus*) who reigned 55 years and odde Moneths; *the Lamb of God came into the world*, aged 30 *in the fifteenth of Tiberius reign* (Luke, & C.) so that the aforesaid the 55 years and six Months, to Moneths 666 amounts the Grigean Account put into the reckoning since which Empires rising (1600 compleat).[97]

Davies's figures, elaborate to the extreme, suggest, if nothing else, an insistent and apparently inexhaustible impetus to make things fit – to decipher the indecipherable. In her reckonings, even Britain's various coats of arms become proof positive that Daniel's "Vision of the Four Beasts" is in the process of being fulfilled.

The extremity of Davies's connections illustrates a perspective in which "There *is* nothing so secret, That shall not be discovered [my emphasis]." Given her fondness for epigram and elaborate metaphor, the ambiguity of the texts themselves seems more appropriate, the tangential asides far less arbitrary. Davies promises comprehension to her readers, but only if they are skillful and sufficiently well-versed in biblical allusion. She writes, "Although *pend* somewhat hastily or imperfectly . . . I shall the lesse need to excuse [my text] unto such as have a full knowledge of the Scriptures."[98] Her texts expect a great deal. They demand a tremendous *personal* response; individual readers must authorize her work through their interpretations of it. Like the Gospels that her texts describe, Davies's writings are worthy of exegesis. In Davies's writings, national accountability for the English has been textually refigured to insist on an absolute and unified interpretation – one that everyone must share in acknowledging her authority.

In addition to reminding her readers of her prophetic skill through rhetorical enigma, Davies also reorders experience to position herself and her prophecies at the center of all action, thus shifting the dynamic of reform onto the texts themselves. In *The Everlasting Gospel*, she presents related events and experiences as close to synchronically as she can. Describing an early tract of hers that was ill-received, Davies conflates its reception with a second event – prophesying the end of a plague. Moving from discussions of text, to plague, to text, and then back again to plague, she associates the arrival of plague with the failure of her audience to appreciate her textual warnings and the cessation of that same plague with the presentation of her text in the first place. In this account, the plague becomes both the result of her text's reception and the cause of its writing, evidence of both the fulfillment of her prophecies and the failure of her audience to heed them.

Throughout, the circuitous nature of Davies's narrative allows for the conflation of events and intents.[99] Her text, "Great Britain's Blow forshewing" – rejected on page 4 by "Priest and Elders . . . [who] endeavor to stop the peoples mouths" – on page 5, "occasion[s] the Cities unparalleled Plague." On page 7, that same text, "its mouth the Oracle," is delivered to Archbishop Abbot "in presence of no few; with this for a Token given, *the plague presently to cease*."[100] The plague's meaning has been altered in Davies's account. For her, successful reform means neither defending the New Model Army nor supporting parliamentary action against the king; instead, it is simply a willingness to listen.

Davies's status as a woman in a culture that delineates most acceptable female behavior as "chaste, silent, and obedient,"[101] suggests an authorial manipulation and design that allows for the legitimacy of individual interpretation regardless of gender qualification and necessitates recognition of her authorial significance in that interpretation; it suggests writing techniques that privilege Davies's secrets and demand their attention and discovery by observant readers.

Davies uses the third person to recount her prophecies, only rarely combining it with a narrative acknowledgment of her own voice. This structure effectively separates the volitional subject agent – Davies as avenger and victim – from the rather more passive narrative that encloses it. Threat and intimidation (holy hatred) and Davies's ability to manipulate both are generally at a safe remove from the "I" who controls the discourse. To a certain extent, this separation authorizes Davies's actions. The deaths of her adversaries (husband, bishop, and king) are carried out by another person – a prophet who is made credible *and* successful by her author. The separation between "I" and "she," however, also mirrors a dislocation in Davies's aggressive stance. She expresses anger at immediate offenders (offenders within the domestic circles that she frequents)[102] and in secondary sorts of ways (she did it; I did not).

An overlapping of cause and effect (in most male-authored accounts this relationship is unidirectional) diffuses any direct confrontation with anger in Davies's texts.[103] In numerous instances throughout, she refers to events or people, obscuring intent and motivation. Often it is difficult to make distinctions between the actors and those who are acted upon, between the antagonists and protagonists in her battles. At the word level, this confusion is often simply a matter of an ambiguous preposition or the absence of identifying pronouns. Setting up a parallel between herself and Joseph, Davies at one point de-emphasizes the punitive in her actions by keeping her phrasing sufficiently vague. Describing Joseph she writes, "This JOSEPH, and about to take his flight, hated hetherto, for the Evill-report brought of his Brethren."[104] According to the same passage in Genesis (37.2),[105] the action being described is fairly straightforward. Joseph brings his father report of his brothers' intemperate behavior – "their evil saying." Davies's presentation, settling on the rather less distinct "of" and neglecting an additional "he" to mark direction, instead confounds it. Her commentary should perhaps read instead, "This JOSEPH . . . about to take his flight [is] hated hetherto, for the Evill-report [he] brought [concerning] . . . his Brethren."

In Davies's handling of the material, it is not clear whether Joseph is the abused or the abuser, whether he has heard ill of his brothers or they of him. That she uses the analogy to emphasize her own mistreatment seems obvious. Joseph, we are certain, is the one who is "hated hetherto." As proclaimer of his brothers' sins, however, her Joseph is rather less straightforward. Certainly Davies's own position as informant is critical in this passage. As apocalyptic writer, it is she who must warn her readers of the punishments that will befall them if they continue to sin; it is she who must reveal their indiscretions to a doubting world. (Her anagram, after all, explains her position – Reveale O Daniel.) As a woman, however, writing in a culture that is only beginning to recognize women as moral guardians and educators, and then only within the secure confines of a patriarchal household, perhaps Davies is responding to issues of conformity by hedging her bets, by including yet de-emphasizing that status. Presumably less free to express anger or enact punishment than the majority of her counterparts, who have, if nothing else, women and servants to practice upon, Davies must handle her subject far more carefully, filtering it through her own experience of restricted and circumscribed voice.

One last narrative peculiarity evident in Davies's texts is her tendency to withhold the action of a particular description until the end of the sentence or group of sentences – in some cases, dropping it altogether. The resulting construction, reliant on the concluding statement for its impetus, parallels the classical Latin in formation. (If Davies's biblical source is Latin, then her own apocalyptic texts may consciously imitate Latinate constructions.) The deferral of action, however, also echos restrictions and uncertainty in access to legitimate, socially acceptable action for women. When Davies hypothesizes a confrontation with the Devil, his actions are immediate and hers, deferred. "And so this but the truth of it . . . *How* Satan because he knows his reigne or time to be short: is ready to devoure the Woman even for the truth of the Resurrection time revealed, *as most proper to be performed by that sex, a Woman by whom death came to be the Messenger of Life.*"[106] Defending her status as prophet, Davies relies on passive voice and delayed action. "The truth of the Resurrection time" is passively "revealed" and "performed" *by* a woman. The verb ("revealed") follows both its object ("truth") and a prepositioned phrase ("of the Resurrection"). In contrast, Satan's action is considerably more direct in both construction and structure. He is actively "ready to devoure" her for her prophetic warnings. Again and again Davies's stylistic considerations are emblematic of a recurring trend in her writings to postpone action and/or neutralize its force making it safe, acceptable, and blameless.

Davies's stylistic presentation problematizes her relationship to her audience. In fact, given the various distancing techniques that I have described, techniques that diffuse anger, disallow agency, and refocus reader energy onto the act of interpretation itself, Davies's writings are almost without audience, regardless of whom she addresses. Switching readership from individuals (Mr. Mace, the Elector Palatine, Lucy Hastings, and Oliver Cromwell) to groups of individuals (parliament) to entire populations (all nations), Davies's texts rarely involve much direct interaction with her identified audience. In *The Lady Eleanor Her Appeal*, audience absence is made literal when Davies admits, "Your Silence on all sides . . . concludes consent" (19). Certain that her writings will remain unacknowledged, Davies, instead, reads indifference as approval.

Only in her account to her daughter, Lucy, does Davies seem to negotiate a relationship with any degree of success. Here her words reinforce the connection between a mother and child explicitly and poignantly. "To you dedicated," she writes, "that so punctually have discharged that duty of the first commandment with promise, in so much and such dishonor endured, have bene your mothers Copartner, even You, her alone and sole support under the Almighty" (*From the lady Eleanor*, 38). It is perhaps to be expected that the one relationship that Davies is able to establish with her audience in a conventional (masculinist) sense is inextricably linked to the private domain, to the socially acceptable relationship she is allowed as a mother to her daughter.[107]

Some final considerations

Legitimate action is personalized in Davies's construction of subjectivity. Interpretation, in and of itself, should be enough of a response given each text's own value system. Clearly, however, this is not the case. Though Davies's contemporaries allowed her a certain notoriety, they frequently found her texts inadequate. Written for the most part during the English Civil War, her prophecies do intimidate and threaten her adversaries; they do attribute personal guilt to national cause and mete out punishment accordingly. As gendered texts, however, struggling with issues of voice and authority in a predominantly masculine genre, Davies's writings realign that anger, positioning it in ways that may seem inappropriate for a readership that demands an absolute hierarchy between individual and state concerns. Where Davies's thematic interests direct anger away from the national despite its almost pervasive presence in her accounts, her formal interests, framed by gender, neutralize her ability to express that anger legitimately or ensure her audience's response to it. Accordingly, Davies's writings refocus audience obedience from state obligation to an individual acknowledgment of their author that is inappropriate according to most apocalyptic standards of the time.

At the same time, Davies's construction of subjectivity is, by the early years of the English Civil War, so dependent on a gender-coding of discursive identity that she must call on the prophet Daniel for authorization to speak of England's ills, authorization that has little to do with her status as aristocratic wife, and even less to do with the kinds of restrictions that she faces because of her gender. In fact, the prerequisites required to speak politically and to speak as a woman have, to a large degree, become mutually exclusive. Davies's formulation of holy hatred will no longer accommodate the gendering of her concerns. Accordingly, her writings and the subjectivity that they construct are almost uniformly dismissed as bedlam.

Because Davies must respond to cultural requirements already in place, her rhetoric constructs an alternative version of seventeenth-century subjectivity. Because her writing foregrounds personal authority and offers articulations of guilt and anger separate from those of the majority of her contemporaries, her texts realign and refocus the relationship between national and individual allegiance. Davies's writings address specific social concerns – concerns that can be materially identified in women's restricted status, expectation, and mobility but, nevertheless, remain unspoken and unacknowledged in a conventional (masculinist) rhetoric. To this extent, her texts do reveal a distinctly gendered voice – a voice that delineates permissible behavior for women, at one and the same time that it attempts to defy those strictures. Accordingly, Davies's writing, as an example of one available female voice in the seventeenth century, is compromised both by the material obstacles that she faces as a woman writer and by a rhetoric of holy hatred that foregrounds her disobedience at the expense of her authority.

5   Connections, qualifications, and agendas

The preceding explorations suggest a few of the various depths of cultural field that one might consider in interrogating gender- and state-formation in early modern England. From contract law to court examination, from saint's life to sermon, the texts within these analyses illustrate some of the many constructions of English identity available in the sixteenth and seventeenth centuries. Each refocuses our line of critical vision to consider different strategies and alternative authorities. Each extends our scope of understanding about the English state and its subjects. It is tempting and, I think, politically relevant, in positioning these various studies chronologically, to trace patterns of gender and state negotiation between them and to imagine cultural directives at work in the particularity of their shaping.

In one sense I can identify, as a result of these analyses, the formation of what appears to be a gendered conscience – a conscience consonant with first private and then public ideas of state citizenship. Certainly, in my opening exploration I see little evidence of this formulation. Askew, in resisting traditional authorities within the Henrician government, can only gesture toward a singular notion of conscience. She can claim a certainty of conviction via the self and establish her right to write only sporadically. At the same time she offers no elaboration of identity in her descriptions of that self. In Askew's writings, the domain of private conscience remains barely fleshed out – mostly unstated. In contrast, Clitherow's historic moment seems far more willing to concede to some sense of acknowledged interiority – to identity as individualized and worthy to be announced as such. It is in fact Mush's insistent discursive separation of Clitherow from others, evoked in the uniqueness of her religious perseverance and faith, that will finally define her, and, to a certain extent, that celebrated separation illustrates a shifting in ideological definitions of private identity.

By the early decades of the seventeenth century these refigurings appear, I think, even more marked and codified. In the writings of authors like Ester Sowernam, private identity translates to personal responsibility. In Sowernam's tract, selfhood means a domestic and a directive conscience – a recognition of identity that derives in part from an ability to establish and heed one's own moral codes. In addition, once the singular has retreated behind closed doors, once it has made its way into the safe and secure "propriety" of the newly framed English home, yet another complication occurs. As a result of a geographic marking of privacy's utilitarian effect, the domain of conscience, with all of its attendant responsibilities, falls to women. Women, if only within the confines of their husbands' households, become for a time the guardians of men's minds.

In Davies's prophetic warnings to the English people at mid century we can see a further set of dislocations in identity formation. Here we can identify the appearance of a "civic" perception of conscience as separate from and superior to the moral domestic. Recognizing greater and greater needs to direct and motivate behavior at both the local and regional levels, civil-war writers like Davies frame their understandings of conscience broadly. They posit two distinct realms of interiority: civic interiority – a congregationally motivated concern for one's own well-being within the broader spectrum of one's public fellows (determined by religious affiliation, government office, status allegiance, and masculine right) – and domestic interiority – a concept of private identity that is gauged in personal terms, both by virtue of its relegation to the domain of the private household and by virtue of its by now inviolable "protected" status as separate from and lesser to its civically defined counterpart. During the Civil War, private conscience blends with national, the part with the whole, in order to coerce English citizens to civic action from both within and without. However, attention to one's self or family loses significance in conjunction with a civic monitoring of one's neighbors. Conscience, defined this time in congregational terms, asks for a fragmenting of personal responsibility along both national and singular lines, and this splitting further reifies boundaries between gendered responsibilities. The moral domain of the *civic* self belongs to men alone.

Much has changed within the shifting landscapes of England's political, religious, and social economies as we move from sixteenth to seventeenth century, from Reformation to Civil War, still more in the ideological networks that have held those various allegiances intact. Key have been the processes whereby English subjects have come to understand themselves and their nation in national terms, as English citizens. Key as well has been that sense of identity that establishes itself through differentiation and alterity – the impetus to distinguish one from another, this person from that person, and all women from all men. These definitions, mutually reinforcing, operate within bodies as well as outside them, enabling English subjects to create boundaries around and through various aspects of their life and identity and to recognize, despite such categorical differences, some understanding of each self as self.

At the level of nation and state, this sense of totality allows for broader constituencies, for the belief, however erroneous, that wider networks of cooperation and shared interest are not only possible but inevitable. Once England acquires a stable and cohesive national status, the perceived duties and obligations of its remote shires become synonymous with those of London, despite the very real imbalances in effect that might occur when decisions about both are made unilaterally. Broader constituencies, in turn, pave the way for more invasive and pervasive hierarchies of power and domination. The tidy directionalism of feudal obligation, no longer sufficient in and of itself to organize social relations, gets replaced by more flexible mechanisms of social control and invigilation. Labor, law, land, finance, title, profession, family, education – gender – all become potentially discrete and effective sites of cultural coercion. The proliferation in social registers, however, also offers additional opportunity for contradiction and contestation; it provides more spaces in which to define oppositional identity and defend singular prerogative. Because roles are being announced in ever more particular spheres of influence and effect, women can strategically deploy different aspects of those roles, pitting one against another to imagine resistance and rewrite existing narratives in newer forms.

At the more immediate level of the subject individual, we can see further echoes of this kind of definitional paradox. Here the formulation of self as "self-contained" can occur only at that point where the integrated whole becomes the sum of its parts. Social, singular, secular, sacred – the various categories of conscience that define and complicate identity reinforce it as an imagined whole and render it fictively unique. In the years leading up to and including England's first civil war, they also order it. At one and the same time when there is no interest but self-interest, when writers like Thomas Hobbes can assert that the only reason that we only "do unto others as we would have done unto ourselves" is because we are afraid not to, English subjects can still passionately insist that private desire be subordinate to public duty, personal prerogative, to parliamentary process.[1] At those very moments when individuals are deemed masters of their own minds, ethically and spiritually responsible for both moral choices and secret sins, the New Model Army can usurp that mastery by force, and one's religious fellows can appropriate it by fiat.[2]

The political consequences of such narrative reframing can be seen in the historical legacies of post civil-war England, but its traces extend as far back as we choose to go. Mapping lines between faith and loyalty, between spiritual integrity and secular allegiance, sixteenth-century writers like Anne Askew were only beginning to unsettle the univocality of church and state. That religion and religious belief need not be coterminous with political hierarchy, that one may, in fact, have a deleterious effect on the other, will be a rallying cry of later centuries, but the elements of that making are evident in even these brief attempts to speak identity outside established parameters and to justify behavior according to different and often dissonant cultural registers. Proclaiming moral virtue the preeminent domain of chaste women, Ester Sowernam and others like her offer financial leverage and didactic authority to seventeenth-century England's middling-rank maids, wives, and widows. She extends the scope of the domestic to include behaviors both within and outside that domain. That same attribute, however, reified in later philosophical, educational, and medical discourses, will eventually come to determine female identity in far more absolute and restrictive terms. Denied the possibility of erotic desire, rendered vulnerable and dependent on the well-meaning and attentive men who must protect them *and* heed their warnings, women will lose what they have gained in other fronts and across different boundaries. Less mobility and more; a greater likelihood for resistance with fewer chances of success as its result; rapidly changing social structures, and yet constant and recurring sameness within their formulaic oppressions – the cultural paradoxes that write the befores and afters, the earliers and laters, are surprisingly recursive and yet amazingly diverse.

Tracing developmental lines between the various subject configurations that I have posed is both possible and politically sound. Within the textual studies that I consider, such chronologies do reflect the various permutations of identity that occur. There is a catch, however. The assumption of absolute links and linear progressions across English history from specific cultural moments and the micro-histories written about them is compromised before it begins. As we have seen from the discussion of Reformation narratives in chapter 1, chronologies erase as much as, if not more than, they reveal because they selectively ignore the unrecorded shifts and intrusions, the countless mitigating circumstances – that are not and can never be factored into any single theory of state- or gender-formation.

We shouldn't forgo theories, of course. Chronology does matter. Judgment does count. Such relational understandings are integral to the work that critics are asked to do in deciphering a history of the present. They are necessary, persuasive, and essential. In fact, a justified suspicion of such pronouncements is both reflective of and at odds with one of the more significant motivations behind this discussion – an insistence on critical theory as political strategy, on criticism as goal-oriented reform. Accountability in academic interrogation in some sense presupposes the belief that things can improve. Political responsibility assumes the inevitability of change – of continual change – but it also imagines the possibility of determining or at the very least reconfiguring some of those courses, of recognizing our complicity and then attempting to disrupt its many narratives. Pragmatically speaking, academic criticism can never provide, in and of itself, legitimate and transformative social action. While discussions of cause and effect may unsettle notions of absolute normativity and remind us of erased memories, such interrogations will never claim a unique or socially significant voice in evincing cultural change (at least no more unique or socially significant than any other). Instead, theorizing is, at best, one critical element in a larger process of determining which energies we ought to be rallying in our material engagements within and beyond academic discourses; what concerns we ought to be expressing in the other social, political, and economic affiliations that we embrace as participants of those varied groupings.

Tactics imply direction and intent. A tactically directed criticism cannot simply fill in isolated moments or reconfigure previously covert relationships as to do so foregrounds stasis; it neutralizes political responsibility. It seems to me crucial that we account for both *movement* and *moment* in order to exaggerate the possibilities of tactical investment. We need to emphasize tactical strategies that trace movements between positions and uncover the histories of those connections. Locating critical points of reference in the gaps or fissures between stable concepts or among temporally distinct moments foregrounds process and context and allows for the possibility of a more politically vested and accountable critical discourse. At the same time, emphasizing temporality reminds us that there is a certain troubling and comforting constancy to status quo social connections. Erased memories and excluded relationships, inequalities in power and authority continue to exist, not simply because a minority of people possess a majority of social control, but also because the sheer numbers of cultural groupings and their manifold connections to one another render them familiar and secure in already established (albeit unequally established) reciprocities. Accordingly sameness across time needs to be reconsidered, as well as difference.

Calling on whole-centered and historically attentive critical practices may indeed seem to reinvoke the very teleological narratives that we ought to be undermining. Such judgments have been traditionally figured in terms of the linear, as either forward- or backward-looking, epicly forgetful in all of the pieces that do not and will never fit. Political accountability assumes interpretive direction and universal principles as well – movement toward something or away from it, a willingness to form judgments and make choices that order and categorize. We cannot dismiss the unsettling ramifications of these paradigms and the positions that they imply, but we need not abandon them either. Timelines need not begin and end. They need not run in parallel or continuous directions. There is always a question of degree. If we can recognize these constructions as historically and holistically fluid and theorize about them both inside and outside academics in the material practices of our research and our lives, then, I think, we are on the right track (or at least one of them).

Some qualifications

I have tried, through a variety of different "takes," to explore the cultural writing of identity in transition, as process. The discussions here, however, are only a beginning – a fragmentary beginning at best. It is my hope that they can provide the groundwork for what should be a continuing dialogue – a dialogue that will demand multiple speakers, frames, and critical perspectives.[3] That this project is one of the earlier voices in that conversation should remind us that much of the careful critical work has yet to be done. Filling out the contours of early modern gender- and state-configuration will extend well beyond the scope of this book. In fact, while the methodological strategies that I employ in my research allow for a particular kind of lucidity, they are hardly absolute in negotiating these concerns. Subject formation is both complex and contradictory. No single focus can account for all of the problems and possibilities inherent in constructing a feminized state identity for sixteenth- and seventeenth-century Englishwomen. Accordingly, this approach should be considered as one among many – its discoveries as much a result of the editorial decisions that I have made along the way as of a comprehensive interrogation of gender- and state-formation during this period.

The studies in this book focus on singular material representations of subject construction at identifiable moments in time.[4] Sowernam's use of a particular gendered appositive on the title page of her pamphlet tells us a great deal about how *she* imagines gender roles to function, *within* controversy writings, *in* 1617, *amongst* London apprentices. Her unique construction of a gendered subjectivity can point to a more generalized historical trend but cannot assume it directly. A considerable body of research, making use of a wide variety of disparate "histories," has been brought to bear on these writings and the issues they engage. My explorations are not serendipitous or idiosyncratic. I have selected these topics and the writers who employ them because they are representative *and* because they are unique. I have also selected them because they have compelling stories to tell us – because those stories, repeated and reprinted, have made them the stuff of history and of literature.

I bring up the material fact of my own editorial "choices" to remind readers that disciplinary boundaries similarly determine or direct our definitions of what counts. Literature is scripted, much like any other field that privileges documentation, to understand itself and the cultural artifacts that it studies by virtue of their textuality – their ability to be written down, recorded, and interpreted. We need to remember, then, that the medium of analysis (the written word), as much as any critical voice within that medium, necessarily limits and directs our explorations. To talk about absences in terms of what has been left unstated ought simultaneously to remind us that the histories we announce are first determined by what can be written and what is left unwritten, by actions that have been recorded and those that have been assumed unworthy of note.

One unfortunate side effect of this dependence on textual evidence can be found in the limitations that it imposes on the subjects that we study.[5] There are few non-elite women in my explorations. Because writing is predominantly a leisured activity during the sixteenth and seventeenth centuries, there are few writers, if any, who are not without some form of economic advantage. While we can find the occasional shop keeper who writes, most authors from this period claim social status in terms of property and inheritance. The problem of finding non-elite writing is geometrically compounded when the voices under consideration are those of early modern women – women who faced additional restrictions in their access to reading and writing. This critical and theoretical "bias" excludes voices marginalized by ethnic, racial, or geographical considerations as well. In privileging available discourses and disciplinary boundaries, I am necessarily compounding these exclusions.

Reformulating the criteria for critical evaluation may alleviate some of the difficulties inherent in accounting for absence.[6] To imagine hypothetically an authorized position from which to speak or a program of action where no action has been documented can open up historical representation to the traditionally unwritten.[7] My discussion, in chapter 2, of Clitherow's resistances, attempts such a construction. In reinventing notions of history to account for absent voices and redraw their many outlines, comparative analysis can be particularly effective. A comparative approach may permit us to create and construct absent voices by relying on the materially specific, yet historically variable influences and concerns within any given cultural moment. It can also provide a template for further evaluation. Shared subject positions such as gender, social rank, ethnicity, and religious affiliation offer established points of departure. These created "categories," however, are hardly absolute or identical, and differences as well as similarities need to be taken into account. In every case, comparisons must be framed simultaneously and not hierarchically.

Current material debates over the primacy of social rank, ethnicity, or gender in determining identity have the unfortunate effect of further limiting what can be said about unwritten subjectivities. In each privileging, hierarchical analysis proves counter-productive. To argue that economic status should override gender consideration or ethnic background invariably simplifies the complex intersections between a wide range of subject positions. It is true that a woman of the middling ranks like Margaret Clitherow will not share the same social affiliations as a queen. Elizabeth Tudor would have little in common with this butcher's wife, and their differing economic and cultural situations would no doubt ensure that disparity. At the same time, however, let us remember that Clitherow's ideological concerns are not simply or absolutely her husband's either. That the whole of her religious life depends on keeping that life a secret and side-stepping her husband's authority is telling. Clitherow's recognition of herself as a woman influences both the social practices that she participates in and the ways in which she is able to defy those social practices in the first place. The very fact of her "womanness" can at times extend beyond her status and beyond her Catholicism to direct action and determine identity. This gender sameness allows for the possibility of comparative projects regardless of difference. Though Askew's and Clitherow's writings are separated by oppositional religious platforms, material histories, and generic concerns, and despite the very real and palpable divergences between each woman's account, substantial elements of their discourses are, nevertheless, *shared* as a result of their cultural gendering. Those discursive similarities are suggestive and can provide evidence of authority and resistance where, in fact, no documented voice remains.

New directions

At present this project takes as its point of focus 100 years of English history and culture – from Henry VIII's break with the Roman Catholic Church to the English Civil War. Despite this breadth, I have been careful in the preceding chapters to consider issues and writers within narrowly defined material frames. The specificity of this kind of approach necessarily leaves a great deal of ground uncovered. Accordingly I would like to suggest a few directions that future projects might take in order to "fill in the gaps."

Salient moments worth considering could include the 1550s and the first years of the seventeenth century, with their authorial concerns over succession and political leadership. Later analyses might begin to take into account a wider range of status groups. We could greatly complicate and expand our understanding of gender construction with more specific attention to non-elite writers, though these discussions will likely involve us in hypothetical speculations about women whose voices we see only in response to high-culture law or policy. Attention to the particularities of region and location can and should be foregrounded as well. Considering writers whose lives are informed by different realms of cultural and geographic experience will allow us to form distinctions between local desires and national affiliations. Studies that highlight such comparisons might include colonial perspectives from the Americas, British national perspectives from Ireland and Scotland, and expatriate perspectives from Europe, as well as more particular regional distinctions among English voices.

Finally, we might also look at other kinds of state practices. A wide range of cultural fields and disciplinary categories are beginning to codify and particularize during this period, notable among them the sciences,[8] education, and the liberal arts. Jane Sharp, writing soon after the Civil War, offers a detailed defense for midwifery that begs further analysis.[9] In 1616, Dorothy Leigh delineates a program of instruction for her children which calls upon current assumptions about men's and women's separate educations.[10] Numerous other early modern women writers, Ladies Clifford and Mildmay among them, suggest through their diaries what it means to preside over house and home in Tudor and Stuart England.[11] All of these arenas of cultural redefinition are worthy of analysis and have been largely left out of literary critical analyses because they do not fit into pre-established generic or discursive categories.

Culture in process

Understanding the ways in which subjectivities are multiply coded – the ways in which they respond to and develop from a wide range of often disparately weighted ideological imperatives – informs my ability to evaluate my own actions and to recognize their embeddedness within cultural practice. As a result of this more materially aware understanding, I can recognize the cultural dynamics *within* subject construction, even if I cannot anticipate its directions. A decision to privilege a particular "gendered" response may have radically diverse repercussions in how it is taken up within a particular cultural moment. That skewing, while it can never be absolutely or finally traced, can, in fact, be hypothetically imagined. It is possible, as a result of this kind of material critique, to suggest, or at least begin to suggest, the cultural dynamics that inform gender and state definitions – past, present, and future.

Notes

INTRODUCTION

1 Margaret Cavendish, "Margaret Cavendish: From *A True Relation of my Birth, Breeding and Life, 1656*," in *Her Own Life: Autobiographical Writings by Seventeenth-Century Englishwomen*, ed. Elspeth Graham, Hillary Hinds, Elaine Hobby, and Helen Wilcox (London, 1989) 90. Cavendish's memoir was first published in 1656. For an account of Englishwomen's autobiographies in the seventeenth century, see Graham, Hinds, Hobby, and Wilcox, *Her Own Life*, 1–27.

2 For later versions of this argument, see Nancy Armstrong, *Desire and Domestic Fiction: A Political History of the Novel* (New York, 1987); Ruth Bloch, "Untangling the Roots of Modern Sex Roles: Four Centuries of Change," *Signs* 4 (1978) 237–52; and Catherine Hall, "The Early Formation of Victorian Domestic Ideology," in *Fit Work for Women*, ed. Sandra Burman (London, 1979) 15–32.

3 One of the first extant diaries/memoirs written by a woman is that of Lady Margaret Hoby. Entries date from August 1599. Hoby's journal was apparently suggested by her minister as an exercise "for the sake of religious discipline" (Charlotte Kohler, "Elizabethan Woman of Letters, the Extent of her Literary Activity," Ph.D. diss. [University of Virginia, 1936] 370). Two other early seventeenth-century women "diarists" are Lady Grace Mildmay and Lady Anne Clifford. For modern editions, see *Dairy of Lady Margaret Hoby, 1599–1605*, ed. Dorothy M. Meads (Boston, 1930); *With Faith and Physic: The Life of a Tudor Gentlewoman Lady Grace Mildmay, 1552–1620*, ed. Linda Pollock (New York, 1995); and *The Diaries of Lady Anne Clifford*, ed. D. J. H. Clifford (Stroud, 1990).

4 One of the more culturally focused accounts to trace state processes in early modern England, *The Great Arch: English State Formation and Cultural Revolution* (Oxford, 1985) by Philip Corrigan and Derek Sayer, offers a sociological macro-survey of English state-making from the eleventh to the late nineteenth centuries. Integrating discussions of England's political, economic, and religious upheaval with an eye toward the development of a concurrent moral ethos, Corrigan and Sayer make a persuasive case for reading English history as cultural revolution. Less willing to commit to the kind of "big picture" narrative or polemical frames that *The Great Arch* repeatedly asserts, most historians do, nevertheless, posit significant shifts in

institutional and ideological supports from the sixteenth to the seventeenth centuries. Some notable examples include G. E. Aylmer, *The King's Servants: The Civil Service of Charles I, 1625–1642* (London, 1974), and *Rebellion or Revolution? England, 1640–1660* (Oxford, 1986); C. G. A. Clay, *Economic Expansion and Social Change: England 1500–1700* (Cambridge, 1984) 2 vols.; A. G. Dickens, *The English Reformation* (New York, 1964); G. R. Elton, *Policy and Police: The Enforcement of the Reformation in the Age of Thomas Cromwell* (Cambridge, 1972), and *Reform and Reformation – England, 1509–1558* (Cambridge, 1977); Christopher Hill, *Change and Continuity in Seventeenth-Century England* (London, 1974), and *The World Turned Upside Down: Radical Ideas During the English Revolution* (New York, 1972); David Loades, *Politics and Nation, 1450–1660: Obedience, Resistance and Public Order*, 4th edn. (London, 1992); Alan G. R. Smith, *The Emergence of a Nation-State: The Commonwealth of England, 1529–1660* (London, 1984); Lawrence Stone, *The Causes of the English Revolution, 1529–1642* (New York, 1972); and Penry Williams, *The Tudor Regime* (Oxford, 1979). Patrick Collinson (*The Birthpangs of Protestant England: Religious and Cultural Change in the Sixteenth and Seventeenth Centuries* [London, 1988]), Claire Cross (*Church and People, 1450–1660: The Triumph of the Laity in the English Church* [Atlantic Highlands, NJ, 1976]), Eamon Duffy (*The Stripping of the Altars: Traditional Religion in England, c. 1400–c. 1580* [New Haven, 1992]), Christopher Haigh (*English Reformations: Religion, Politics, and Society under the Tudors* [Oxford, 1993]), William Lamont (*Godly Rule: Politics and Religion, 1603–1660* [London, 1969]), and Keith Thomas (*Religion and the Decline of Magic: Studies in Popular Beliefs in Sixteenth- and Seventeenth-Century England* [London, 1971]) explore these same state processes through the framework of English religious history.

5 See Thomas N. Tentler for a discussion of the confessional as a site of regulation (*Sin and Confession on the Eve of the Reformation* [Princeton, 1977] and "The Summa for Confessors as an Instrument of Social Control," in *The Pursuit of Holiness in Late Medieval and Renaissance Religion; Papers from the University of Michigan Conference* [Leiden, 1974] 103–25). In chapter 2 of this book I discuss the unusual dynamics of the priest/penitent relationship in English recusancy.

6 Roger Chartier, ed., *A History of Private Life* (vol. III, *Passions of the Renaissance* [Cambridge, MA, 1989]) documents the numerous and multiple irruptions of privacy to appear in the sixteenth and seventeenth centuries.

7 P. Williams, *The Tudor Regime*, 238–39. For an overview of early modern English legal history, see Alan Harding, *A Social History of English Law* (Baltimore, 1966) esp. pts. 1 and 2.

8 Chartier, *A History of Private Life*, esp. vol. III, ch. 3.

9 P. Williams, *The Tudor Regime*, esp. chapters 1–4.

10 Joan Thirsk, *Economic Policy and Projects: The Development of a Consumer Society in Early Modern England* (Oxford, 1978). See also Clay, *Economic Expansion and Social Change*, vol. II, 98–102.

11 Joan Kelly Gadol's landmark early essay "Did Women Have a Renaissance?" (*Becoming Visible: Women in European History* [Boston, 1987] 175–201)

reconsiders the supposed "rebirth" of Renaissance culture in terms of its impact on women.

12 Clay, *Economic Expansion and Social Change*, vol. II, 230–31, 234–35.

13 See chapter 3 for a discussion of the intersections between these regulatory practices.

14 In his book *Forms of Nationhood: The Elizabethan Writing of England*, Richard Helgerson acknowledges connections between writing national identity and writing the self. Focusing specifically on the forms (discursive and political) that shaped those identities for sixteenth- and seventeenth-century English writers, Helgerson only briefly alludes to the inevitable gendering that such pursuits fostered (Chicago, 1992, esp. 295–301). See also Claire McEachern, *The Poetics of English Nationhood, 1590–1612* (Cambridge, 1996).

15 To my knowledge, no one has yet considered adequately the transitional character of a state-inflected gender-coding during this historical period. Critics who address connections between gender and state in later periods include: Varda Burstyn, "Masculine Dominance and the State," in *Socialist Register 1983* (London, 1983) 45–89; Hall, "Formation"; Catherine A. MacKinnon, "Feminism, Marxism, Method and the State," *Signs* 7.3 (1982) 515–44; Mary McIntosh, "The State and the Oppression of Women," in *Feminism and Materialism: Women and Modes of Production*, ed. Annette Kuhn and Ann Marie Wolpe (London, 1982) 254–89; and Jeffrey Weeks, *Sex, Politics and Society: The Regulation of Sexuality Since 1800* (London, 1981). Benedict R. Anderson (*Imagined Communities: Reflections on the Origin and Spread of Nationalism* [London, 1983]) provides one of the more explicit discussions of the link between ideological and material circumstances in constructing national identity.

16 The Women Writers Project at Brown University continues that pursuit on an ongoing basis, copying and editing previously unavailable texts. Together with WWP, Oxford University Press has published numerous editions of early modern women's texts, including Aemilia Lanyer's poems, Lady Arbella Stuart's letters, Anna Weamys's continuation of the *Arcadia*, and, more recently, a wide selection of Lady Eleanor Davies's prophetic tracts and Anne Askew's *Examinations*. These newly edited works are part of a series entitled Women Writers in English 1350–1850. Works anthologizing early modern Englishwomen's writings include Katherine Usher Henderson and Barbara F. McManus, eds., *Half Humankind: Contexts and Texts of the Controversy about Women in England, 1540–1640* (Urbana, IL, 1985); James Fitzmaurice, Josephine A. Roberts, Carol Barash, Eugene R. Cunnar, and Nancy A. Guitierrez, eds., *Major Women Writers of Seventeenth-Century England* (Detroit, 1997); Graham, Hinds, Hobby, and Wilcox, *Her Own Life*; Germaine Greer, ed., *Kissing the Rod: An Anthology of Seventeenth-Century Women's Verse* (London, 1988); Charlotte F. Otten, ed., *English Women's Voices: 1540–1700* (Gainesville, FL, 1992); and Betty S. Travisky, ed., *The Paradise of Woman: Writings by Englishwomen of the Renaissance* (Westport, 1981).

17 For comprehensive bibliographies of recent studies in early modern women's writings, see Sara Jayne Steen, "Women Writers of the Seventeenth Century, 1604–1674," *English Literary Renaissance* 24 (1994) 243–74; and Georgianna

M. Ziegler, "Women Writers of Tudor England, 1485–1603," *English Literary Renaissance* 24 (1994) 229–42. Elizabeth H. Hageman's bibliographic reviews in *English Literary Renaissance* ("Recent Studies in Women Writers of the English Seventeenth Century [1604–1674]," 18 [1988] 138–67, and "Recent Studies in Women Writers of Tudor England," 17 [1987] 409–25) can provide an overview of earlier research.

18 Some noteworthy examples include Clare Brant and Diane Purkiss, eds., *Women, Texts and Histories, 1575–1760* (London, 1992); S. P. Cerasano and Marion Wynne-Davies, eds., *Gloriana's Face: Women, Public and Private, in the English Renaissance* (Detroit, 1992); Isobel Grundy and Susan Wiseman, eds., *Women, Writing, History, 1640–1740* (Athens, GA, 1992); Margaret P. Hannay, ed., *Silent but for the Word: Tudor Women as Patrons, Translators, and Writers of Religious Works* (Kent, OH, 1985); Anne M. Haselkorn and Betty S. Travitsky, eds., *The Renaissance Englishwoman in Print: Counterbalancing the Canon* (Amherst, 1990); Carole Levin and Jeannie Watson, eds., *Ambiguous Realities: Women in the Middle Ages and Renaissance* (Detroit, 1987); and Betty S. Travitsky and Adele F. Seeff, eds., *Attending to Women in Early Modern England* (Newark, 1994).

19 See Elaine V. Beilin, *Redeeming Eve: Women Writers of the English Renaissance* (Princeton, 1987); Constance Jordan, *Renaissance Feminism: Literary Texts and Political Models* (Ithaca, 1990); Tina Krontiris, *Oppositional Voices: Women as Writers and Translators of Literature in the English Renaissance* (London, 1992); and Barbara Lewalski, *Writing Women in Jacobean England* (Boston, 1993). For studies focusing on the social histories of Renaissance women, see Susan Dwyer Amussen, *An Ordered Society: Gender and Class in Early Modern England* (Oxford, 1988); Patricia Crawford, *Women and Religion in England, 1500–1720* (London, 1993); Margaret George, *Women in the First Capitalist Society: Experiences in Seventeenth-Century England* (Urbana, 1988); Margaret L. King, *Women of the Renaissance* (Chicago, 1991); Phyllis Mack, *Visionary Women: Ecstatic Prophecy in Seventeenth-Century England* (Berkeley, 1992); Mary Prior, ed., *Women in English Society 1500–1800* (London, 1985); Retha M. Warnicke, *Women of the English Renaissance and Reformation*, Contributions in Women's Studies 38 (Westport, CT, 1983); and Linda Woodbridge, *Women and the English Renaissance: Literature and the Nature of Womankind, 1540–1620* (Urbana, 1984).

20 Catherine Belsey's *The Subject of Tragedy: Identity & Difference in Renaissance Drama* (London, 1985) offers one of the more provocative discussions of female subjectivity to depend on already canonized male writers (see especially 129–91). Even here, however, relying on dramatists like Webster to characterize women's lives, Belsey's study is limited in the real options that it can legitimately address.

21 Megan Matchinske, "Credible Consorts: What Happens When Shakespeare's Sisters Enter the Syllabus?" *Shakespeare Quarterly* 47 (1996) 434.

22 *Writing Women's Literary History* (Baltimore, 1993) 4. Refusing such models, critics like Stephanie Jed ("The Tenth Muse: Gender, Rationality and the Marketing of Knowledge," in *Women, "Race" and Writing in the Early Modern Period*, ed. Margo Hendricks and Patricia Parker [New York, 1993]

195–208) manage a temporary "suspension" of critical and documentary judgment by breaking with scholarly tradition to envision new dialogues. See also Patricia Fumerton's *Cultural Aesthetics: Renaissance Literature and the Practice of Social Ornament* (Chicago, 1991). Fumerton argues for a historically grounded notion of early modern aesthetics in social ornamentation and cultural marginalia.

23 Ezell offers a persuasive critique of the ways in which modern feminisms unintentionally foreclose discussions of early modern women writers (*Writing Women's Literary History* – see esp. chapters 2 and 3).

24 A number of recent studies foreground the conditional nature of resistance for early modern women. Barbara Lewalski's "Introduction: Women, Writing, and Resistance in Jacobean England" (*Writing Women in Jacobean England*, 1–11) provides one of the more materially aware overviews on this subject. See also Brant and Purkiss, "Introduction: Minding the Story," in their *Women, Texts and Histories*, 1–12; and Wendy Wall, *The Imprint of Gender: Authorship and Publication in the English Renaissance* (Ithaca, 1993) 279–340.

25 For suggestive readings of the gender dynamics inherent in half a century of Elizabethan rule, see Susan Frye, "The Myth of Elizabeth at Tilbury," *Sixteenth Century Journal* 23 (1992) 95–114, and *Elizabeth I: The Competition for Representation* (Oxford, 1993); John King, "Queen Elizabeth I: Representations of the Virgin Queen," *Renaissance Quarterly* 43 (1990) 30–74; Carole Levin, *"The Heart and Stomach of a King": Elizabeth I and the Politics of Sex and Power* (Philadelphia, 1994); and Louis A. Montrose, *"A Midsummer Night's Dream* and the Shaping Fantasies of Elizabethan Culture: Gender, Power, Form," in *Rewriting the Renaissance: The Discourses of Sexual Difference in Early Modern Europe*, ed. Margaret W. Ferguson, Maureen Quilligan, and Nancy J. Vickers (Chicago, 1986) 65–87, and "The Work of Gender in the Discourse of Discovery," *Representations* 33 (1991) 1–41. Other women such as Mary Sidney and Lucy Russell exerted a tremendous amount of "court" influence during their lifetimes as well. See Barbara Lewalski's *Writing Women in Jacobean England*, and Retha M. Warnicke's *Women of the English Renaissance and Reformation*, for discussions of some of England's more "politically persuasive" women.

26 Linda Alcoff, "Cultural Feminism versus Post-Structuralism: The Identity Crisis in Feminist Theory," *Signs* 13 (1988) 433. Alcoff's position is persuasively critiqued in Teresa de Lauretis, "The Essence of the Triangle or, Taking the Risk of Essentialism Seriously: Feminist Theory in Italy, the US, and Britain," *Differences* 1 (1988) 10–13. De Lauretis concurs with Alcoff that we must begin both to "theorize experience in relation to practices" and to understand "gendered subjectivity as an emergent property of [that] historicized experience" (12).

27 For some early materialist discussions within the subject/structure debate, see Theodore W. Adorno, *Negative Dialectics* (New York, 1973); Stanley Aronowitz, *The Crisis in Historical Materialism* (New York, 1981); Michael H. Best and William E. Connolly, "Politics and Subjects," *Socialist Review* 9 (1979) 75–99; Pierre Bourdieu, *Outline of a Theory of Practice*, trans. Richard Nice (Cambridge, 1977); Anthony Giddens, *Central Problems in Social Theory:*

Action, Structure, and Contradiction in Social Analysis (Berkeley, 1979); Jorgen Habermas, "Psychic Thermidor and the Rebirth of Rebellious Subjectivity," *Berkeley Journal of Sociology* 24 (1980) 1-12; Stephen Heath, "The Turn of the Subject," *Cine-Tracts* 8 (1979) 32-48; Julian Henriques, *Changing the Subject: Psychology, Social Regulation and Subjectivity* (New York, 1984); Fredric Jameson, *The Political Unconscious* (Ithaca, 1981); Dominick LaCapra, *Rethinking Intellectual History* (Ithaca, 1983); Ernesto Laclau and C. Mouffe, *Hegemony and Socialist Strategy* (London, 1985); Georg Lukacs, *History and Class Consciousness* (Cambridge, 1971); D. Morely, "Texts, Readers, Subjects," in *Culture, Media, Language: Working Papers in Cultural Studies, 1972-79* (London, 1980) 163-76; P. Wexler, "Structure, Text and Subject: A Critical Sociology of School Knowledge," in *Cultural and Economic Reproduction in Education: Essays on Class, Ideology, and the State*, ed. Michael W. Apple (London, 1982) 275-303; P. Willemen, "Notes on Subjectivity," *Screen* 19 (1978) 41-69; and Raymond Williams, "Problems of Materialism," *New Left Review* 109 (1978) 3-17.

28 Paul Smith, *Discerning the Subject* (Minneapolis, 1988) xxxiv.

29 It is during the sixteenth and seventeenth centuries that English medical treatises begin to describe, with some frequency, female and male genitalia as inherently different. For a provocative and troubling rereading of the whole of western history in same sex/different sex terms, see Thomas Laqueur, *Making Sex: Body and Gender from the Greeks to Freud* (Cambridge, 1990). Accounts that focus more particularly and, I think, more accurately on the complex social history of English medicine and the gendering of anatomy can be found in Audrey Eccles's *Obstetrics and Gynaecology in Tudor and Stuart England* (Kent, OH, 1982); Carolyn Merchant's *The Death of Nature: Women, Ecology, and the Scientific Revolution* (New York, 1980); and Merry E. Weisner's "Early Modern Midwifery: A Case Study," in *Women and Work in Pre-Industrial Europe*, ed. Barbara A. Hanawalt (Bloomington, 1986) 94-113.

30 From an involvement with the poor and a regulation of the London labor market via patents of monopoly, to a reorganization of privy council and a more coherent and complex method of calendar-keeping, sixteenth-century English government seems to intensify and consolidate its participation in extended social networks. For a discussion of an evolving privy council, see P. Williams, *The Tudor Regime*, 27-33; poor laws: E. M. Leonard, *The Early History of English Poor Relief* (Cambridge, 1900) chapters 5, 7; and patents: Thirsk, *Economic Policy and Projects*, esp. chapters 2 and 3. The *State's* active involvement in these directives mirrors the more "informal" *state* practices that I will consider in this book.

31 For discussions of subjectivity in performative terms, see Belsey, *The Subject of Tragedy*; Stephen Mullaney, *The Place of the Stage: License, Play, and Power in Renaissance England* (Chicago, 1988); and Karen Newman, *Fashioning Femininity and English Renaissance Drama* (Chicago, 1991).

32 For an overview of this transition in European contexts, see Chartier, *A History of Private Life*. A less history-specific reading of the private can be found in Barrington Moore, Jr., *Privacy: Studies in Social and Cultural History* (Armonk, NY, 1984).

33 In *Private Matters and Public Culture in Post-Reformation England* (Ithaca, 1994), Lena Cowen Orlin identifies the particular and, as yet, ill-defined attributes of the early modern domestic scene. See Don E. Wayne's *Penshurst: The Semiotics of Place and the Politics of History* (Madison, 1984) for discussions of a developing notion of "property" and "propriety" in early modern England.

34 Corrigan and Sayer define "moral regulation" as "a project of normalizing, rendering natural, taken for granted, in a word 'obvious,' what are in fact ontological and epistemological premises of a particular and historical form of social order" (*The Great Arch*, 4). I want to emphasize the importance that gender accrues in this regard in relation to both state and self.

35 See chapter 4 for a detailed discussion of the connections between "universals" and "particulars" in state formation.

36 In "Ideology and Ideological State Apparatuses" (*"Lenin and Philosophy" and Other Essays* [New York, 1971] 127–88), Louis Althusser identifies the state as *"State"* – as a specifically defined set of institutions and related institutional practices. He includes among this list, both offices of the State (its government) and extra-official apparatuses of the State (its system of education). I am defining the *"state"* more broadly than Althusser. I am also loathe to see its various practices as all of one piece. I do, however, want to stress an Althusserian "hegemony of effects" in the way that economic and cultural processes frequently support one another, even outside the more formally constituted offices of Althusser's *State*.

37 Corrigan and Sayer, *The Great Arch*, 7, in turn quoting Karl Marx, *Capital*, vol. I (London, 1967) 77. See Bob Jessop (*Capitalist State: Marxist Theories and Methods* [New York, 1982]) for an argument *against* a general theory of the state.

38 I owe John McGowan a debt of gratitude for reminding me that there are different registers of state regulation and that those registers are not equally weighted. For an attention to degree in our political responses within the post-structural debate, see his book *Postmodernism and Its Critics* (Ithaca, 1991), esp. chapters 1 and 4.

39 A statute issued in 1536 consolidates judicial power under royal jurisdiction, leaving the appointment of all judges and justices throughout the realm to the king. Another injunction issued in 1538, by Cromwell, requires the keeping of registers in every parish in the kingdom to record baptisms, marriages, and burials. These records allowed for more effective taxation of English subjects and began to document title of inheritance (Elton, *Policy and Police*, 259–60; P. Williams, *The Tudor Regime*, 254).

40 It is estimated that the dissolution of the monasteries brought the crown 10 percent of the landed wealth in England (£136,000), together with the first fruits and tenths (approximately £40,000), and plate and bullion worth an estimated £1 million (Loades, *Politics and Nation, 1450–1660*, 174).

41 If anything, Cromwell's chief contribution to state-making came in the overhaul of parliamentary office and a reformulation of its decision-making responsibilities (Corrigan and Sayer, *The Great Arch*, 52).

42 Here I am talking about a select group of "vested" men – men who by

education, economic status, and occupation recognize in those allegiances justification to act for and on behalf of government.

43 Mark Breitenberg ("The Flesh Made Word: Foxe's *Acts and Monuments*," *Renaissance and Reformation* 25 [1989] 385) reminds readers that the oft-held belief that Foxe's *Acts and Monuments* was a fixture in every parish church has no extant substantiation.

44 Plays performed at the Red Bull for largely non-aristocratic audiences catered to a clientele different from that of court masques or poetry in manuscript. Accordingly, generic difference is often compounded by specific and distinct political agendas and platforms.

45 John Mush, as author of Clitherow's life, controls both the direction and force of her claims to legitimacy. We cannot assume that her options are more restricted than Askew's simply because Mush says so. Even if we had in our possession an extant manuscript by Clitherow, making such assumptions would be risky. Still, I think it is possible to defend a historical claim to a narrowing (or should I say a particularizing) of cultural options as we move into the Elizabethan period.

46 Corrigan and Sayer, focusing on the 1640s, remind us that "religion was not, in the seventeenth century, a disposable set of rationalizations, it was a vital element in the framework within which people thought: including thinking their politics. Protestantism, like the place of Parliament or the rule of law, was an integral part of a political culture which was by this time both coherent and distinctively (and proudly) English" (*The Great Arch*, 77).

47 Riley, *Am I that Name?: Feminism and the Category of "Women" in History* (Minneapolis, 1988) 16. Unfortunately, because Riley speaks so broadly, her discussion frequently recategorizes "woman" at the very same instant that it deconstructs "women."

48 I am thinking here of Teresa de Lauretis's description of her own critical encounters with cinema as looking "through a critical lens with variable focus" (*Alice Doesn't: Feminism, Semiotics, Cinema* [Bloomington, 1984] 11).

1 RESISTANCE, REFORMATION, AND THE REMAINING NARRATIVES

1 Anne Crawford, Tony Hayter, Ann Hughes, Frank Prochaska, Pauline Stafford, and Elizabeth Vallance, eds., *The Europa Biographical Dictionary of British Women: Over 1000 Notable Women from Britain's Past* (London, 1983) 19. I would to thank Betty Travitsky for her generous and life-saving help in tracking down this quotation.

2 I want to stress here both the unusual status that Askew has among other sixteenth-century English Protestant martyrs and her typicality. As a privileged and educated gentlewoman, Askew is alone in writing her defiance of Henrician religious policy. There are no others. Nevertheless, from the intensity of her assertions to the inquisitorial format in which she positions them, Askew shares much with her contemporaries. Her placement within the larger frameworks of polemicists like Foxe and Bale reinforces that similarity, continually stressing comparison and precedent, repetition and sameness.

3 Nineteenth- and twentieth-century novelists found Askew's account worthy

of dramatic presentation. See, for instance, Anne Manning, *The Lincolnshire Tragedy: Passages in the Life of the Faire Gospeller, Mistress Anne Askew* (London, 1866; New York, 1966), and Alison Macleod, *The Heretic* (Boston, 1966).

4 In "An Essay to Revive the Ancient Education of Gentlewomen" (1673), Bathshua Makin makes the connection absolute, calling Askew "a person famous for learning and piety, who so seasoned the Queen and ladies of the Court, by her precepts and examples, and after sealed her profession with her blood, *that the seed of reformation seemed to be sowed by her hand* [my emphasis]" (*The Female Spectator: English Women Writers Before 1800*, ed. Mary Mahl and Helene Koon [Bloomington, 1977] 134).

5 In *The Reformation in Historical Thought*, A. G. Dickens and John Tonkin offer a descriptive historiography of the Reformation from its first speakers to its last, suggesting that it has, from its earliest moments, always been conceived as a historical project (Harvard, 1985).

6 See also Thomas Brice's *Compendious Register in Metre* (1559). Other mid-century martyr-writing reformists included Ludwig Rabus, Jean Crespin, and Adrian Cornelis van Haemstede (Dickens, *The Reformation in Historical Thought*, 41).

7 "To commemorate his fellow Augustinian and friend at Wittenberg, Henrich of Zutphen[, Luther published in 1525] . . . *The Burning of Brother Henry in Dithmarschen*": William Tyndale followed it with *The Obedience of a Christian Man* (1528), and his edition of the Lollard *Examination of Thorpe and Oldcastle* and *The Testament of William Tracie* (1535). Published in 1616, *Les tragiques* by D'Aubigné was apparently begun sometime in 1577 (Dickens and Tonkin, *The Reformation in Historical Thought*, 40, 41, 43).

8 *The Acts and Monuments of John Foxe*, ed. George Townsend (New York, 1965) vol. I, xxiv.

9 For other Reformation historians who explicitly name Askew in their accounts, see Reverend James Anderson, *Ladies of the Reformation: Memoirs of Distinguished Female Characters Belonging to the Period of the Reformation in the Sixteenth Century* (London, 1855) vol. I, 136–79; John Stow, *The Annales of England . . . untill this present yeere 1592* (London, 1592) 999; John Strype, *Ecclesiastical Memorials* (London, 1721) vol. I, 387–88.

10 In "A Challenge to Authority: Anne Askew" (*Redeeming Eve*, 29–47) and "Anne Askew's Self-Portrait in the Examinations" (*Silent but for the Word*, 77–91), Elaine V. Beilin attends to gender specifically. Beilin's studies of Askew are foundational. It is largely through her work that students are beginning to encounter the Askew document outside its traditional reformist boundaries. Beilin's recent edition of Askew's *Examinations* (*The Examinations of Anne Askew* [Oxford, 1996]) includes the 1546 and 1547 editions with Bale's commentary as well as Foxe's 1563 edition in *Acts and Monuments* (English version).

11 The two fullest contemporary accounts are Bale's and Foxe's. The standard biography is Derick Wilson's *A Tudor Tapestry: Men, Women and Society in Reformation England* (Pittsburgh, 1972). See also Beilin's introduction (*The Examinations of Anne Askew*, xv–xliii).

12 Parliamentary decrees, the first in 1543 and the second in 1544, sought for

redress and moderation in the penalties originally proscribed for defiance of the Act of Six Articles. First-time and repeat offenses were to be treated differently, with both penalties to focus on symbolic rather than corporal punishment (John Guy, *Tudor England* [Oxford, 1988] 193–4). Askew's execution was, according to these decrees, illegal. See Paula McQuade ("'Except that they had offended the Lawe': Gender and Jurisprudence in *The Examinations of Anne Askew*," *Literature & History* 3 [1994] 1–14) for a discussion of other irregularities in the Askew trial.

13 The six articles included rulings on transubstantiation, communion in one kind, vows of chastity, votive masses, clerical celibacy, and auricular confession (Haigh, *English Reformations*, 152).

14 The controversy over this one theological principle cannot be underestimated; it extended back to the days of Wycliffe and the early Lollards, and continued on well into the seventeenth century (Haigh, *English Reformations*, 51).

15 Historian Barbara Harris reminds me that gentlewomen traveling alone were not as unusual as we might first suppose and that many carried out family business in their travels to and from London. Nevertheless, the kind of activity in which Askew was engaged was clearly taboo. The Act for the Advancement of True Religion (1543) prohibited men under the rank of "gentleman" and *all* women from reading the Bible. While a proviso in the act did stipulate that noble and gentry women might read the Bible privately, Askew's gospelling placed her well outside those parameters (Haigh, *English Reformations*, 161).

16 While I shall speak in a general sense of a single "division" between a reformed and a traditional perspective in Renaissance England, there was no single "reformist" or "traditionalist" platform. While all members of Henry VIII's privy council had, by 1534, sworn allegiance to the king, that allegiance did not necessarily mean support for the "new" religion or even acknowledgment of the same terms of debate in its regard (Elton, *Policy and Police*, 222). The Reformation brought with it an endless number of religious reconfigurations. Accordingly, my comparisons, limited as they are to the binary split between major religious camps, will address general principles at the risk of erasing specific considerations within them.

17 One can trace an almost geometric rate of preferment for Protestant "upstarts" in the early years of Henry VIII's struggles with the church; new, often less well-placed, men like Cranmer rose quickly and forcefully into positions of close confidence with the king (Penry Williams, *The Tudor Regime*, 424). The awarding of these appointments was to change markedly in later years (from reformist to conservative) with traditionalists receiving their own share of the spoils from Henry's break with Rome.

18 Despite a nominal allegiance to the king, Bishop Gardiner maintained an avowedly Catholic slant in his religious and political allegiances. See Haigh, "From Monopoly to Minority: Catholicism in Early Modern England," *Transactions of the Royal Historical Society* 5th ser. 31 (1980) 131.

19 Other supporters in the Gardiner faction included another participant in the Askew inquest, Sir Thomas Wriothesley (Secretary to the Council), the Duke of Norfolk (Lord Treasurer), the Earl of Southhampton (Lord Privy Seal), and Cuthburt Tunstall (Bishop of Durham). Chief among the opposition

were, in addition to Cranmer, Lord Audley (Lord Chancellor), the Duke of Suffolk (Great Master of the Household), the Earl of Hertford (Lord Great Chamberlain), Viscount Lisle (Lord Admiral), Sir Anthony Denny (Chief Gentleman of the Privy Chamber), and Sir Ralph Sadler (Secretary to the King in the Privy Chamber) (Elton, *Reform and Reformation*, 116–18, 328–32; Guy, *Tudor England*, 197–99; and David Starkey, *The Reign of Henry VIII: Personalities and Politics* [London, 1985] 133).

20 The most notable example of Henry VIII's even-handedness in persecuting religious offenders can be seen in the execution of six men – three reformists, three Catholics – on July 30, 1540 (Wilson, *A Tudor Tapestry*, 126).

21 In a public display of his continued orthodoxy, Henry VIII took an active role in the 1538 trial of John Lambert. Involving himself intimately in Lambert's prosecution, Henry supposedly announced, "if you do commit yourself unto my judgment you must die, for I will not be a patron unto heretics" (Foxe, *Acts and Monuments*, vol. V, 234).

22 In early 1543, King Henry VIII ratified a treaty with Catholic Spain. May of that year saw an official statement of the monarchy's position on religious faith in *The Necessary Doctrine and Erudition for any Christian Man*. That document, known as the King's Book, was, by and large, a revised edition of the earlier Bishop's Book and clarified Henry VIII's position on transubstantiation, sacramental penance, etc. Gardiner's influence in this work cannot be overstated (Wilson, *A Tudor Tapestry*, 139, 143).

23 Starkey (*The Reign of Henry VIII*) persuasively documents the political factionalism of court/council battles in the last years of Henry VIII's reign. See especially pp. 124–67. See also Starkey, "Court and Government," in *Revolution Reassessed*, ed. Christopher Coleman and Starkey (Oxford, 1986) 29–58, and *Rivals in Power: Lives and Letters of the Great Tudor Dynasties* (New York, 1990).

24 While Protestant sympathizers had been persecuted since the early days of the Reformation, forced to perform public penance and witness the burning of controversial books, few were to lose their lives at the stake until More's appointment as Chancellor in 1529 (Haigh, *English Reformations*, 67). From that point onward and at almost regular intervals, Henry's government would remind English subjects of the dangers of the heresy by focusing on isolated, London-based and court-attached offenders. Men like Robert Barnes, Thomas Garrett, and William Jerome, all of whom died in the aftermath of Thomas Cromwell's 1540 execution, lost their lives not so much for their beliefs as for their unfortunate connections (Haigh, *English Reformations*, 154).

25 Wilson, *A Tudor Tapestry*, 115–16, 34, 159. While Suffolk was "tolerant of unorthodoxy," he was far from a radical himself. He did, nevertheless, support Cromwell and take an active role in the persecution of Catherine Howard, no doubt making a few enemies in the process (S. J. Gunn, *Charles Brandon, Duke of Suffolk, c. 1484–1545* [Oxford, 1988] 104, 197).

26 Beilin, *The Examinations of Anne Askew*, xvii.

27 John Bale, ed., *The lattre examinacyon of Anne Askewe, lately martyred in Smythfelde, by the wycked Synagoge of Antichrist, with the Elucydacyon of Johan Bale* (Marpurg [Wesel], 1547) 43A–B. All future citations are from the

first edition (British Library copy) and will be identified simply as *lattre examinacyon*. For the definitive modern edition, see Beilin, *The Examinations of Anne Askew*. An earlier edition can be found in Reverend Henry Christmas, ed., *Select Works of John Bale, D.D. Bishop of Ossory, Containing the Examinations of Lord Cobham, William Thorpe, and Anne Askew*, and *The Image of Both Churches* (Cambridge, 1968) 185–248.

28 All of these women had direct and unmediated *household* access to the reform-minded queen, and several of them husbands who were advisors to the king. Lady Denny's husband, Anthony Denny, was one of the most influential and powerful men in the kingdom (Starkey, *The Reign of Henry VIII*, 162). For a study that focuses on women's political participation in Henry VIII's court, see Anne Somerset, *Ladies in Waiting: From the Tudors to the Present Day* (New York, 1984) 12–46. Somerset speculates that Askew was an occasional participant in the queen's devotional meetings (45). See also John King, "Patronage and Piety: The Influence of Catherine Parr" (Hannay, *Silent but for the Word*, 43–60).

29 The circumstances surrounding the scripting of the king's final will have been the subject of much speculation. With no signature but the Dry Stamp, erroneous dating, and only William Paget's avowal "on his honour that he was privy to the beginning, proceeding and ending of the same," the king's will was very much the creation of those closest to Henry VIII in his last few months, namely the very men who attended the king in his privy chambers (Starkey, *The Reign of Henry VIII*, 159–67).

30 For additional information regarding Lascelles, see A. G. Dickens, *Lollards and Protestants in the Diocese of York, 1509–1558* (London, 1959) 33–34; Foxe, *Acts and Monuments*, vol. V, 551–52; and Charles A. Wriothesley, *A Chronicle of England During the Reigns of the Tudors, from A.D. 1485–1559* (Westminster, 1875–77) vol. I, 169.

31 Lascelles and Huick were initially arrested for dissuading the radical preacher, Dr. Walter Crome, from recanting. Askew's arrest followed soon after (Starkey, *The Reign of Henry VIII*, 142). Lascelles and Askew were burned together at Smithfield sometime in June or July. Foxe places the execution in June; Bale identifies a precise date: July 16, 1546 (Anderson, *Ladies of the Reformation*, vol. I, 174).

32 The Pilgrimage of Grace in 1536, with uprisings in Askew's own Lincolnshire, and the Exeter Rebellion in 1538 were evidence of reactions *against* the religious changes that Askew and Bale represented, and were themselves choreographed by an educated elite. To many English women and men the only visible signs of the king's religious debate came in the closing of local monasteries, the removal of vestments and plate from parish churches, and the eviction of friends and relatives from long-established religious office (Madeleine Hope Dodds and Ruth Dodds, *The Pilgrimage of Grace, 1536–1537, and the Exeter Conspiracy, 1538* [London, 1971] 14; Joyce Youings, *The Dissolution of the Monasteries*, Historical Problems, Studies, and Documents [London, 1971] vol. XIV, 178). J. J. Scarisbrick cites wills and legacies as *prima facie* evidence of the continuing recalcitrance of the English people to abandon traditional religious practices even in the face of religious upheaval (*The Reformation and the English People* [London, 1984], 1–18). For

one of the more persuasive recent studies to foreground the sustained belief in traditional church practices that was to occur in the early years of the Reformation, see Eamon Duffy, *The Stripping of the Altars.*

33 According to Bale, these anonymous merchants were also present at Askew's burning. The uncertain transmission of the texts from London to Wesel lends fuel to long-standing masculinist claims that these texts could not possibly have been authored by a woman. Still, the hazy circumstances surrounding the transmission of the Askew texts ought not to provoke suspicion in and of themselves. A number of Reformation historians acknowledge the centrality of merchant middle-men in the religious information exchange (Protestant and Catholic) between England and the continent. See for instance, John Bossy, "The Character of Elizabethan Catholicism," *Past & Present* 21 (1962) 39–59, and Mary Jane Barnett, "Tyndale's Heretical Translation: Lollards, Lutherans, and an Economy of Circulation," in *Renaissance Papers, 1996*, ed. George Watten Williams and Philip Rollinson (Columbia, SC, 1996), 1–12. Barnett's research indicates that books from Protestant exiles made their way into England along well-established and rarely monitored trade routes for much of Henry VIII's reign. In any event, stylistic differences between Askew's commentary and Bale's responses to it are epic enough to discredit the claim for single authorship.

34 Gardiner was, at the time of this writing, perilously close to the end of his own career, ousted in Edward VI's reign for precisely those sentiments that he expresses here.

35 Foxe, *Acts and Monuments*, vol. VI, 30–31.

36 As a participant in Askew's inquest, Gardiner was personally implicated in Bale's supposed "misreportings"; after the trial he was *labeled* a martyr-killer. Accordingly Gardiner's anxieties about the power of words seem particularly apt.

37 Bale will be no less of a stickler for hard and fast lines between correct interpretations and their blasphemous counterparts. He too will try to neutralize the ability of the word to metamorphose with each new audience or presentation.

38 Leslie P. Fairfield, *John Bale, Mythmaker for the English Reformation* (West Lafayette, IN, 1976), 142. John Bale's *The vocacyon of Johan Bale to the bishoprick of Ossorie in Ireland his persecucions in the same and finall delyveraunce* (Wesel?) was published in 1553.

39 Andrew Hadfield notes that Bale desires not the execution of the king or a call to arms but rather national unity under a godlike, god-fearing monarch (*Literature, Politics and National Identity* [Cambridge, 1994] 80).

40 In Henrician England, matters of church and matters of state are largely inseparable. Accordingly, when I refer to political motivation or religious justification, I am foregrounding one aspect of an always integrated understanding. Distinctions between church and state, between spiritual and secular, become key, however, in the subtle shifting of allegiances that occurs in identity formation.

41 John King locates the actual publication in Wesel, suggesting that Marpurg is an intentional red herring, named both to mislead Bale's adversaries as to his whereabouts and to designate him as "apostolic successor to William

Tyndale" who also used the Marpurg colophon (*English Reformation Literature: The Tudor Origins of the Protestant Religion* [Princeton, 1982] 72); Beilin, *The Examinations of Anne Askew*, xxxiii, 51n. By the end of Edward VI's reign, 4 new editions (combining both *Examinations*) had been printed in England, 3 of which omitted Bale's commentary. Fairfield estimates that as many as 3,500 separate copies of the *Examinations* were in circulation during Edward VI's reign (*John Bale*, 135). While Fairfield's estimates may be optimistic, the high number of extant copies suggests an extensive readership. Foxe's version in *Acts and Monuments* was not published in English until 1563.

42 John Bale, *The first examinacyon of Anne Askewe, lately martyred in Smythfelde, by the Romysh popes upholders, with the Elucydacyon of Johan Bale* (Marpurg [Wesel] 1546) 5A–B. All future citations are from the first edition (British Library copy) and will be identified simply as *first examinacyon*. For other editions, see Beilin (*The Examinations of Anne Askew*) and Bale (*Select Works of John Bale*, 135–84).

43 In 1520 the first Papal Bull against Luther's writings had been issued in England. This regulation was followed by a second in 1524, requiring exhibition of all copy before Episcopal authorities prior to publication. A third proclamation in June, 1530, gave Episcopal powers the ability to monitor certain books "printed beyonde the see" (A. W. Reed, "The Regulation of the Book Trade Before the Proclamation of 1538," *Bibliographic Society* 15 [1917–19] 162). Despite the church's increasing worry over religious and political heterodoxy in the press, the proclamations themselves seemed to have little effect. In her discussion of Tynedale's New Testament, Barnett ("Tynedale's Heretical Translation" 6–7) writes that there were ample opportunities for texts to slip through the cracks. Only during isolated periods of concerted action, when authorities took on the task of discovering specific texts, did any effective form of censorship occur.

44 Bale, *The Image of bothe churches after the moste wonderfull and heavenly Revelation of Sainct John the Evangelist* (Wesel, 1541) pt. 1, Preface. For a modernized edition, see Bale, *Select Works of John Bale*, 254–55.

45 While I do not intend to pursue this line of resistance in any depth, it is worth noting that discussions of nationhood develop their most detailed accounting when subjects begin to speak from outside national borders. Take, for example, the more intense evoking of national identity that is to occur in the years preceding the English Civil War when religious dissidents are relocating to New England.

46 For traditionalist discussions of this theological question, see Stephen Gardiner, *A detection of the devils Sophistrie, wherewith he robbeth the unlearned people, of the true byleef in the sacrament of the aulter* (London, 1546); and William Peryn, *Thre notable and godley sermons* (London, 1546).

47 *lattre examinacyon*, 39A. Shaxton delivered the sermon at Askew's burning. That sermon was refuted in Robert Crowley's *The confutation of xiii articles* [1548] (J. W. Martin, *Religious Radicals in Tudor England* [London, 1989] 47).

48 While professional authorship was hardly a viable claim in 1546, the relative ease of publication, and the numbers of well-born, educated readers who had access to books, no doubt encouraged perceptions of selfhood in specifically

discursive terms. Bale's own voicing of authorial prerogative grew out of his discursive obligations as a student at Cambridge, his involvement in civil law and debate, and the early patronage of Cromwell and Essex who undoubtedly recognized his "literary" talent primarily because his politics happened to be coincident with their own. That Bale accepted religious office and later proceeded to the degree of Doctor in Divinity situates his status as "author" within the broader religious and secular contexts surrounding it.

49 *lattre examinacyon*, 51A–B. The strain of apocalysm apparent in Bale's threats to his enemies will reemerge in more strident terms in the years preceding the English Civil War. See Paul Christianson's *Reformers and Babylon: English Apocalyptic Visions from the Reformation to the Eve of the Civil War* (Toronto, 1978) for a charting of the history of apocalyptic thought in England from Reformation to Civil War. See also John R. Knott, *Discourses of Martyrdom in English Literature, 1563–1694* (Cambridge, 1993).

50 That Bale imagines Askew's accounts worthy of scriptural merit does authorize her writing in significant ways. Bale's interest in Askew's work implies at the very least that he believes that women can be religiously inspired and rhetorically capable.

51 *lattre examinacyon*, 60A–B. Bale must be referring here to *A mysterie of inyquyte contained within the heretycall Genealogye of Ponce Pantolabus* (Geneva, 1545). To my knowledge, *The myracles of the Masse* never appeared as such. In his catalogue, Bale does list two works of his own composition on the Mass, but neither has been traced (Jesse W. Harris, *John Bale: A Study in the Minor Literature of the Reformation*, Illinois Studies in Language and Literature, vol. 25, no. 4 [Urbana, 1940] 63).

52 Indeed, Dickens repeatedly stresses the close relationship among early Reformation martyrologists, "all [of whom were] members of an international movement and in most cases forced into exile by religious persecution" (Dickens and Tonkin, *The Reformation in Historical Thought*, 48).

53 Beilin positions Askew's responses squarely within the reformist camp, stressing Askew's "piety, constancy, learning, and fortitude" ("Challenge to Authority," in *Redeeming Eve*, 32). While Beilin is correct in recognizing Askew as inspired by her religious beliefs, I want to suggest that Askew's rendering of religiosity leaves much to be desired, especially if we choose to read her in terms of other reformist voices on trial in the 1540s. See, for example, John Frith, "A Letter of John Frith to his Friends" (Foxe, *Acts and Monuments*, vol. V, 11–14); John Lambert, "The Answers of John Lambert to the Forty-five Articles" (vol. V, 184–225); and Master George Wisehart, "The Examination of Master George Wisehart" (vol. V, 628–36). While the format of the trial transcript necessarily insists on a certain amount of evasion, in each of these cases doctrine takes precedence. Respondents clarify rather than confound their religious positions on key issues such as confession, fasting, and priestly marriage. Earlier martyr accounts using these same strategies include the "Examination and Death of Lord Cobham (1413)" (Bale, *Select Works of John Bale*, 15–59); and the "Examination of Master William Thorpe (1407)" (64–133). Foxe believes the latter to be the work of William Tyndale (62n).

54 As Askew supposedly signed a retraction of her beliefs at the end of her first

trial, critics suggest that the written *Examinations* offer both an explanation and a denial of that document. See, for example, Retha M. Warnicke, *Women of the English Renaissance and Reformation*, 64–65.

55 *first examinacyon*, 31B. Askew was likely referring to the passage in the Coverdale Bible (London, 1539) or perhaps to Tyndale's more recent translation of the New Testament (1544) that read, "Let your wives keep silence in the congregations. For it is not permitted unto them to speak; but let them be under obedience, as saith the law. If they will learn any thing, let them ask their husbands at home. For it is a shame for women to speak in the congregation" (William Tyndale, *Tyndale's New Testament*, ed. David Daniell [New Haven, 1989] 1 Corinthians xiv, 257.

56 *first examinacyon*, 10A–B. As early as 1436, Margery Kempe navigated this same set of constraints in her spiritual autobiography. When reprimanded for speaking the word of God, she replied, "I preach not, sir; I come into no pulpit. I use but communication and good words, and that I will do while I live" (Margery Kempe, *The Book of Margery Kempe*, ed. W. Butler-Bowden (London, 1936) 189.

57 *first examinacyon*, 4A (my emphasis).

58 *first examinacyon*, 5A (my emphasis).

59 A century later Lady Eleanor Davies felt no such compunction, equating her own voice with that of the prophet Daniel.

60 For a detailed analysis of the connections between an early English prose style and scriptural precedent, see Janel Mueller's *The Native Tongue and the Word: Developments in English Prose Style, 1380–1580* (Chicago, 1984). Mueller's study reminds us of the very real differences between Askew's presentation and those of her reformist supporters, including Bale.

61 Foxe's *Acts and Monuments* includes numerous women, many of them martyred during Mary's reign. For accounts which mirror the question-and-answer format used in the *Examinations*, see, for instance, Joyce Lewes (vol. VIII, 401–4), Katherine Hut (vol. VIII, 143), and Elizabeth Young (vol. VIII, 537–45).

62 While the question-and-answer format becomes generically set in Foxe's repeated use of court testimony as evidence of Protestant martyrdom for *both* men and women, I do want to stress the particular appropriateness of such a format for English women with no legitimate discourse history of their own.

63 Status could also exclude one from established writerly communities. While inadequate funding or educational opportunity rather than inappropriate anatomy would define the specific lines of separation, it seems likely that the move toward interiorized resistance may very well be the same.

64 Askew's account consistently avoids comparison. At no point does she imagine herself within the ranks of other reformist authors (even privileged ones) or attempt to justify her own actions in terms of others.

65 *first examinacyon*, 6A. Not until the *lattre examinacyon*, when at the end of Askew's narrative she is forced to locate her convictions and draw things to a close, does the vocabulary change to direct assertion.

66 Askew is released at the close of her first trial when she signs a confession denying her beliefs. She puts her name to the document, however, only after she has altered its meaning with the following addition: "I Anne Askewe do

beleve all maner thynges contayned in the faythe of the Catholyck churche"
(*first examinacyon*, 38A). In Askew's appended text, "*Catholyck*" refers to the
universality of the "true" church. While the confession holds, and Askew is
temporarily released, her additions render the whole of the retraction somewhat ambiguous.

67 Foxe reiterates this certainty in his introduction to the Askew material: "here
    next followeth . . . the true examinations of Anne Askew . . . by the which, if
    thou marke dilligently . . . thou mayest easily perceive the tree by the fruit
    and the man by his work" (*Acts and Monuments*, vol. V, 537).

68 In *Drama of Dissent* (Chapel Hill, 1986), Ritchie Kendall notes Bale's
    consistent desire to "limit the degree of play permitted between a word and
    the object it describes" (100). Kendall recognizes in this maneuver a histori-
    cally specific and religiously marked attempt to control rhetorical meaning,
    rendering words less ambiguous. This move toward clarity, echoed in much
    reformist literature of the time, serves to underscore the unusual positioning
    that we find in Askew's evasion.

69 See especially chapter 2 for discussions of such a framing.

70 The "subversion"/"containment" debate is, I assume, a familiar one. Can
    individual subjects successfully intervene in (subvert) processes of political
    and ideological transformation or are their local actions already "contained"
    by the very forces they seek to defy? For some useful originary voices, see
    Stephen Greenblatt, Introduction to "The Forms of Power and the Power of
    Forms in the Renaissance," *Genre* 15 (1982) 3–6; Jean E. Howard, "The New
    Historicism in Renaissance Studies," *English Literary Renaissance* 16 (1986)
    13–43; Louis A. Montrose, "Renaissance Literary Studies and the Subject of
    History," *English Literary Renaissance* 16 (1986) 5–12; and Edward Pechter,
    "The New Historicism and Its Discontents," *PMLA* 102 (1987) 292–303.

71 Michel Foucault, *Power/Knowledge: Selected Interviews & Other Writings
    1972–1977*, ed. Colin Gordon, trans. Leo Marshall, John Mepham, and Kate
    Soper (New York, 1980) 136. Foucault's question was first posed in a 1977
    interview with the editorial collective of *Les révoltes logiques* – Jean Borreil,
    Geneviève Fraisse, Jacques Rancière, Pierre Saint-Germain, Michel Souletie,
    Patrick Vauday, and Patrice Vermeren.

2   FRAMING RECUSANT IDENTITY IN COUNTER-REFORMATION ENGLAND

1 Mary Claridge, *Margaret Clitherow [1556?–1586]* (New York, 1966) 45.

2 Pressing to death, *peine forte et duro*, was the prescribed punishment for those
   who, "mute of malice," failed to plead in criminal cases. The practice of
   loading recalcitrant prisoners with increasing weights was apparently introduced sometime between 31 Edward III and 8 Henry IV (John Mush, ed.,
   "The Life of Margaret Clitherow," in *The Troubles of our Catholic Forefathers*, vol. III, 438n.

3 Born in Yorkshire in 1552, in the diocese of Chester, John Mush studied at
   Douai and was sent to Rome to finish philosophy and theology in the newly
   founded English College (Godfrey Anstruther, *The Seminary Priests: A
   Dictionary of the Secular Clergy of England and Wales, 1558–1850* [Ware

(Herts.), 1969] 240; Richard Challoner, *Memoirs of Missionary Priests* [Manchester, 1803] 463). Mush returned to England in 1581 after his ordination and began his missionary work in and around York. As Clitherow's chaplain, Mush encouraged her beliefs and wrote a vernacular account of her life upon her execution. In the years following her death, Mush was one of four priests chosen to present the case for the appellants in Rome (Anstruther, *Seminary Priests*, 241). Accusing the Jesuit mission of disloyalty and political subversion, the appellants sought a practical alliance with the English monarchy against their religious brothers (Caroline M. Hibbard, "Early Stuart Catholicism: Revisions and Re-Revisions," *Journal of Modern History* 52 [1980] 24). In fact, Mush signed a declaration of allegiance to Elizabeth in the last year of her reign. He died in 1617 of unknown causes (Anstruther, *Seminary Priests*, 241).

4 Despite the hundreds of titles authored by English women from 1500 to 1700, few works were published during the 1580s. Anne Wheathill (*A handfull of holesome though homely hearbes, gathered out of the godly garden of Godes most holy word*, London, 1584) is perhaps the most familiar to literary scholars, though Jane Anger (*Jane Anger her Protection for Women*, London, 1589) provides a more explicit discussion of gendered experience during those years. See also Anne Dowriche, *The French Historie. that is; a lamentable discourse of three of the chiefe and most famous bloddie broiles that have happened in France for the gospell of Jesus Christ* (London, 1589).

5 In her anthology, *"Glow-Worm Light": Writings of 17th Century English Recusant Women from Original Manuscripts* (Salzburg, 1989), Dorothy L. Latz provides excerpts from several previously unpublished accounts of seventeenth-century recusant English women. Most of the writers included in this edition were associated in one manner or another with conventual life on the continent.

6 Claridge mentions a number of recusant women, among them Anne Killingale, Anne Lawnder, Dorothy Neville, Agnes Taylor, and Anne Tesh. These women were with Clitherow at various points during her days at York Castle prison (*Margaret Clitherow [1556?-1586]*, 75–77).

7 Even the labeling of crimes reveals this divide. In a Henrician government still nervous about flaunting its own newly proclaimed demands for absolute allegiance from its subjects, heresy may be a much safer charge to levy against detractors than outward defiance to royal command. In contrast, Elizabeth I's monarchy has little trouble denouncing the same kind of transgression as treason, and rather more awkwardness when religious preference is the stated issue.

8 In chapter 3 of this book, I discuss the material connections between moral regulation and middling-rank female identity that were to occur in the early years of the seventeenth century.

9 In my essay, "Credible Consorts," I argue that an issue-centered approach is most successful in breaking masculinist patterns of history and history making.

10 In her provocative essay, "The Tenth Muse," Stephanie Jed discovers/constructs extra-textual documentation to illustrate the unwritten and unrecorded history of women's voices. Her essay has been pivotal in framing this chapter.

11 There has been a recent trend in cultural studies to emphasize stasis and continuity rather than its opposite (this, I think, to offset an earlier critical impulse toward fictive periodization, and the teleology of much historical narrative). This "will toward sameness" carries obvious contemporary appeal (a renewed interest in the familiar may provide coping strategies for our own end-of-century angst). Unfortunately uniformity downplays opposition, and it does not lend itself to a very thorough understanding of social transformation. I want, instead, to stress change, if only to recognize, in what seems like sameness, the microscopic shifts in power and privilege that are always occurring and the attendant recalculations of behavior and choice that follow in their wake.

12 Elizabeth I took advantage of this prerogative at the start of *every* parliamentary election, warning her subjects to keep their discussions away from matters pertaining to religion (J. E. Neale, *Elizabeth I and her Parliaments, 1559–1581* [New York, 1958] vol. II, 438–39; T. E. Hartley, *Elizabeth's Parliaments: Queen, Lords and Commons, 1559–1601* [Manchester, 1992] 4, 81–103).

13 Elizabeth I's Privy Council was predominantly Anglican and latitudinarian in composition. This relative homogeneity kept the subject of religion from outwardly disrupting council authority. "Latitudinarians" generally saw religion as a matter of expediency – a convenient way to administer the church – and Episcopal rule as "a thing indifferent" (Warnicke, *Women of the English Renaissance and Reformation*, 144).

14 Cecil wrote *The Execution of Justice in England* (1583), justifing royal policy toward Catholic missionaries (P. Williams, *The Tudor Regime*, 274).

15 P. Williams, *The Tudor Regime*, 454–58.

16 John Bossy, *The English Catholic Community, 1570–1850* (London, 1975) 175.

17 London was the site of numerous highly publicized Catholic martyrdoms. One seminary priest, lamenting his continued safety, imagined orders for his own London execution (Haigh, "From Monopoly to Minority," 135).

18 In June of 1580, the queen's Privy Council sent a letter to the commission in the north, admitting that "if those parts were well furnished with a competent number of good, learned preachers, they would be inwardlie in harte as conformable as they be outwardlie in Bodie" (Francis Peck, *Desiderata curiosa: or a Collection of Divers Scarse and Curious Pieces Relating Chiefly to Matters of English History*, 2 vols. [London, 1779] vol. II, 3.18.92).

19 These Catholics, usually of lesser status, with few local connections and insufficient funds, ended up overcrowding English prisons and putting additional strain on local communities to support them (William Raleigh Trimble, *The Catholic Laity in Elizabethan England, 1558–1603* [Cambridge, 1964] 76).

20 The English Colleges at Douai and Rome, the former established in 1568, the latter in 1578, provided religious training for missionary priests intent on returning to England (Arnold Pritchard, *Catholic Loyalism in Elizabethan England* [Chapel Hill, 1979] 5).

21 Trimble, *Catholic Laity*, 68.

22 John Hungerford Pollen, *The English Catholics in the Reign of Queen*

Elizabeth: A Study of their Politics, Civil Life and Government (New York, 1971) 161–70, 175–79. Robin Clifton draws a correlation between the sporadic intensification of anti-Catholic sentiment and specific economic and political crises besetting the country ("The Popular Fear of Catholics During the English Revolution," *Past & Present* 52 [1971] 23–55). Events like the Northern Rising, and the Babington and the Gunpowder Plots, that announced their Catholic allegiances explicitly, rekindled national fears (Bossy, "The Character of Elizabethan Catholicism," 42; Patrick McGrath, *Papists and Puritans Under Elizabeth I* [London, 1967] 161–204).

23 Mary D. R. Leys, *Catholics in England 1559–1829: A Social History* (New York, 1961) 35. These measures reveal a widespread English anxiety about the likelihood of an extra-national Catholic invasion. See Patrick McGrath, "The Bloody Questions Reconsidered," *Recusant History* 20.3 (1991) 305–19, for the range of responses and respondents on the Catholic conflict between allegiance to crown and allegiance to pope.

24 The enactment of this piece of legislation ensured the eventual conviction and execution of Mary Stuart in 1587 (Neale, *Elizabeth I and her Parliaments*, 15).

25 For a more thorough discussion of anti-Catholic sentiment during this period, see Robin Clifton, "The Popular Fear of Catholics"; Lacey Baldwin Smith, *Treason in Tudor England: Politics and Paranoia* (Princeton, 1986); and Carol Z. Wiener, "The Beleaguered Isle. A Study of Elizabethan and Early Jacobean Anti-Catholicism," *Past & Present* 51 [1971] 27–62.

26 Where Henry VIII's religious dissenters were tried primarily in ecclesial courts, headed up by an acting and newly powerful church hierarchy, Elizabeth I's were dealt with through any of three separately authorized courts of law: through the church (archbishops' courts, diocesan courts and visitations handled most church-related issues, from disciplining the clergy to deciding the appropriate type of wafer for the sacrament), through the state (assizes and quarter sessions could punish offenders for ecclesiastical disobedience or impose recusancy fines), and finally through a body beholden to both church and state (Elizabeth I's ecclesiastical commissions combined both lay and clerical members and dealt specifically with recusancy and its related problems) (P. Williams, *The Tudor Regime*, 263). For more detailed history on the Elizabethan courts, see J. S. Cockburn, *A History of English Assizes, 1558–1714* (Cambridge, 1972); Ralph A. Houlbrooke, *Church Courts and the People During the English Reformation: 1520–1570* (Oxford, 1979); and Wilfred R. Prest, *The Inns of Court under Elizabeth I and the Early Stuarts: 1590–1640* (London, 1972).

27 In 1598, another woman, Jane Wiseman, receiving the same sentence, apparently fared better with a royal hearing. On learning how "for so small a matter [Wiseman] should have been put to death, [the queen] rebuked the justices of cruelty, and said she should not die" (Don Adam Hamilton, *The Chronicle of the English Augustinian Canonesses Regular of the Lateran, at St. Monica's in Louvain (1548–1625)*, 2 vols. (Edinburgh, 1904) vol. I, 83.

28 Reformers faced fewer direct attacks of religious conscience in outward conformity than did their Catholic counterparts, especially when it came to oath taking. For a complete list of anti-Catholic statutes adopted under Elizabeth I, see William MacCaffrey, *Queen Elizabeth and the Making of*

Policy, 1572–88 (Princeton, 1981); and J. A. Williams, "English Catholicism Under Charles II: The Legal Position," *Recusant History* 7 (1963) 123–43.

29 Even the metaphor of "conformity" reinforces the impetus to sameness that became central to Elizabethan attitudes on religion.

30 P. Williams, *The Tudor Regime*, 277; Claridge, *Margaret Clitherow [1556?–1586]*, 57–58.

31 P. Williams, *The Tudor Regime*, 278.

32 Claridge, *Margaret Clitherow [1556?-1586]*, 120.

33 While many of the initial letters to the newly constituted York Commission are salutary, as the letters continue we get a sense of the Privy Council's increasing frustration at the inadequacy of the searches and the perceived threat they are failing to alleviate. One letter, written in 1580, deals with the centralization of recusant prisoners so as not to infect the prison population at large. A second reiterates the queen's support for all commission activities. "Her majestie is fullie resolved to proceid rowndly against such obstinate Recusants as refused Conformities: soe as you shall not need doubt, but from hence to receive all good Encouragement & Assistance" (Peck, *Desiderata Curiosa*, 3.18.92).

   Letters from 1582 to 1584 offer a more mixed response from the Privy Council. Clearly the queen's council is annoyed at finding its orders carried out so ineffectually. It counters, sending veiled warnings admonishing commission members to shape up. One letter, rebuking the commission for its failure to do what is required, details the particulars that the council would like to see on each and every recusant recorded (3.24.96). Demanding a thorough sweep of every diocese, shire, village, and county within the commission's jurisdiction, the council presents a list of fifteen questions to be answered in full by each recusant brought in (3.25.97). The points addressed include the number of household members who share papist beliefs, and more specifically a description of yearly living and goods possessed. These regulatory practices reveal the extent of government intrusion into the lives of its subjects. They also point to the economic motivations at work in extending state control.

34 Ironically, late sixteenth-century versions of priest/lay relations suggest that the government's focus on high-status Catholicism was misplaced. Established gentry chaplains and the houses that supported them were, as a result of their own economic well-being, increasingly unwilling to risk either recusancy persecution or the consequences of extra-national invasion. Certainly Catholic gentry had more at stake when it came to charges of recusancy or treason. Accordingly, by the time of William Allen's *Admonition* in support of the Spanish invasion, many leading Catholic gentlemen were declaring their allegiance to Elizabeth I (Bossy, "The Character of Elizabethan Catholicism," 51). Because only financially solvent recusants were legally liable for their failure to conform to church policy, only a small proportion of the total national population was technically affected by the Act of 1581 (Elliot Rose, *Cases of Conscience: Alternatives open to Recusants and Puritans under Elizabeth I and James I* [Cambridge, 1975] 23ff.).

35 "From the beginning, the leaders of the [Catholic] mission envisaged a reconstruction of English Catholicism along seigneurial, rather than parochial or congregational, lines" (Haigh, "From Monopoly to Minority," 136).

Returning priests were to focus their energies first and foremost on the gentry, with the idea that conversion would filter down. Missionaries in and around York (where recusancy figures were high) were unique in that the majority of their parishioners were middling- to low-rank. Significantly, despite an emphasis on Catholics of high standing, the effects of anti-Catholic legislation (in terms of both fines and imprisonment) fell disproportionately in impoverished areas (York being one of them) and, notably, on recusant women (J. C. H. Aveling, *Catholic Recusancy in the City of York, 1558–1791* [St. Albans, Herts., 1970] 65, 68).

36 This list appears in the anonymously written "Notes by a Prisoner in Ousebridge Kidcote" (Morris, *The Troubles of our Catholic Forefathers*, vol. III, 237).

37 The Archbishop's list raises that figure to £20 (Claridge, *Margaret Clitherow [1556?–1586]*, 68).

38 Investigation at the local level was hardly far-reaching or consistent. The sporadic nature of much regional prosecution probably had a good deal to do with local political clout. Caroline Hibbard reminds us that the enforcement of punitive religious measures was often a question of "personality, property, and prestige" ("Early Stuart Catholicism," 4). For a useful discussion of the differences between anti-Catholic legislation on paper and in practice, see Rose, *Cases of Conscience*, 11–22.

39 Morris, "The Life of Margaret Clitherow [introduction]," in Morris, *The Troubles of our Catholic Forefathers*, vol. III, 352.

40 "As late as 1601, a number of men who were prepared to protect Catholics, had Catholic wives and family members, and many of whom must themselves have been church papists, sat in Parliament – in the House of Commons as well as in the House of Lords" (Hibbard, "Early Stuart Catholicism," 21n).

41 Persecution in the Clitherow case was likely as much a jurisdictional struggle as it was a religious conflict. It reflects a more exhaustive attempt by central authorities to introduce policy and procedure in outlying areas and a more vocally announced, state-imposed understanding of the limits of government. Such wide-ranging pronouncements were unlikely during the Henrician period as governmental structures were not in place to carry them out nor was the impetus in governing there to support them.

42 William of Orange was assassinated in this year (L. B. Smith, *Treason in Tudor England*, 16–17). Wiener addresses this extra-national/regicidal threat in what she categorizes as the "outsider" component to fear about Catholics in Elizabethan and Early Jacobean England ("The Beleaguered Isle," 33ff.).

43 When I say "ideological perspectives" here, I am not thinking of a set of beliefs that can be accepted and discarded at the level of conscious thought, nor am I describing in them an illusory representation of a reality outside and above social relations. Rather I want to insist that *the ideological is the real* insofar as we can ever *know* the real. Ideologies are not something that social beings falsely believe but rather the very matter that constitutes social being in the first place. The content of the ideological then is the content of knowing and making known all that appears coherent, stable, and socially relevant in human society. For the background to this understanding, see introduction, note 27.

44 It is my contention that each of these "categories" was less resonant – carried less authority – at the time of Askew's persecutions. In announcing them as discrete, though, I have simplified what was no doubt a far more amorphous and at best tangentially related series of historic dislocations.

45 P. Williams, *The Tudor Regime*, 280.

46 David Loades (*Politics, Censorship and the English Reformation* [London, 1991] esp. chapters 9 and 10) and F. S. Siebert (*Freedom of the Press in England, 1476–1776* [Urbana, 1952]) discuss the increasing stringency of governmental censorship during Elizabethan rule.

47 P. Williams, *The Tudor Regime*, 281.

48 William Fulke listed forty-one Catholic titles printed at home or abroad in 1580, and recent scholarly tallies now put the total for Elizabeth I's reign at 223 (P. Williams, *The Tudor Regime*, 280).

49 Mush, "Life," 365. All future in-text citations are from this edition and will be identified simply as "Life."

50 For a detailed discussion of Bale's authorial largess, see chapter 1, especially pp. 35–40.

51 The *Acta Sanctorum* offers a complete record of all canonized saints. Numerous "private" (restricted) documents have been gathered on figures awaiting beatification or additional church perusal. Clitherow, while never sainted, retains the title "Venerable."

52 For useful summaries of English Catholic writings, both printed and in manuscript, see A. F. Allison and D. M. Rogers, eds., *A Catalogue of Catholic Books in English Printed Abroad or Secretly in England, 1558–1640* (London, 1968); Peter Milward, *Religious Controversies of the Elizabethan Age: A Survey of Printed Sources* (Lincoln, 1977); John R. Roberts, ed., *A Critical Anthology of English Recusant Devotional Prose, 1558–1603* (Pittsburgh, 1966); Leona Rostenberg, *The Minority Press and the English Crown: A Study in Repression, 1558–1625* (Nieuwkoop [The Netherlands], 1971); and A. C. Southern, *Elizabethan Recusant Prose, 1558–1582* (London, 1950).

53 "Nothynge at all shall it terryfye us, nor yet in anye poynt lett us of our purpose, that our bokes are now in Englande condempned and brent, by the Byshoppes and prestes with their frantyck affynyte, . . . But it wyll from hens forth occasyon us, to set fourth in Latyne also, that afore we wrote onlye in the Englysh, and so make their spirytuall wyckednesse and treason knowne moche farther of" (Bale, *first examinacyon*, 5B).

54 Mush's completion of the "Life" verified the efficacy of missionary work in England. It became the recorded illustration of a job well done. Clitherow's Catholic allegiances, nourished in large part by a small contingent of continental priests, proved steadfast despite concerted persecution. Accordingly, Mush's scripting of her life came to define an ideal that recusant women might emulate – a material example of successful late sixteenth-century English Catholicism. In a more remunerative economic sense, however, Mush's written "Life" was also at least partly responsible for his later nomination to the post of assistant to the Archbishop of Rome – no small honor considering his humble origins and nationality. One of the few writers to script a Catholic life during the early years of the Counter-Reformation, Mush must also have been known as a martyr-maker and a minor Catholic apologist. On his return to the

continent, Mush composed additional books on the English mission, one of them being *An Account of the Sufferings of Catholics in the Northern Parts of England* (Challoner, *Memoirs of Missionary Priests*, 103).

55 The peculiar organization of the Catholic enterprise in England contributed to Mush's public exposure as well, and this has interesting implications for our understandings of both subject definition and the directives at work behind cultural transformation. Career possibilities for priests like Mush expanded even as the persecutions against them increased. As a result of its unstructured and largely unsupervised nature, the English mission attracted a more socially diverse grouping of men than might otherwise have been possible. The early founders of the English colleges at Douai and Rome were generally clerks not gentlemen. Many recruits were in fact transplanted Oxford clerks who left their fellowships to study abroad (Bossy, "The Character of Elizabethan Catholicism," 45ff.). Younger and less economically secure than their predecessors, these men were formative in determining the geography of the new English Catholicism and establishing their place within it. Priests returning to England from the continent arrived with something like guerrilla status. They could stretch the limits of church governance by claiming religious identities that they had no legal business claiming. In England, they could assert special powers of absolution and perform rituals that were generally considered outside lay priest jurisdiction. Those who sought English missionary work could also avoid the more regimented discipline of either established Catholic institutional authorities or their equivalent within the secular realm. Beholden to a Catholic laity for their protection and free of traditional institutional chains of command, English missionary priests might literally reframe their identities to enhance their status value in the eyes of their protectors (Hibbard, "Early Stuart Catholicism," 24). Bossy writes that "the priest arrived in England without either exterior signs of his priesthood or the structure of a clerical order behind him; he did not appear as a priest, but as a gentleman, a soldier, or a servant" ("The Character of Elizabethan Catholicism," 51). A less sympathetic version can be found in Thomas Fuller's account of seminarists: "He who on Sunday was a priest or Jesuit was on Monday a merchant, on Tuesday a soldier, on Wednesday a courtier, etc., and with the shears of equivocation (constantly carried about him) he could cut himself into any shape he pleased" (*The Church History of Britain; from the Birth of Jesus Christ until the Year 1648*, [1655] new edn. [Oxford, 1845] vol. III, 19).

56 I use the word "domestic" advisedly. I am not talking here about a discrete home space (hardly available at this historic juncture); nevertheless, Mush does posit Clitherow as homemaker, mother, and wife, situating each in expressly locational terms. For Mush, Clitherow's marital duties occur within a domestic community of similarly constituted families and within a boundaried household of servants, apprentices, and children.

57 Suzanne W. Hull's catalogue of conduct books (*Chaste, Silent, and Obedient: English Books for Women, 1475–1640* [San Marino, CA, 1982]) reveals a good number of fairly restrictive and pointed advice about female behavior during the middle years of Elizabeth I's reign – advice that had been neither as comprehensive nor as directive in the 1540s. Beginning in 1579 with *the*

schoole of honest and vertuous lyfe and followed immediately by *the mirrhor of modestie* (1579), *a watchword for wilfull women* (1581), *the widowe's treasure* (1582), *the first and second parts of the good huswife's jewell* (1585), (1587), and *the good hous-wives treasurie* (1587), the surviving publications focus on the repeated articulation of a perfect and submissive woman and wife (Hull, *Chaste, Silent, and Obedient*, 68).

58 While Catholic doctrine acknowledged religious equality between the sexes, it was only within the polemical literature of the reform movement that the assertion began to appear with any frequency; it was also largely within the context of Protestant ideology that the idea of a patriarchal (privatized) authority became paramount. Historians like Christopher Hill have argued that this emphasis played into concurrent changes in the economy (shifts in capital accumulation, etc.), in government (increasing bureaucratization), in contractual agreement, and in definitions of private and public. See, for instance, Hill's early landmark essay on this subject, "Protestantism and the Rise of Capitalism," in his *Change and Continuity in Seventeenth-Century England*, 81–102.

59 Philip Stubbes scripts his own Protestant hagiography of the life and death of his wife in 1592, entitled *a Crystal Glas for Christian Women* (London). The attention to domestic identity in both Catholic and Protestant accounts is astonishing. This was hardly the case in Bale's 1546 account of Askew's martyrdom. Both a wife and a mother, Askew is only once referred to as such, and she herself makes no mention of those ties. While Askew's separation from husband and children would compromise any overt discussion by either writer, there seems to be far less of a need for a domestic disclaimer in this earlier work.

60 Such configurations remind us that making absolute claims about women's condition during the Renaissance is to erase the strategic, regional, and definitional nature of power configurations and who is advantaged by them.

61 The scriptural word possessed a fairly restricted historic role in Catholic ritual. Eileen Power underscores this emphasis in her discussion of late medieval English nunneries. The Latin Masses repeated by convent sisters in the years preceding the dissolution were frequently learned by rote – their meanings indecipherable and insignificant to the ritual itself (*Medieval English Nunneries, c. 1275–1535* [Cambridge, 1922] 246).

62 Historians like Carolyn Walker Bynum locate Catholicism's most marked materiality in the later Middle Ages – 1200–1500 – and connect it up with a direct increase in the number of female mystics and saints (*Holy Feast and Holy Fast: The Religious Significance of Food to Medieval Women* [Berkeley, 1987] and *Jesus as Mother: Studies in the Spirituality of the High Middle Ages* [Berkeley, 1982]). Bynum sees the celebration of materiality as playing into an already established patriarchal binary that understood the female as body and the male as spirit. The inversion of status, legitimating female sanctity, then, paralleled a simultaneous privileging of the corporeal body. While I would be loathe to see so regimented or absolute a split between terms and categories, these correspondences are nevertheless compelling in delineating female sainthood. See also Richard Kieckhefer, *Unquiet Souls: Fourteenth-Century Saints and their Religious Milieu* (Chicago, 1984).

63 "Life," 421 (my emphasis). That the Elizabethan Settlement recognized this framing as dangerous can be seen in the nature of its Catholic persecutions. Authorities were looking for bodies not books.

64 Within the Catholic Church, the only available "word" is the priest's: "If you speak the word, I am ready to obey it" ("Life," 380).

65 Refer to Claridge, *Margaret Clitherow [1556?–1586]*, 146ff., and "Notes by a Prisoner," in Morris, *The Troubles of our Catholic Forefathers*, 308–9.

66 Obviously, the nature of the hagiographical format directs Mush's handling of acceptable spirituality for women. Certain features remain constant (i.e., the iteration of examples of chastity, poverty, and humility). Indeed, earlier saints' lives provide numerous variations on the theme of Suzanne Hull's by now infamous "chaste, silent and obedient" woman. Mush is also writing the "Life" with an understanding that his work must be approved by hierarchical superiors – that it must find its way through the rather exclusive mechanisms of the Roman Curia. This more narrowed sense of genre and audience complicates what he can and cannot say in a way that Bale never needed to consider.

67 See, for instance, Margaret J. M. Ezell's excellent exposition of the problems that we are likely to encounter in using inappropriate historiographical models to figure feminist literary history (*Writing Women's Literary History* 1993).

68 Despite assertions to the contrary, there are a considerable number of early modern texts written by women, in print as well as manuscript. In my own informal cataloguing of English women's writings between 1500 and 1700 (not counting translations or letters), I have found over 650 separate works.

69 Any discussion of Clitherow's negotiations will be problematic despite my access to Askew's written maneuvers. My reconstructions must depend for their substance on only those elements that Mush has chosen to foreground. These procedural limitations do not mean, however, that exploration is useless. Refusing to consider marginal voices because they have been marginalized, because they cannot be theoretically accounted for, is to beg the issue, to reinforce the dominant again in a second silencing.

70 Clitherow's resistances cannot be mapped in tidy opposition to Askew's. One woman's dependence on a particular cultural directive to legitimate her actions does not necessarily ensure the other's inattention to that directive. The cultural valences of each encounter suggest a different, not simply an oppositional, weighing of choices and outcomes. As I want to stress the fluidity of exchange and the variety of combinations rather than the historical polarities that are its occasional result, I will explore issues between both women generally, not comparatively.

71 When I talk about Clitherow's actions in this section, I am understanding them in representational terms.

72 Social status, no doubt, affects the location of these sites. Clitherow, as a middling-rank tradeswoman with marital obligations that spanned from supervising household servants to physical labor in dressing meats for sale, bookkeeping, etc., faces restrictions far different from those of a gentlewoman.

73 One of Clitherow's prison sentences was remitted due to pregnancy (Claridge,

Margaret Clitherow [1556?–1586], 34). *The Lawes Resolutions of Womens Rights* ([London, 1632] 206ff.) outlines this legal loophole (available in the sixteenth as well as the seventeenth century). "Benefit of the womb" could only be claimed once, but it took precedence over other criminal sentencings. Numerous dramatic references to such remittances occur throughout the period (compare, for instance, Claudio's death penalty and Juliet's disposing "to some more fitter place" in William Shakespeare's *Measure for Measure*, ed. J. W. Lever, Arden Shakespeare [London, 1986] 2.2.17).

74 I am here making the rather obvious distinction between Clitherow's socially engendered status as a woman and the biological fact of that status as it is revealed in pregnancy.

75 William Trimble (*Catholic Laity*, 250) notes an unusual correspondence between lower-status Catholic populations in England (primarily in the north) and an increased incidence of petty persecution (fines and prison sentencings). While lay offenders faced more frequent sentencing in these areas, seminary priests were more vulnerable in the larger urban centers, especially London. Punishments imposed on priests were also far more dramatic (Haigh, "From Monopoly to Minority," 135). Pritchard (*Catholic Loyalism in Elizabethan England*, 8) observes that of 803 seminary priests sent to England, 377 were imprisoned, and 133 were executed.

76 Mush mentions the *Rheims New Testament* (1582) and William Peryn's *Spiritual exercises and ghostly meditations, and a near way to come to perfection and life contemplative* (1557) as two of Clitherow's favorite readings ("Life," 393).

77 "Life," 395. Numerous traitors were executed at the gallows at Knavesmire. According to Mush, Clitherow considers the place a shrine, visiting it whenever she can get away from other responsibilities.

78 "Of the fifteen recusant wives of tradesmen in Christ Church Parish [officially listed in 1576], seven were the wives of butchers, and one the wife of a 'pennyman,' who specialized in the dressing of meat." Within the next year three more butchers' wives would be reported to the Privy Council as recusants (Claridge, *Margaret Clitherow [1556?–1586]*, 68).

79 One of the more fascinating recent discussions of Catholic privacy can be found in Janet E. Halley's article, "Equivocation and the Legal Conflict over Religious Identity in Early Modern England" (*Yale Journal of Law & the Humanities* 3 [1991] 33–52). Discussing English concerns over the problem of Catholic equivocation in the early years of the seventeenth century, Halley notes an assertion by captured Jesuit priests of a private identity so complete that these priests can claim internal dialogue as paramount in the act of confession. Halley points out that those being interrogated can withhold part of their response from outside listeners, by continuing their answers within their own minds. Citing an example from *A Treatise of Equivocation* (ed. David Jardine [London, 1851] 52), Halley explains that a priest might answer a question about a fugitive in this way: "I did not see Father Gerard [*ut tibi dicam*] [i.e., in order to tell you about him]" ("Equivocation," 35). Halley's description of confessional equivocation provides a perfect illustration of the increasingly insular nature of privacy that I am describing here. What was in 1546 an interpretive debate over the exact meaning of spoken words between

two separate speakers/writers, has, by 1606, literally moved within, to an already established and legitimate space of secret thoughts and private conversations. Here, Polonius's advice – "to thine own self be true" – takes on an entirely different meaning. See Ronald J. Corthell, " 'The Secrecy of Man': Recusant Discourse and the Elizabethan Subject," *English Literary Renaissance* 19 (1989) 272–90, and Katharine Eisaman Maus, "Proof and Consequences: Inwardness and Its Exposure in the English Renaissance," *Representations* 34 (1991) 29–52, for additional discussions of Renaissance "privacy." Chapter 3 of this book offers a comprehensive exploration of interiority, in gendered terms.

80 The priest–penitent relationship was frequently depicted in anti-Catholic polemic as sexually charged. Anthony Tyrell, a perjured priest, illustrates this stereotype in terms his Protestant accusers encouraged and/or constructed: "but among all other things one of the principal causes of my spoiling was in not keeping my heart always pure and clean as at the beginning it was, and long had the enemy practised with me to desire to be conversant much with women, and this under the colour of holiness and piety . . . And therefore let all good men beware of this snare" (Challoner, *Memoirs of Missionary Priests*, 464).

81 The irony of this stance in a country governed by a female head of state cannot be overemphasized. The increasing discursive interest in theories of absolute rule in the late sixteenth century illustrates the precarious nature of all of Elizabeth I's rhetorical and political maneuvers (though it is probably largely the result of her own compromised position as female ruler that such articulations do not become as egregious to her subjects as they will for her successors). In order to maintain authority in a manner acceptable to her culture, Elizabeth I fostered contradictory images of her self as female monarch. Calling on her joint status as mother, virgin, and mistress, Elizabeth I slid back and forth between definitions, proving the exception to an otherwise firm rule. For discussions of Elizabeth's royal iconography, see; Frye, "The Myth of Elizabeth at Tilbury," and *Elizabeth I*; Helen Hackett, *Virgin Mother, Maiden Queen: Elizabeth I and the Cult of the Virgin Mary* (New York, 1995); J. King, "Queen Elizabeth I: Representations of the Virgin Queen" and Carole Levin, *'The Heart and Stomach of a King*." See also Montrose, "*A Midsummer Night's Dream* and the Shaping Fantasies of Elizabethan Culture: Gender, Power, Form," for one of the first studies of this kind.

82 According to Mush, Clitherow's ennobling refusal to plead rests in her allegiance to both family and religious obligations. She does not want her children to have to give evidence and is unwilling to burden her judges with the sin of her condemnation ("Life," 436). If Clitherow were to acknowledge publicly her wrongs, her husband would be liable for her crimes, losing his property to the courts. At the same time, her inquisitors could insist as part of Clitherow's admission of guilt that she provide the names and locations of all other guilty parties (i.e., the priests whom she had been harboring). Her silence, then, reinforces her domestic, spiritual, economic, *and* social commitments simultaneously.

83 Clitherow's final apprehension was supposedly the result of testimony by a

young boy who claimed that he had seen priests in her home. Mush makes a point of identifying the child as non-English ("Life," 412).

84 Father John Gerard, *The Condition of the Catholics under James I: Father Gerard's Narrative of the Gunpowder Plot*, ed. J. Morris (London, 1872) vol. II, 283, qtd. in Haigh, "From Monopoly to Minority," 141.

85 In the Act of the year 27 Elizabeth (1585), legislation was put in place dealing expressly with the problem of children sent to seminaries abroad. Families who sent children "into any the parts beyond the seas out of her Highness's obedience" were to forfeit £100. Parents sending money to children already abroad were to incur the penalties of *praemunire* (J. R. Tanner, *Tudor Constitutional Documents AD. 1485–1603 with an Historical Commentary* [Cambridge, 1951] 157).

86 Henry died at Viterbo, date unknown (Claridge, *Margaret Clitherow [1556?–1586]*, 188).

87 St. Ursula's English archives were transferred to St. Monica's, also in Louvain, in 1609 and relocated again in the late nineteenth century to Newton Abbot (Hamilton, *The Chronicle of the English Augustinian Canonesses Regular of the Lateran*, vol. I, x–xi).

88 Another book found in the collection carries the title, *An Abstracte of the Life and Martirdome of Mistress Margaret Clitherowe, who suffered in the year of our Lorde 1586, the 25 of March. At Mechline, 1619*, and is dedicated "To the virtuous and devout religious Sister, Sister Ann Clitherowe of the Order of St. Augustin, at Louvain" (Hamilton, *The Chronicle of the English Augustinian Canonesses Regular of the Lateran*, vol. I, 22).

89 Still in colloquial use in and around York, the term "warch" roughly equates to "ache." I would like to thank Ruth Campbell for her help in translating some portions of the manuscript. Ms. Campbell generously transcribed a number of other Yorkist colloquialisms for my benefit as well.

90 Campbell translates "thrung" as "crowded."

91 I have never been to St. Augustine's Priory or seen its library of the convent, And Devon is still one place among many that I dearly wish to visit.

92 Actually, Clitherow's letter has been co-authored. My good friend, writer Lynn York, brought this text to life, animating it with the imagined spirit of Margaret Clitherow. Would that these two women had been able to meet.

3 LEGISLATING MORALITY IN THE MARRIAGE MARKET

1 Ester Sowernam, *Ester hath hang'd Haman* (London, 1617). All citations are from this edition. The pamphlet has been reprinted in Simon Sheperd, ed., *The Women's Sharp Revenge: Five Women's Pamphlets from the Renaissance* (London, 1985) 85–124.

2 For a general discussion of other texts responding to Swetnam, see Louis B. Wright, *Middle-Class Culture in Elizabethan England* (Chapel Hill, 1935) 481–99. The *Araignment* went into ten editions before 1634. Additional editions came out in 1690, 1702, 1707, 1733, and 1807. Two Dutch translations were published in Amsterdam in 1641 and 1645 (487). Sowernam's text had only a single printing (Hull, *Chaste, Silent, and Obedient*, 115).

3 *Women and the English Renaissance: Literature and the Nature of Womankind,*

1540–1620 (Urbana, 1984) 93. Woodbridge's hypothesis about male author-ship is given further credence in the anonymity of the writer. Because *Ester hath hang'd Haman* was published under a pseudonym, the possibility of authorial gender-bending and/or multiple authorship exists. While I argue that Sowernam's defense displays gender-specific attributes in the way that it positions women and men (the male-authored defenses that I have en-countered tend to focus on a generalized ideal of femininity to a much greater degree), the stance that the anonymous author has taken, regardless of gender, constructs itself as female and as such establishes itself in those terms. For a persuasive reading of this text as both single-voiced and female-authored, see Henderson and McManus, *Half Humankind*, 20–24. For a useful reminder of what is at stake in these claims, see Diane Purkiss, "Material Girls: The Seventeenth-Century Woman Debate," in Brant and Purkiss, *Women, Texts and Histories*, 69–101. "Because [texts like this one] purport to be by women, they seem to offer a visible female self-consciousness about gender," Purkiss suggests. "But because what is at stake in these texts seems at first glance so familiar and understandable, it is possible that their estranging or culturally autonomous aspects may not be fully noticed" (70).

4 "Counterattacks on 'the Bayter of Women': Three Pamphleteers of the Early Seventeenth Century," in Haselkorn and Travitsky, *The Renaissance English-woman in Print*, 53.

5 The earliest theatrical reference that I have found is in George Peele's *The Old Wives Tale* (1595). See Sacrapant's riddle, lines 448–49 (*The Old Wives Tale*, ed. Patricia Binnie [Baltimore, 1980] 60).

6 The term "middle-class" is not only anachronistic but also imprecise. Sowernam's audience, addressed in her dedications as gentlewomen on the one hand and London apprentices on the other (themselves a wide and financially diverse grouping), consists of a vast range of professions and incomes, most of which operate outside and in opposition to anything as homogenized and all-encompassing as a singular "middle class." Accordingly, I will use the term only in quotes to underscore a sense of *middle* ground and *in-between* status among these various groupings.

7 Drama is perhaps the most visible forum during this period to recognize marriage as a site of cultural instability. See, for instance, *How a Man May Choose a Good Wife from a Bad* (London, 1602) and *The London Prodigal* (London, 1604); Francis Beaumont and John Fletcher, *The Double Marriage* (London, 1620), *Four Plays or Moral Representations in One* (London, 1612), and *The Spanish Curate* (London, 1622); Robert Dabourne, *The Poor Man's Comfort* (London, 1617); Thomas Dekker, *The Honest Whore, Parts I and II* (London, 1604–5), *The Noble Spanish Soldier* (London, 1623), and *The Welsh Ambassador* (London, 1623); William Rowley, *All's Lost by Lust* (London, 1622); and William Sampson, *The Vow-Breaker, or the Fair Maid of Clifton* (London, 1625).

8 *Swetnam the Woman-Hater* is an obvious choice here in that it uses the Swetnam debate to tell its story. The original edition of the play was published anonymously in 1620. Wright argues that its author was Thomas Heywood. Wright sees the "language, dialogue, and clownery" in *Swetnam the Woman-Hater* as reminiscent of Heywood's work. In the introduction to A. B.

Grosart's 1880 reprint of the play, Grosart speculates that either Heywood or Dekker was the play's likely author (Wright, *Middle-Class Culture*, 490n). Throughout this analysis, I am presuming male authorship. Regardless of the genetic makeup of its author, this play nevertheless presents itself from a masculinist viewpoint. Its central narrative imagines a connection to male audience members and locates its sympathies accordingly.

9 Sowernam's defense is no less vexed, no more "savvy," in its claims than either of the male-authored plays. It too regulates as it revises, and codifies as its constructs. In a contractual catch-22, Sowernam advocates for women a program of chaste behavior and moral guardianship that will continue to generate greater and more precise categorizations of female regulation, categorizations that will be called to service as the English state embraces the domestic as a site of potential invigilation and control.

10 In exploring the relationships between these writings, I want to prioritize the interplay between assumed voice and the situating of that voice within a particular and gender-specific history. As Sowernam's defense is the only female-announced text of the three works that I am considering, it is my intent to privilege that status in my explorations. In order to highlight the gendering that is critical to all three works, I will foreground Sowernam's writing, using her defense as a sounding board against which to examine both male-authored works.

11 During the London "season," sons and daughters of the gentry could occasionally meet without adult supervision. These unobserved trysts allowed for the infrequent but not altogether uncommon exchange of "secret vows" (Keith Wrightson, *English Society, 1580–1680* [New Brunswick, 1982] 74).

12 There are two distinct types of spousals recognized in early marriage law: spousals *de futuro* that promise eventual marriage but can be broken for just cause, and spousals *de praesenti* that are immediately binding and ostensibly irrevocable. In the above scenario I am assuming that spousals *de praesenti* have been exchanged, but in either case once consummation has occurred, marriage vows are final. For a more detailed analysis of English marriage law, see Carroll Camden, "The Marriage Contract, Marriage, Marriage Customs," in her *The Elizabethan Woman: A Panorama of English Womanhood, 1540–1640*, rev. edn. (New York, 1975) 77–106; Martin Ingram, "Spousals Litigation in the English Ecclesiastical Courts, c. 1350–1640," in Outhwaite, *Marriage and Society*, 37–39; and Chilton Latham Powell, *English Domestic Relations, 1487–1653: A Study of Matrimony and Family Life in Theory and Practice as Revealed by the Literature, Law, and History of England* (New York, 1972) 3–5. For early modern discussions of court procedure and accepted jurisprudence, see Henry Conset, *The Practice of the Spiritual or Ecclesiastical Courts* (1685); Sir Thomas Smith, *De Republica Anglorum*, ed. Mary Dewar (Cambridge, 1982) 78–144; Henry Swinburne, *A Treatise of Spousals or Matrimonial Contracts* (London, 1685); and T. E., *The Lawes Resolutions of Womens Rights* (1629).

13 I use the more general term "friends" here as many transplanted London women of marriageable age did not reside within a "nuclear" family during their stay in the city. "Friends," then, refers to any number of consanguinal

or affinal ties, from an apprenticed brother or distant relative to a godparent or local patron.

14 According to Stone, early Stuart dowries generally equaled one year's income (*The Crisis of the Aristocracy, 1558–1641* [London, 1967] 291). I have placed Sowernam's hypothetical portion at £150 as this figure generally represents a typical mid-range income for merchant families at the time of Sowernam's writing.

15 Shakespeare, *Measure for Measure*, xxxi. All future references to *Measure for Measure* are from this edition.

16 Risking accusations of essentialism, I want to stress the importance of reading these texts as gender-coded. For other critics who talk about the problems of re-negotiating the much-trodden terrain of the English Renaissance in gendered terms, see Marilyn Boxer and Jean H. Quataert, "Introduction: Restoring Women to History," in *Connecting Spheres: Women in the Western World, 1500 to the Present*, ed. Marilyn J. Boxer and Jean H. Quataert (New York, 1987) 3–18; Ann D. Gordon, Mari Jo Buhle, and Nancy Schrom Dye, "The Problem of Women's History," in *Liberating Women's History: Theoretical and Critical Essays*, ed. Berenice A. Caroll (Urbana, 1976) 75–92; Jordan, *Renaissance Feminism*, 1–10; Hilda Smith, "Feminism and the Methodology of Women's History," in Carroll, *Liberating Women's History*, 369ff.; and Gary F. Waller, "Struggling into Discourse: The Emergence of Renaissance Women's Writing," in Hannay, *Silent but for the Word*, 241ff.

17 Two other texts published within months of Sowernam's, both ostensibly authored by women and written in response to Swetnam's *Araignment*, are Constantia Munda's *The Worming of a Mad Dogge* (London, 1617), and Rachel Speght's *A Mouzell for Melastomus* (London, 1617).

18 L. B. Wright outlines a number of the more prominent voices in the debate (*Middle-Class Culture* 465–507). Other writers who discuss the controversy and offer additional bibliographical material are Barbara J. Baines, "Introduction," in *Three Pamphlets on the Jacobean Antifeminist Controversy*, ed. Barbara J. Baines (Delmar, NY, 1978); Elaine V. Beilin, "Redeeming Eve: Defenses of Women and Mothers' Advice Books," in her *Redeeming Eve*, 247–85; Diane Bornstein, "Introduction," in *Distaves and Dames: Renaissance Treatises for and about Women*, ed. Diane Bornstein (Delmar, NY, 1978); Coryl Crandall, "The Cultural Implications of the Swetnam Anti-Feminist Controversy," *Journal of Popular Culture* 2 (1968) 136–48, and *Swetnam the Woman-Hater: The Controversy and the Play* (Purdue, 1969), 1–21; Sara J. Eaton, "Presentations of Women in the English Popular Press," in Levin and Watson, *Ambiguous Realities*, 165–83; Henderson and McManus, *Half Humankind*, esp. 381ff.; Jones, "Counterattacks," 45–62, and "Nets and Bridles: Early Modern Conduct Books and Sixteenth-Century Women's Lyric," in *The Ideology of Conduct: Essays on Literature and the History of Sexuality*, ed. Nancy Armstrong and Leonard Tennenhouse (New York, 1987) 39–72; Jordan, "Gender and Justice in Swetnam the Woman-Hater," *Renaissance Drama* 18 (1987) 149–69, and *Renaissance Feminism*; Purkiss, "Material Girls: The Seventeenth-Century Woman Debate"; Sheperd, *The Women's Sharp Revenge*; Betty S. Travitsky, "The Lady Doth

Protest: Protest in the Popular Writings of Renaissance Englishwomen,"
English Literary Renaissance 14.3 (1984) 255–83, and Travitsky, ed., *The
Paradise of Woman: Writings by Englishwomen of the Renaissance* (Westport,
1981) 97–113; Francis Lee Utley, *The Crooked Rib; An Analytical Index to the
Argument about Women in English and Scots Literature to the End of the Year
1568* (Columbus, 1944); and Woodbridge, *Women and the English Renaissance*.

19 Woodbridge (*Women and the English Renaissance*, 13–14) contends that these
authors approach their topic as an intellectual game, a classical exercise that
assumes a certain level of educational expertise (see esp. 13–18). Woodbridge's recovery of rhetorical control for women like Sowernam is a
necessary component in refiguring female authorial voice, but she tends to err
in the opposite extreme by diminishing the very real and powerful political
ramifications of these supposed "literary exercises" for English women *outside*
the text in the realm of lived experience and desire. Woodbridge's disclaimer
erases the social impact of misogynistic practices on women of the period and,
very possibly, on Sowernam herself.

20 Powell, *English Domestic Relations*, 2.

21 The ordinance, entitled *Reformatio legum ecclesiasticarum* (32 Henry VIII, ca
38), was not established permanently until 1601 and even then to little
purpose (Powell, *English Domestic Relations*, 62).

22 Powell, *English Domestic Relations*, 73ff.

23 While "ecclesiastical law did not recognize parents' right to determine their
children's choice of spouses . . . [p]arents' opposition to what they felt to be
unsuitable marriages probably lay behind much matrimonial litigation"
(Houlbrooke, *Church Court*, 62–63). Houlbrooke cites one example of a
pregnant maidservant whose master threatened her lover with summary
proceedings if he failed to marry her. The lover apparently refused, making an
offer to a second woman who was accorded contract free and clear (64).

24 Although it was necessary to the securing of a valid contract, consummation
did not legally mark the moment that legitimacy was conferred. If such a
moment could be identified in English law, it was synonymous with the
exchange of vows (Ingram, "Spousals Litigation," 39).

25 Ralph A. Houlbrooke, *The English Family, 1450–1700* (London, 1984) 80.

26 R. H. Smith, "Marriage Processes in the English Past: Some Continuities," in
Bonfield, Smith, and Wrightson, *The World We Have Gained*, 71.

27 John Rushworth, *Historical Collections*, vol. IV, 212, in Powell, *English
Domestic Relations*, 36. See S. F. C. Milsom (*Historical Foundations of the
Canon Law*, 2nd edn. [London, 1981] 314–60) for the history of contract law
in England.

28 The cases tried within the courts were almost invariably high-status
(Wrightson, *English Society*, 100).

29 In the upper echelons of the peerage, the years 1598–1620 were particularly
illustrative of broken contract. Stone writes that "something like one-third of
the older peers were estranged from or actually separated from their wives"
during this period (*Aristocracy*, 297). Following Stone's lead, Wrightson
recognizes the late sixteenth and early seventeenth centuries as formative in
the construction of formalized English marriage law. He notes a growing

recognition of public ceremony to legitimate marriage (*Poverty and Piety in an English Village: Terling, 1525–1700* [New York, 1979] 127). See also Camden, "The Marriage Contract, Marriage, Marriage Customs," in her *The Elizabethan Woman*, 92ff.

30 For general discussions of *Measure for Measure* as it relates to spousal conventions, see J. Birje-Patil, "Marriage Contracts in *Measure for Measure*," *Shakespeare Studies* 5 (1969) 106–11; Davis P. Harding, "Elizabethan Betrothals and *Measure for Measure*," *Journal of English and Germanic Philology* 49 (1950) 129–58; S. Nagarajan, "*Measure for Measure* and Elizabethan Betrothals," *Shakespeare Quarterly* 14 (1963) 115–19; Alan W. Powers, "'Meaner Parties': Spousal Conventions and Oral Culture in *Measure for Measure* and *All's Well That Ends Well*," *Upstart Crow* 8 (1978) 28–41; Ernest Schanzer, "The Marriage Contracts in *Measure for Measure*," *Shakespeare Survey* 13 (1960) 81–89; and Karl Wentersdorf, "The Marriage Contracts in *Measure for Measure*: A Reconsideration," *Shakespeare Survey* 32 (1979) 129–44. Most of these discussions assign a legal definition to the lovers' negotiations and accordingly fail to consider the cultural imperatives that might necessitate Shakespeare's dramatic imaginings in the first place.

31 The specific circumstances surrounding each of these "partnerships" seems to have little bearing on their legitimacy in the eyes of the state. In *Measure for Measure*, the higher the status of the encounter, the more binding its marital ties.

32 In *Swetnam the Woman-Hater*, one of the two lovers is to be executed; the other banished. This "double" sentence paves the way for a related plot device – trying to ascertain whether women provoke men to sin or men provoke women.

33 Both Duke Vincentio's friar and Prince Lorenzo's Amazon are "strangers" to the court, "other" in terms of gender, religion, or country. This position outside traditional power centers permits a limited critique of traditional authority but does so only by erasing the reality of marginalized "others" who are without such dual status.

34 Crandall, *Swetnam*, 5.3.169–70. All future references are from this edition.

35 Lorenzo's refusal to take the king's word offers a simultaneous critique on kingship and royal promises.

36 The *OED* (*Oxford English Dictionary*) defines "steward" as "an administrator and dispenser of wealth, favours, etc.; esp. one regarded as the servant of God or of the people . . . dispensator." This joint definition, current in the early seventeenth century, alludes to both biblical and civil precedents and seems most apt here. Related definitions see a steward as "an officer of a royal household," a "deputy-governor, vice-gerent," or a "public administrator" (prepared by J. A. Simpson and E. S. C. Weiner, 2nd edn. [Oxford, 1989], vol. xvi, 665).

37 Despite the fact that Sowernam's account manages to articulate anxieties about the nature of the marriage contract so forcefully, anticipating the legal ramifications of that negotiation by thirty-five years (five generations according to English property law), it is a creature of its time. Sowernam understands the sanctity of marriage to come primarily from its ecclesial ties. In Sowernam's elaboration of God as a triumvirate of English authorities

(father, priest, steward), it is the office of priest that enables him to tie "so inseparable a knot." Accordingly, although she uses a pseudo-legal discourse to arraign Swetnam and other contract-breaking mercantile husbands and seems to embrace the righteousness of civil litigation in the marriage market, she nevertheless fails to recognize or articulate that bond as specifically the domain of the state. (This is true of other conduct writers publishing at this time: William Whateley, in his 1617 publication of *A Bride-Bush, or A Wedding Sermon* [London], uniformly equates state and church authority in marriage.) Sowernam's reformulation of civil and domestic relationships, then, suggests anxieties inherent in "middle-class" culture about the status of marriage but does not, in and of itself, advocate a secular overhaul of marriage policy. In contrast, *Swetnam the Woman-Hater* locates the authority to legitimate marriage squarely within the state. King Atticus never even considers the possibility of a church service. He never insists that a friar "do . . . the office" (*Measure for Measure*, 5.1.376) or a priest "tie . . . a knot." "As we are King of Sicil," he declares, "[this royal match] 'tis confirm'd / Firm, to be revoked never, / Untill death their lives dissever." (5.3.171–73).

38 For a comprehensive overview of the kinds of crimes and cases tried in the church courts, see F. G. Emmison, *Elizabethan Life: Morals & the Church Courts* (Chelmsford, 1973).

39 Vivien Brodsky Elliott, "Single Women in the London Marriage Market: Age, Status and Mobility, 1598–1619," in Outhwaite, *Marriage and Society*, 81.

40 Powell, *English Domestic Relations*, 16–17.

41 Elliott, "Single Women," 84.

42 Only one-sixth of all marriages in the London diocese between 1598 and 1619 were licensed. People of low to middle status who could not afford the cost of securing a license generally married by banns or troth-plight, often without witness from either church or state (Elliott, "Single Women," 82).

43 Wright, *Middle-Class Culture*, 8. Less than 10% of the great Elizabethan and Stuart merchants in London were born there (Wrightson, *English Society*, 28). In fact, migration to the city was the norm rather than the exception. In families of high status, as many as 34.7% of their daughters migrated to London to reside with kin while looking for marriage partners (Elliott, "Single Women," 94).

44 Arguing for the legitimacy of divorce, Milton saw unfitness of mind as a just cause for separation. That understanding, though not entirely atypical, remained conceptually outside the law for over 200 years (Powell, *English Domestic Relations*, 100). In his polemical writings, Milton produced four tracts that dealt specifically with questions of divorce: *Doctrine and Discipline of Divorce* (1643); *The Judgment of Martin Bucer Concerning Divorce* (1644); *Tetrachordon*; and *Colasterion* (both 1645). For an interesting counterpoint to my argument in Milton's divorce tracts, see Olga Lucia Valbuena, "Milton's 'Divorsive' Interpretation and the Gendered Reader," *Milton Studies* 27 (1992) 115–37.

45 Sir Thomas Smith notes that early modern English courts were generally accepting "of unsolemnized marriage as lawful in so far as the inheritance of the offspring of such unions was concerned," but he goes on to add that "the

matter of the wife's property rights in such unions [was] far less certain" (*De Republica Anglorum,* 62).

46 Sir Thomas Smith writes,

> Whatsoever [wives] have before mariage, as soone as mariage is solemnized is their husbandes, I meane of money, plate, juelles, cattaile, and generally all moveables . . . and what soever they gette after mariage, they get to their husbandes. They neither can give nor sell anie thing either of their husbandes, or their owne . . .
>   This which I have written touching mariage and the right in moveables and unmoveables which commeth thereby, is to be understoode by the common law when no private contract is not more particularly made. *If there be any private pacts, covenants, and contracts made before the mariage* betwixt the husbande and the wife, by themselves, their parents, or their friends, *those have force and be kept according to the firmitie and strength in which they are made* [my emphasis]. (*De Republica Anglorum,* 133–34)

Land inheritance operated somewhat differently in that it was generally tied to specific rights of succession.

47 According to Stone, the legal position of women did improve between 1580 and 1640. During this time, successive Lord Chancellors rendered judgments that affected married women's property rights with the creation of the doctrine of the Wife's Separate Estate. As its result, the economic penalties of separation substantially diminished for women (*The Family, Sex and Marriage in England 1500–1800* [New York, 1977] 297). To what extent this doctrine actually affected women of the middling ranks, Stone does not say. The conjunction between perceived injustices and legal responses to them would, however, account for both Sowernam's continued anxiety and limited restitution for women in general.

48 Vivien Brodsky, "Widows in Late Elizabethan London: Remarriage, Economic Opportunity and Family Orientations," in Bonfield, Smith, and Wrightson, *The World We Have Gained,* 142. The few women allowed membership within the London guilds (generally widows who carried on in their husbands' businesses) were, in the early seventeenth century, often physically excluded from entering guild halls, forced to sit at separate tables once there, and denied voting privileges. While the presence of women within guilds was never officially remarkable (current research suggests that their numbers were so few as to be almost negligible), the legislation enacted against the possibility of their future membership does suggest a growing awareness of the marketplace as an inappropriate arena for women.

49 For additional early seventeenth-century texts that discuss female and male obligations within marriage, see Kathleen Davies, "Continuity and Change in Literary Advice on Marriage," in Outhwaite, *Marriage and Society,* 66ff.

50 Jane Anger (*Jane Anger her Protection for Women*) also warns her readers not to trust in men's words, but Sowernam's defense specifically directs that warning into the material circumstances of marriage negotiation, insisting on legal retribution for failure to uphold the contract and a recognition of specific status and property rights in demanding restitution in a literal court of law.

51 Henderson and McManus, *Half Humankind,* 39.

52 To my knowledge, Sowernam's use of an actual trial is the first within the

controversy. Both playwrights share her fascination with the legal implications of female/male relationships.

53 Sheperd, citing the *OED* definition of "Stafford law" from Breton's *Will of Wit* (1599), describes it as "martial law, killing and hanging" (*The Woman's Sharpe Revenge* 120). While military authority was clearly outside early modern women's domain, women of the middling ranks were also denied access to more traditional forms of legal and political authority: "Women are excluded from all civil and public offices; and thus they may not be judices, nor magistrates, nor advocates; nor may they intervene on another's behalf in law, nor act as agents" (Andrea Alciato, *Digest, De verborum significatione*, qtd. in Ian MacLean, *The Renaissance Notion of Woman: A Study in the Fortunes of Scholasticism and Medical Science in European Intellectual Life* [Cambridge, 1980] 77).

54 With the publication of the *39 Articles* in 1552, marriage lost its actual standing as a sacrament. Nevertheless, the church still retained full power over the rites and offices of marriage, and both church and lay writers continued to refer to marriage in those terms (Powell, *English Domestic Relations*, 40).

55 Cromwell's 1652 Marriage Act mandated (if only in writing) what no other legislation had before it. It limited the means by which a marriage could be made legal (only a magistrate could perform it and only by following a uniform set of procedures). It also specified the actual moment that legality was conferred. The document reads:

> the said Justice of Peace may and shall declare the said man and woman to be from thenceforth husband and wife; and from and after such consent so expressed, and such Declaration made, the same . . . shall be good and effectual in Law; And no other Marriage whatsover . . . shall be held or accompted a Marriage according to the Laws of England. (Henry Scobell, *A Collection of Acts and Ordinances of Parliament, 1640–1656* [London, 1658] vol. II, 237)

With the passage of the Marriage Act, marriage was accounted legal only in the presence of a public official and at a clearly announced moment, not behind closed doors in the marriage bed where promises once uttered might conveniently be forgotten. Cromwell's act did not, however, completely alleviate marriage controversy in England as clandestine marriages continued to occur, some of them in neighboring Scotland. It was not until the passage of Lord Hardwicke's Marriage Act in 1753 that English marriage policy acquired the form it was to carry into the twentieth century (Ingram, "Spousals Litigation," 40).

56 In her essay on Mary Wollstonecraft's *Rights of Women*, Cora Kaplan reminds us that reevaluations of gender difference are always historically distinct and categorically specific, and that the questions we ask about them must in some sense always take these factors into account. She writes, "history offers no final resolution, only the constant sexual division of labour. The questions for the historian of feminism are why at some moments does sexual difference and division take on a political significance – which elements in the organization are politicized, what are the terms of the negotiation and between whom?" (*Sea Changes: Essays on Culture and Feminism* [London,

1982] 35). Noting a constant political reevaluation of gender division and organization, Kaplan traces a few of these configurations through nineteenth-century gender debates. Her insights, both written and spoken, have, in large part, provided me with a way to "read" this text – a methodology that can account for both the reformist possibilities within Sowernam's defense and the limitations created by those very reforms.

57 Barbara J. Baines offers a close reading of this play in terms of chastity's power that in many respects parallels my own ("Assaying the Power of Chastity in *Measure for Measure*," *Studies in English Literature* 30 [1990] 283–301).

58 Angelo recognizes the impulse to sin as his alone. "It is I," he admits, "That, lying by the violet in the sun, / Do as the carrion does, not as the flower, / Corrupt with virtuous season" (2.2.165–68).

59 In all four source accounts for *Measure for Measure* the woman relents, sacrificing her chastity to save a man's life (*Measure for Measure*, xxxv). Shakespeare's translation of the narrative, from violated maiden to legitimate stand-in, both underscores the inviolability of the marriage contract (Angelo's unheeded promise to Mariana must eventually come due) and articulates the potential threat of a chastity (Isabella's) that refuses to yield.

60 *Measure for Measure*, 5.1.489. The Duke's last lines in the play underscore the "value" that Isabella will possess when she accepts his offer of marriage. He tells her:

> dear Isabel,
> I have a motion much imports your good;
> Whereto if you'll a willing ear incline,
> What's mine is yours, and what is yours is mine.   (5.1.531–34)

61 Ideologies of chastity are so familiar and assumed that my declaration of them may seem unnecessary. I emphasize them, however, not to argue their presence (which is a given), but rather to point out how they (and other culturally promoted sexualities) are able to serve various agendas simultaneously. Seventeenth-century women actively promote concepts of chaste living, despite the restrictions that attend such positionings.

62 *Swetnam the Woman-Hater*, like *Ester hath hang'd Haman*, announces its status allegiances in popular terms. The play, initially performed at the Red Bull (itself an avowedly popular venue), no doubt drew in the same apprentice population that Sowernam solicits in her account (Crandall, *Swetnam*, 26, 33–35; Andrew Gurr, *Playgoing in Shakespeare's London* [Cambridge, 1987] 60, 61, 64–65, 76). *Measure for Measure*, in contrast, includes a more elite audience than either Sowernam's tract or the anonymous *Swetnam*, if only by virtue of its announced performance at court and its numerous allusions to King James (*Measure for Measure*, xxxiff.). For connections between commercial trade and the theater, see Jean-Christophe Agnew, *Worlds Apart: The Market and the Theater in Anglo-American Thought, 1550–1750* (Cambridge, 1986).

63 Actually, the depiction of a potentially disruptive transgression secures and delineates class lines more emphatically. Women of the middling ranks do not get pregnant before marriage; their social inferiors do.

64 In *A Mirror for Magistrates*, George Whetstone explicitly connects sexual incontinence with status breakdown. He explains that "Dice, Drunkennesse and Harlots, ha[ve] consumed the wealth of a great number of ancient Gentlemen, whose Purses [a]re in the possession of vile persons, and their Landes at morgage with the Marchants . . . The Gentlemen ha[ve] made this exchaunge with vile persons: they [a]re attyred with the Gentlemens brauerie, and the Gentlemen disgraced with their beastly manners" (qtd. in Thomas C. Izard, ed., *George Whetstone: Mid-Elizabethan Gentleman of Letters* [New York, 1942] 135). Not surprisingly, what is hinted at in *Measure for Measure* is made explicit in *Swetnam*.

For one of the more provocative discussions of Shakespeare's play to date, see Jonathan Dollimore, "Transgression and Surveillance in *Measure for Measure*," in *Political Shakespeare: New Essays in Cultural Materialism*, ed. Jonathan Dollimore and Alan Sinfield [Ithaca, 1985] 79). Dollimore's argument parallels my own in its focus on Shakespeare's play as a reworking of early modern disciplinary regimes and political methodologies. It is also owing to Dollimore's essay that I here revisit both Whetstone and, in what is to follow, Richard Hooker.

65 Hooker, in the preface to *Of the Laws of Ecclesiastical Polity* (1593), condemns those of the "Calvinist Discipline" for their naïveté in ascribing greater religious insight to women. While he argues that women's "eagerness of affection" not their judgment makes them prime candidates for zealous faith, his language seems to acknowledge as well women's "natural" propensities for avoiding sin and "drawing their husbands, children, servants, friends, and allies the same way" (London, 1969, vol. I, 103–4). It is interesting to note that Hooker's associations have been both reclaimed and, to a large extent, secularized by the time Ester Sowernam publishes her tract in 1617.

66 In the Fifth Book of *Ecclesiastical Polity*, Hooker notes, albeit dismissively, the disciplinary uses to which religious authority has been put when he asserts that "men fearing God are thereby a great deal more effectually than by positive laws restrained from doing evil; inasmuch as those laws have no farther power than over our outward actions only, whereas unto men's inward cogitations, unto the privy intents and motions of their hearts, religion serveth for a bridle" (vol. II, 19).

67 By the civil-war years the connection between gender and morality is both overt and restrictive. Women may be keepers of conscience, but that effect has been limited to issues of household education. In addition, global ideas of nationhood and common cause are undermining female guardianship, replacing a family-based morality with an even smaller unit of regulation – the national subject. Sowernam's positioning of seventeenth-century wives as prototypic "secret" police, uncovering "true" motivation in recently invigilated realms of inner discourse, is itself a nervous and unsatisfying gesture. The ability to find someone out, to discover the intent behind the words or acts, is something the new state is very much anxious to possess. Given a growing English population and the literal economic and physical impossibility of controlling their behavior via either an inadequate court system or its nebulous and often unenforceable penal codes (prosecuting offenders in the

early years of the seventeenth century was a long and frequently futile process), state bureaucracies are no doubt willing to embrace any and all solutions that happen along.

68 Allowed scope outside the house within the community, wives can potentially divulge domestic secrets.

69 Indeed, Sowernam's chief complaint against Rachel Speght's *A Mouzell for Melastomus* is that it fails to take a strong position. According to Sowernam's account, the earlier text is so tentative in its stance that it rather condemns women than defends them. She writes, "whereas the Maide doth many times excuse her tendernesse of yeares, I found it to be true in the slendernesse of her answer, for she undertaking to defend women, doth rather charge and condemn women" (dedication).

70 For a statistical breakdown of crime in England during the early Stuart period, see J. S. Cockburn, *Crime in England, 1550–1800* (Princeton, 1977).

71 Within the ecclesiastical courts, public shame and the threat of excommunication were the only real punitive measures available (though fines were occasionally levied as well). These types of punishment depended for effect on the subject's willingness to recognize her or his behavior as wrong (Emmison, *Elizabethan Life*, 300). Thus, the inability to enforce any type of moral legislation with certainty became particularly worrisome. In "Proof and Consequences" (33), Maus usefully notes that the legal relationship in early modern England between "pact and act" – between inward truth and its public display – was fairly complex and not altogether clear.

72 Ivo Kamps reminds us that *Measure for Measure*'s movement toward benevolent resolution is greater than the "anxieties" that it generates in the process. Despite its amibivalence, the play does eventually restore "justice" to concepts of monarchical rule and assuage audience fears about governmental corruption ("Ruling Fantasies and the Fantasies of Rule: *The Phoenix* and *Measure for Measure*," *Studies in Philology* 42.2 (1995) 248–73.

73 The duke's skill at setting things to rights parallels the state's anticipated/ supposed authority to do the same.

74 Although there are occasional references to confessional boxes during the fifteenth century, the first verifiable enclosed (screened) confessional was used in Flanders in the seventeenth century and in Belgium not before the middle of the sixteenth (Thomas N. Tentler, *Sin and Confession on the Eve of the Reformation* [Princeton, 1977] 82n). For detailed information on the place of the confessional in state making, see also *Sin and Confession*, 57–133, and Tentler, "The Summa." The latter specifically addresses the regulatory aspects of religious confession.

75 *Measure for Measure*, 3.2.264. Sowernam acknowledges the inappropriateness of such exposure. Of men who are too public with their private thoughts, she writes, "it is as shame for a man to publish and proclaime household secrets, which is a common practise amongst men, especially Drunkards, Lechers, and prodigall spend-thrifts" (*Ester hath hang'd Haman*, 44).

76 Justice in *Measure for Measure* is imagined as both credible and male-focused in its dealings. Isabella and Mariana must beg for hearing before the duke. *His* power alone will resolve their plight. At the same time their own apparent intransigence is coded as derivative; we are twice reminded that they have

been "suborn'd" and are "instruments of some more mightier member" (5.1.109, 236).

77 A returning interest in religious ritual and heightened church authority in the years preceding the Civil War may have addressed problems of moral regulation as well.

78 In 1634, John Milton will bring to center stage a later version of chaste conscience in *The Masque at Ludlow*: "Thou canst not touch the freedom of my mind / With all thy charms, although this corporal rind / Thou hast immancl'd" (in *John Milton: Complete Poems and Major Prose*, ed. Merritt Hughes [New York, 1957] 663–65).

79 While *Swetnam the Woman-Hater* reminds its viewers that the king's laws may punish bodies but cannot command minds, the logic of the play nevertheless assumes a real connection between clear conscience and legal innocence. Leonida and Lisandro recognize their sentence as tyrannous, but they do so only because it is coded as tyranny within the play's action. The crime of which they have been accused was never committed, and so their penitence would be inappropriate. This perspective parallels *Ester hath hang'd Haman*'s in its willingness to imagine the mind as knowable and to identify the knowers from those who do not know. What the play does do, to a much greater degree than *Ester hath hang'd Haman* is able, is to suggest a more explicit rejection of the state's ability to "discern" truth without help. Because it locates its authority more emphatically in the person of the king and the king's son and because it addresses the legal ramifications of state power overtly, its criticisms of government and law are more blatantly antagonistic.

80 Jordan sees *Swetnam the Woman-Hater*'s female androgyny as loosely modeled on Sir Philip Sidney's Zelmane in the *Arcadia* ("Gender and Justice," 152). The gender debate offers critical evaluations of cross-dressed men in *Haec-Vir: Or The Womanish-Man* (London, 1620) and *Muld Sacke: Or The Apologie Of Hic Mulier* (London, 1620). A third pamphlet, dealing with female cross-dressers, *Hic Mulier: Or, the Man-Woman* (London, 1620) was published concurrently. All three pamphlets are collected in Baines, *Three Pamphlets*.

81 The construction of the masque as a conscience-catcher would be culturally familiar to Jacobean audiences. From their appearance in medieval morality plays to recreations under the auspices of Inigo Jones, masques explored the relationship between self and state. See Jonathan Goldberg, *James I and the Politics of Literature: Jonson, Shakespeare, Donne, and their Contemporaries* (Baltimore, 1983) 113ff.; and Stephen Orgel, *The Illusion of Power: Political Theater in the English Renaissance* (Berkeley, 1975) 37ff.

82 Before the masque begins, the queen is positioned as its hidden audience. Iago tells her, "Heere, your Grace / May undiscovered sit, and view the Maske, / And see how 'tis affected by the King" (5.3.53–55). As the masque's audience, the queen will be the first to discover the king's thoughts – to search them out and make them public. At the same time, however, that viewing will be privatized. In her role as the king's wife, she will sit undiscovered and out of the king's view when he confesses. Orgel discusses the placement of the royal audience directly on stage as part of the action of the masque. The monarch must not simply witness the masque but must be seen to see it (*The Illusion of*

Power, 10–16). Orgel understands masques as a political means to self-knowledge (59).

83 This sabotaging occurs again and again in the text. Despite a resolution that finds women guiltless of tempting men to sin, Nicanor's final apology ends with this disclaimer: "Your Graces pardon. 'Twas not pride of state, / But [Leonida's] disdaine, that first inspir'd in me / This hope of Soveraigntie" (5.3.209–11).

84 *Swetnam the Woman-Hater* posits the idea of renewing an outdated and ineffectual rule with the coronation of a new king.

85 While cases having to do with questions of conduct and moral regulation were more frequently prosecuted in the first quarter of the seventeenth century than in previous periods (e.g., the church courts were considering bastardy cases where children had been born less than eight months after formal marriage vows), these cases were not considered capital crimes. Most sentences tended to shame rather than debilitate offenders, demanding from them public penance of some variety (stocks, robed display, etc.). See Wrightson, *Poverty and Piety,* 133; and Powers, "'Meaner Parties,'" 34.

86 See, for instance, Wrightson, *Poverty and Piety,* 125–33; and David Levine and Keith Wrightson, "The Social Context of Illegitimacy in Early Modern England," in Laslett, Oosterveen, and Smith, *Bastardy and its Comparative History,* 164.

87 Wrightson, "The Nadir of English Illegitimacy in the Seventeenth Century," in Laslett, Oosterveen, and Smith, *Bastardy and its Comparative History,* 179–80.

88 Interestingly enough, Prince Lorenzo is King Atticus's second son. His older brother (Henry?), much touted for his bravery in battle, has died prematurely, leaving in his stead a less celebrated and prodigal substitute.

4 GENDER FORMATION IN ENGLISH APOCALYPTIC WRITING

1 Eleanor Davies, *Apocalyps, Chap. 11. Its accomplishment shewed from the Lady Eleanor* (n.p., n.d.), 1.

2 I'm taking "millennial" to mean "a future, collective, imminent transformation of life on earth through a supernatural agency" (Christianson, *Reformers and Babylon,* 7).

3 For more information on the influence of Calvinist thought in seventeenth-century English apocalypse, see Hill, *Change and Continuity in Seventeenth-Century England,* 81–102; William Hunt, "Spectral Origins of the English Revolution: Legitimation Crisis in Early Stuart England," in Eley and Hunt, *Reviving the English Revolution,* 305–32; and Lamont, *Godly Rule.*

4 See, for instance, Patrick Collinson, *The Birthpangs of Protestant England*; Corrigan and Sayer, *The Great Arch*; and Margaret Spufford, "Puritanism and Social Control?" in *Order and Disorder in Early Modern England,* ed. Anthony Fletcher and John Stevenson (Cambridge, 1985) 41–57.

5 I would like to thank the Folger Shakespeare Library and the Institute for British Political Thought for their resources, and the members of Esther

Cope's seminar, "Preachers, Prophets and Petitioners" (Folger Shakespeare Library, May 2–June 28, 1990), for their invaluable suggestions. I owe a particular debt of gratitude, first to Esther Cope, who shares my fascination with the enigmatic Lady Eleanor Davies and whose book *Handmaid of the Holy Spirit: Dame Eleanor Davies, Never Soe Mad a Ladie* (Ann Arbor, 1992) provides a historically detailed and sensitive accounting of Davies's life and writings within both social and political contexts. I would also like to thank Stephen Baskerville (another participant in that seminar) for allowing me to see a chapter of his unpublished typescript, "Not Peace but a Sword: The Political Theology of the English Revolution." Baskerville's findings were invaluable in that they offered support to my own and provided a reservoir of pertinent quotes and source material.

6 As sects multiplied, different agendas came to the fore, many of them apocalyptic in scope. Socinians denied the divinity of Christ; Ranters, the immortality of the soul and the literalism of the Resurrection. Diggers mocked the notion of an outward heaven (Thomas, *Religion and the Decline of Magic*, 170), while Anabaptists believed that adults, not infants, should be baptized, that reception should be a voluntary decision, and that property should be owned in common. Familists (Family of Love), in turn, sought to recapture the state of innocence before the Fall and the existence of heaven and hell in this world (Hill, *The World Turned Upside Down*, 22). Some sects, like the Fifth Monarchists, who built their beliefs around a conception of a literal millennium, tended toward prophecy and apocalyptic vision more directly. Nevertheless, the majority of these separatist groups, extreme in their positions relative to the church, envisioned their own empowerment as an immediate result of some sort of apocalyptic revolution. Nor were they alone. Many of those who embraced millennial thought were not separatist at all but rather mainstream puritans who sought reform *within* the English Church.

7 Eleanor Davies, *From the lady Eleanor, her blessing to her beloved daughter* (London, 1644) 3.

8 Hill, *The World Turned Upside Down*, 26.

9 Thomas, *Religion and the Decline of Magic*, 56.

10 Sheila Rowbotham, *Women, Resistance and Revolution: A History of Women and Revolution in the Modern World* (New York, 1972) 28.

11 As it is impossible to gauge the *effect* of millennial writing on all English readers, I want to look, instead, at the formal composition of those writings, particularly at their emphases on holy hatred. I want to see how such writings discursively navigate claims of historical totality and historical particularity for both women and men, and the rhetorical and thematic concerns that they include and omit to achieve those ends.

12 Harry Rushe, "Prophecies and Propaganda, 1641 to 1651," *English Historical Review* 84 (1969) 757.

13 For apocalyptic writing's connection to revolution, see Christianson, *Reformers and Babylon*; and Hill, *The World Turned Upside Down*.

14 For a specific detailing of England's changing state mechanisms during the Civil War period, see Aylmer, *Rebellion or Revolution?*

15 As a result of strict franchise requirements for Parliamentary elections,

determined in large part by status and capital, representation, even symbolic representation, was limited to men of relatively high standing.

16 The irony of this voicing is that it makes its appearance not in support of the English state (loyalty to the king) but in rebellion against it (loyalty to the nation). That Charles I was executed on January 30, 1649, as a "traitor to the state" reveals the slippage that has occurred. In the sentence of the High Court of Justice upon the king, January 27, 1648–49, we are told: "for all which treasons and crimes this Court doth adjudge that he, the said Charles Stuart, as a tyrant, traitor, murderer, and public enemy to the good people of this nation, shall be put to death by the severing of his head from his body" (John Rushworth, vii, 1418, in Samuel Gardiner Lawson, ed., *Constitutional Documents of the Puritan Revolution, 1625–1650*, 3rd edn. ([Oxford, 1962] 380).

17 Henry Parker, *Observations upon som of his Majesties late Answers and Expresses* (n.p., 1642) 20. In the same year Edmund Calamy voices a similar sentiment, addressing parliament: "you are the Nation representatively, virtually, and eminently; you stand in the place of the whole Nation; and if you stand for Gods cause, the whole Nation doth it in you" (*Englands Looking-Glasse* [London, 1642] 45).

18 Obviously, the imposition of alternative systems of control does not ensure their success, nor does it insist on their use exclusively. Regulatory measures were still very much the domain of English law courts. Nevertheless, with an ever-growing inability to maintain successful and economically feasible methods of control through overt coercion, representatives of the law no doubt welcomed these additional and clearly operative forms of social regulation.

19 Michel Foucault, "The Subject and Power," in *Michel Foucault: Beyond Structuralism and Hermeneutics*, ed. Hubert L. Dreyfus and Paul Rabinow, trans. Leslie Sawyer, 2nd edn. (Chicago, 1982) 208–28.

20 Christina Larner, *The Thinking Peasant: Popular and Educated Belief in Pre-Industrial Culture* (Glasgow, 1982) 56, qtd. in Corrigan and Sayer, *The Great Arch*, 80. The Lateran Council of 1215 first instituted the confessional for all Catholic believers. In *Sin and Confession*, Tentler describes the relationship between confessor and penitent as regulatory. The idea of a religious caretaker – the priest – whose concerns rest equally on tending to group and personal salvation, proved particularly amenable to imitation by later state-related powers. For additional exploration of this phenomenon, see chapter 3 of this volume, 110ff.

21 Corrigan and Sayer, *The Great Arch*, 81.

22 Anna Trapnel, *The Cry of a Stone* (London, 1654) 36. Trapnel's focus on the personal in this passage is hardly atypical. All of the tracts that I have encountered take on the "particular" in one form or another. See, for instance, the specificity of such tracts as William Prynne's *Sword of Christian Magistracy Supported* (London, 1647), and Thomas Edwards's *Gangraena* (London, 1646), both of which set out to label and define "secret sins" in respect to their not so secret punishments. Many civil-war sects (even in the early days of their inception) exercised "a close supervision over the personal lives of their members . . . regulating intimate matters with which even the

church courts might have hesitated to interfere" (Thomas, *Religion and the Decline of Magic*, 153). Two items from the agenda of an Independent congregation in Northamptonshire reveal the extent to which sects would go in order to monitor and direct their members' personal lives. Brother Smith is cited "for having no conjugal affection," and Brother Campion "for proffering love to one sister whilst engaged to another" (Thomas, *Religion and the Decline of Magic*, 153).

Judith Richards ("'His Now Majestie' and the English Monarchy: The Kingship of Charles I Before 1640," *Past and Present* 113 [1986] 70–96), Kevin Sharpe ("The Image of Virtue: The Court and Household of Charles I, 1635–1642," in *The English Court: From the War of the Roses to the Civil War*, ed. David Starkey [London, 1987] 226–60), and R. Malcolm Smuts ("The Political Failure of Stuart Cultural Patronage," in *Patronage in the Renaissance*, ed. Guy Fitch Lytle and Stephen Orgel [Princeton, 1981] 165–90) provide material evidence of a growing concern with the personal in the way that Charles I separates the royal household into clearly demarcated spheres of public and private, each with its own duties and obligations.

23 Edward Boughen, *Two Sermons: The first Preached at Canterbury at the Visitation of the Lord* (London, 1630) 4, 14. Nathaniel Ward, Boughen's political opponent, shares the same philosophy, reminding parliament that "unity is the ground of perfection and perpetuity. Order is unity branched out into all parts of consociate bodies to keep them in unity and perfection; where Order failes they are disjoynted and convulsed" (*A Sermon Preached Before the Honourable House of Commons* [London, 1647] 90).

24 Abiezar Coppe, *A Fiery Flying Rolle* (n.p., 1649) unpag. While Coppe's religious vision is clearly radical (as a Ranter he advocates free love and social anarchy), the duality he describes is not. Conservative reformer Edmund Calamy acknowledges the same hierarchical paradox in outlining a program for moderate reform: "as this reformation must be personal, so also it must be national" (*Englands antidote against the plague of civil warre* [London, 1645] 4).

25 This essay foregrounds the self-regulatory "policing" aspects of apocalyptic writing and the way that they map guilt. This does not mean that the rhetoric is absolute in its power or in the way that different readers engage it. "Holy hatred" as a social enforcer is neither as effective nor as directly causal as this reading may make it seem.

26 Early writers like John Bale saw the Antichrist as a threat external to England, a threat which took shape in the pope and the Roman Catholic Church. Gradually, however, the enemy moved onto English soil and into English government, eventually becoming a litigant in a civil dispute between Arminian episcopal rule and sectarian and reformist defiance to it, between allegiance to an unsympathetic king and active rebellion against him. As a result of weakened and eventually nonexistent censorship regulations and the greater pertinency of apocalyptic literature in validating extreme social change during the war, the number of surviving prophecies, both traditional and contemporary, multiplied. Thomas lists just a few of the traditional pieces published in the 1640s: *The Prophesie of Mother Shipton* (1641); *Two strange prophesies* (1642); *Four several strange prophesies* (1642); *Seven several strange*

prophesies (1643); *Nine notable prophesies* (1644); and finally *Fourteen strange prophesies* by the end of the decade (Thomas, *Religion and the Decline of Magic*, 410). George Thomason, a London bookseller, collected over 700 pamphlets in 1645, most of them relating directly to the religio-political situations at home and many overtly apocalyptic in flavor. In the following year he drew in some 2,000 more (Christianson, *Reformers and Babylon*, 182). The 1640s also saw a more strikingly militant form of apocalyptic writing, and it is in this later form that holy hatred becomes most pronounced.

27 Christianson, *Reformers and Babylon*, 9.

28 Drawing distinctions between a sporadic presentation of history in early works like Monmouth's twelfth-century *Historia regum Britanniae* and John Foxe's more fastidious emphasis on historical accuracy and primary sources in the *Acts and Monuments*, William Haller argues that Foxe's epic constitutes a new history for the English people (*Foxe's Book of Martyrs and the Elect Nation* [London, 1963]).

29 Edmund Calamy, *Englands Looking-Glasse*, 44.

30 Eleanor Davies, *Amend, amend; Gods kingdome is at hand* (Amsterdam, 1643) 11.

31 Pilgrims traveling to the New World literalized this connection in its most dramatic form. Conceiving of America as the national fulfillment of an individual religious quest, these puritan settlers referred to themselves as "Little Israel" (Lyle Koehler, *A Search for Power: The Weaker Sex in Seventeenth-Century New England* [Urbana, 1980] 9).

32 Thomas Case, *Two Sermons lately preache at Westminster* (London, 1641) 2.23, qtd. in Baskerville, "Not Peace but a Sword," 193.

33 Foucault, "The Subject and Power," 212.

34 Beginning with Henry VIII's break with the Roman Catholic Church, the relationship between church and state in England became gradually more and more diffuse. Charles I's final decree as king, a last-ditch concession to the opposition, denied bishops the right to hold government office (Christianson, *Reformers and Babylon*, 53).

35 William Bridge, *Babylons Downfall* (London, 1641) 22.

36 Edmund Calamy, *The Noblemans Pattern of True and Real Thankfulnesse* (London, 1643) 51–52.

37 Edmund Calamy, *England's Antidote*, 25.

38 Rawson, *Constitutional Documents of the Puritan Revolution* (my emphasis), 373–74.

39 Stephen Marshall, *Meroz cursed* (London, 1641[1642]). I found Christianson's bibliography of primary sources invaluable in locating writers such as Marshall. For other useful bibliographies on apocalyptic writers, see Bryan W. Ball, *A Great Expectation: Eschatological Thought in English Protestantism to 1660* (Leiden, 1975) 247–59; Baskerville, "Not Peace But a Sword," 235–37; Patricia M. Crawford, *Women and Religion in England*, 232–64; Katharine R. Firth, *The Apocalyptic Tradition in Reformation Britain, 1530–1645* (Oxford, 1979) 255–64; Mack, *Visionary Women*; and Nigel Smith, *Perfection Proclaimed: Language and Literature in English Radical Religion, 1640–1660* (Oxford, 1989) 353–84.

40 Thomas Wilson, *Jerichoes Down-fall* (London, 1643) 40.

41 William Sedgwick, *Zions deliverance and her friends duty* (London, 1642) 39–40.
42 Calamy, *Englands Looking-Glasse*, 10.
43 Sedgwick, *Zions deliverance*, 10–11.
44 Thomas Case, *Gods rising, his enemies scattering* (London, 1644) 34.
45 Beth Nelson points out that Davies wrote and published more in her lifetime than any single English woman had to date ("Lady Elinor Davies: The Prophet as Publisher," *Women's Studies International Forum* 8.5 [1985] 403). For the most complete biography of Davies's life, see Cope, *Handmaid of the Holy Spirit*.
46 Davies's first text, *A Warning to the Dragon*, is 100 pages in length (n.p., 1625).
47 Davies's prophecies of the king's and the archbishop's executions are both corroborated in separate accounts; Laud, himself, recounts her warning of his death in a letter to the king (Theodore Spencer, "The History of an Unfortunate Lady," *Studies and Notes in Philology and Literature* 20 [1938] 53).
48 Spencer, "The History of an Unfortunate Lady," 47–48.
49 B. J. Harris, *Biographical Dictionary of British Radicals in the Seventeenth Century* (Brighton, 1982) 216; C. J. Hindle, *A Bibliography of the Printed Pamphlets and Broadsides of Lady Eleanor Douglas, the 17th Century Prophetess* (Edinburgh, 1934) 3.
50 Esther S. Cope, " 'Dame Eleanor Davies Never Soe Mad a Ladie?' " *Huntington Library Quarterly* 50 (1987) 136. In *Bethlehem signifying the house of bread*, Davies describes the episode in some detail ([n.p., 1652] 4–5).
51 Cope points out that Davies's persecutors continually emphasized the religiosity of her writing over the monarchical issues that it raised ("Dame Eleanor Davies," 137). Though this distinction is endemic to the period, it may also suggest the inability of Davies's peers to recognize female defiance outside an already "gender-coded" religious milieu.
52 Davies's writings have recently been celebrated as powerful examples of seventeenth-century female authority. For accounts that emphasize the empowerment of women's voice during the Civil War, refer to Christina Berg and Philippa Berry, "Spiritual Whoredom: An Essay on Female Prophets in the Seventeenth Century," in *1642: Literature and Power in the Seventeenth Century*, ed. Francis Barker (Essex, 1981) 37–54; Patrick Collinson, "The Role of Women in the English Reformation," *Studies in Church History* 2 (1965) 258–72; Cope, "Dame Eleanor Davies," and *Handmaid of the Holy Spirit*; Patricia M. Crawford, *Women and Religion in England*, and "Women's Published Writings 1600–1700," in Prior, *Women in English Society 1500–1800*, 211–82; Richard L. Greaves, "The Role of Women in Early English Nonconformity," *Church History* 52 (1983) 299–311; Patricia Higgins, "The Reactions of Women, with Special Reference to Women Petitioners," in *Politics, Religion and the English Civil War*, ed. Brian Manning (London, 1973) 179–224; Hilary Hinds, " 'Who May Binde Where God Hath Loosed?': Responses to Sectarian Women's Writing in the Second Half of the Seventeenth Century," in Cerasano and Wynne-Davies, eds., *Gloriana's Face*, 205–27; Elaine C. Huber, " 'A Woman must not Speak':

Quaker Women in the English Left Wing," in *Women of Spirit: Female Leadership in the Jewish and Christian Traditions*, ed. Rosemary Reuther and Eleanor McLaughlin (New York, 1979) 153–82; Peter Lake, "Feminine Piety and Personal Potency: The Emancipation of Mrs. Jane Ratcliffe," *Seventeenth Century* 2 (1987) 143–65; Phyllis Mack, "The Prophet and Her Audience: Gender and Knowledge in the World Turned Upside Down," in Eley and Hunt, *Reviving the English Revolution*, 139–52, *Visionary Women*, and "Women as Prophets During the English Civil War," *Feminist Studies* 8.1 (1982) 19–45; Rosemary Masek, "Women in an Age of Transition: 1485–1714," in *The Women of England from Anglo-Saxon Times to the Present: Interpretive Bibliographical Essays*, ed. Barbara Kanner (Hamden, 1979) 138–82; Ann Marie McEntee, " 'The [Un]Civill-Sisterhood of Oranges and Lemons': Female Petitioners and Demonstrators, 1642–53," in Holstun, *Pamphlet Wars* (London, 1992) 92–111; Brian Patton, "The Women Are Revolting? Women's Activism and Popular Satire in the English Revolution," *Journal of Medieval and Renaissance Studies* 23 (1993) 69–87; Rowbotham, *Women, Resistance and Revolution*, 15–35; Hilda Smith, "Feminism," 3–74; Keith Thomas, "Women and the Civil War Sects," *Past & Present* 13 (1958) 42–62; Rachel Trubowitz, "Female Preachers and Male Wives: Gender and Authority in Civil War England," in Holstun, *Pamphlet Wars*, 112–33; Diane Willen, "Women and Religion in Early Modern England," in *Women in Reformation and Counter-Reformation Europe: Public and Private Worlds*, ed. Sherrin Marshall (Bloomington, 1989) 140–65; Ethan Morgan Williams, "Women Preachers in the Civil War," *Journal of Modern History* 1 (1929) 561–69; and Sue Wiseman, "Unsilent Instruments and the Devil's Cushions: Authority in Seventeenth-Century Women's Prophetic Discourse," in *New Feminist Discourses: Critical Essays on Theories and Texts*, ed. Isobel Armstrong (New York, 1992) 176–96. While these authors make a persuasive case for female written authority during the civil-war years, it is equally important to recognize that such moments are always crossed by a multitude of social and political concerns and that they are not always essentially or inherently liberating. Despite a public avowal of her prophetic authority, Davies was always subject to a recognition of her talent that was based on gender and led, in her case, to repeated incarceration and penury.

53 "Even greater because humbler, she possessed a sublime nature in exceptional form and a singular modesty in charm and kindness" (my translation; S. G. Wright, "Dougle Fooleries," *Bodleian Quarterly Record* 7.3 [1932] 97). For the complete epitaph, see Alexander B. Grosart, "Memorial-Introduction," in Grosart, ed., *The Complete Works of Sir John Davies of Hereford* (New York, 1967) lii–liii.

54 Sir Archibald Douglas, self-proclaimed bastard son of King James I by a daughter of the king's tutor, Sir Peter Young, claimed as part of that lineage an age advantage of several months over Charles I (Esther S. Cope, "The Prophetic Writings of Lady Eleanor Davies" [Midday Colloquium, Folger Library, June 20, 1990] 11, and *Handmaid of the Holy Spirit*, 46–47).

55 Davies, *From the lady Eleanor, her blessing*, 17–18.

56 Davies, *A Warning to the Dragon*, 100. Davies's first husband was a royalist who advocated the divine right of kings, not their populist overthrow by men

of questionable breeding: he writes, "the King doth exercise a double power, viz. an absolute power, or *Merum Imperium,* when he doth use Prerogatives . . . which is not bound by the positive Law" (qtd. in Johan P. Sommerville, *Politics and Ideology in England, 1603–1640* [London, 1986] 37).

57 Davies's first husband, John Davies, apparently revoked her jointure, making her inheritance contingent upon her continuing widowhood. Her rights to both the Englefield and Pirton estates ran afoul when she remarried in 1626. (Cope, *Handmaid of the Holy Spirit,* 42–46).

58 The 1640s saw an amazing surge of women petitioners taking issue on "state" concerns, some of them fairly militant in character. See, for instance, McEntee, "'The [Un]Civill-Sisterhood of Oranges and Lemons'"; and Patton, "The Women Are Revolting?" Most tracts assumed traditional and largely patriarchal forms. While McEntee recognizes in these petitions tentative claims toward English political citizenship, I would argue that the majority of accounts of and by civil-war women suggest that they do not physically bear arms or consider revolution except *as wives and mothers* to men (they still petition for husband and/or family well-being, and consistently remind their readers of the primacy of that role).

59 Eleanor Davies, *The Lady Eleanor Her Appeal. Present this to Mr. Mace the Prophet of the Most High, his Messenger,* n.p., 1646, 11–13.

60 Eleanor Davies, *The Star to the Wise* (London, 1643) 7.

61 Eleanor Davies, *To the most honourable the high court of Parliament assembled* (n.p., [1642]) 2–4.

62 Eleanor Davies, *The restitution of prophecy; that buried talent to be revived* ([London?] 1652) 45.

63 Calamy, *Englands Looking-Glasse,* 10.

64 *The Star to the Wise,* 17–18.

65 For explorations that focus on the changing family and women's status within it, see Collinson, *The Birthpangs of Protestant England,* 60–93; and Spufford, "Puritanism and Social Control?" 41–57. See also chapters 2 and 3 of this book.

66 Emphasizing the temporary authority which was allowed women in religious writings during the civil-war period, Berg and Berry call on Davies as striking in her refusal to define a single subjectivity. Citing the fragmentation of her syntax and her few direct references to self, Berg and Berry suggest that she denies notions of the subject-self altogether ("Spiritual Whoredom," 45). While I agree in the main as to the importance of a subject definition in these works and its implications on gender, the analysis of Berg and Berry fails to consider the already severed subject-self in most millennial writing of the time, both male and female. They neglect to explore the combined pressures of national and individual subjectivity already inherent in the English apocalyptic tradition. Because they do not look at Davies's work within this larger context, they drastically under-emphasize the importance of the personal to her work. Davies's texts, despite their avoidance of first-person pronouns, focus almost exclusively on the self as both subject and object, to a much greater degree, in fact, than do any of her male contemporaries.

67 Davies, *The Star to the Wise,* 8.

68 Eleanor Davies, *The Everlasting Gospel. Apocalpys 14* ([London?] 1649)
   12–13.
69 Thomas M. Lennon poses an interesting parallel to this argument in his
   discussion of an increasing conflict between seventeenth-century rationalism
   and the problem of oracular speech ("Lady Oracle: Changing Conceptions of
   Authority and Reason in Seventeenth-Century Philosophy," in *Women and
   Reason*, ed. Elizabeth D. Harvey and Kathleen Okruhlik (Ann Arbor, 1992)
   39–61.
70 The anonymous *A Prophecie of the life, reign and death of William Laud*
   (London, 1644) makes the connection explicit.
71 Coppe cites one such specific instance in his description of a woman who has
   slighted him: "on this day purses shall be cut, guts let out, men stabb'd to the
   heart, womens bellies ript up, specially gammer Demases, who have forsaken
   us, and imbraced this wicked world, and married *Alexander* the Coppersmith,
   who hath done me much evill" (*A Fiery Flying Rolle*, 3). In Coppe's account,
   however, this framework is the exception rather than the rule.
72 Davies, like many of her puritan contemporaries, claims a religious foundation that is both common to many and unique to herself – reliant on a
   personal interpretation of a communally shared biblical text.
73 Davies, *The Lady Eleanor Her Appeal*, 15.
74 Davies, *The Lady Eleanor Her Appeal*, 15–16.
75 Davies, *The Lady Eleanor Her Appeal*, 22.
76 Davies, *The Lady Eleanor, Her Appeal*, 22.
77 The *OED* offers one seventeenth-century definition of "long Coats" as an
   infant's baptismal clothes.
78 Davies, *The Lady Eleanor Her Appeal*, 24.
79 Davies, *The Lady Eleanor Her Appeal*, 24.
80 Eleanor Davies, *Hells Destruction* ([London?] 1651) 12. I am tempted here to
   bring up a more recent, twentieth-century female evangelist/faith-healer/
   prophet, Ruth Carter Stapleton. Sister to one-time US president Jimmy
   Carter, Stapleton drew her worst detractors from evangelists like Jerry
   Falwell and Pat Robertson, co-religionists who accused her of both witch-
   craft and madness. Stapleton's apocalysm, like Davies's, is surprisingly
   specific in its targets: "[an evangelist] wrote a book about me," she promises
   in an interview during the late seventies, "and two days after it came out, he
   had a heart attack. I sent him a telegraph hoping he'd get well" (Flo
   Conway and Jim Siegelman, *Holy Terror: The Fundamentalist War on
   America's Freedoms in Religion, Politics and Our Private Lives* [New York,
   1982] 226). With over 300 years separating these accounts, the similarity is
   all the more chilling.
81 Michael MacDonald acknowledges that women were believed particularly
   vulnerable to emotional disturbances in the seventeenth century (*Mystical
   Bedlam: Madness, Anxiety, and Healing in Seventeenth-Century England*
   [Cambridge, 1981] 34). The connections between the limitations of female
   roles (as wife and mother) and active rebellion from them in the form of
   unusual behavior and improper action cannot be overemphasized. See also
   R. Porter, *A Social History of Madness: The World Through the Eyes of the
   Insane* (New York, 1987).

82 Cope, "Dame Eleanor Davies," 137; Spencer, "The History of an Unfortunate Lady," 51. For the entire account, see Peter Heylin, *Cyprianus Anglicus: or the History of the Life and Death, of the most Reverend and Renowned Prelate William Laud . . . Lord Archbishop of Canterbury* (London, 1668) 266.

83 Angeline Goreau, *The Whole Duty of a Woman: Female Writers in Seventeenth-Century England* (New York, 1985) 110.

84 Cope, "Dame Eleanor Davies," 138. Cope (*Handmaid of the Holy Spirit*) and Nelson ("Lady Elinor Davies") go a long way in grappling with recent and contemporary charges of madness – Cope by stressing the intersection between Davies's religious convictions and gender constraints, and Nelson by emphasizing contradictions between Davies's gender obligations and literary vocation.

85 Davies continually inserts Latin phrasing into her writing, indicating at least moderate awareness of its English translation.

86 Trapnel (*The Cry of a Stone* and *Strange and Wonderfull Newes from Whitehall* [London, 1654]), writing shortly after Davies's death, echoes the elliptical and often esoteric nature of Davies's narrative form. Trapnel's verse, supposedly spoken in trance, has been recorded by an anonymous "male" reporter (Champlin Burrage, "Anna Trapnel's Prophecies," *English Historical Review* [July 1911] 535). While I would be loathe to insist on an absolute female religious voice in this period, both women share similar syntactic and contextual patterns – patterns that suggest, if nothing else, one *available* discourse for religious women.

87 Eleanor Davies, *Ezekiel, Cap. 2* (n.p. [1647?]) 4.

88 Eleanor Davies, *Ezekiel, Cap. 2*, 14.

89 Eleanor Davies, *Apocalyps, Chap. 11*, 5.

90 Eleanor Davies, *I am the first and the last, the beginning and the ending* (n.p., 1644[1645]) 1.

91 Spencer points out that, between 1594 and 1644, thirty-eight books were published in Latin alone on the subject of anagrams ("The History of an Unfortunate Lady," 45). For more detailed information, see H. B. Wheatley, *Of Anagrams* (London, 1862).

92 As early as King Henry VIII's reign, England saw a series of laws enacted restricting the availability of the Bible for women. In 1543, Henry VIII decreed that no one under the status of gentleman could carry a Bible or read from it to others (this disallowed women of any rank direct contact with the Bible). This legal impediment was historically reinforced in mocking women's involvement in biblical exegesis and prophetic voice for the next hundred years. Francis Beaumont and John Fletcher's *The Prophetess*, published in 1647, provides contemporary evidence of the cultural devaluing of female spirituality that was to occur despite and perhaps because of an increase in women's religiosity during the civil-war years.

93 Davies, *Amend, amend; Gods kingdome is at hand*, 2.

94 Davies, *To the most honourable the high court of Parliament assembled*, 10–11.

95 Davies, *The Star to the Wise*, 9. This plaster may very well be the same one sent to Pym and the House of Commons in 1641. Pamphleteers blamed the

deed on "Romish dragons," and all assumed that the plaster had been taken from a plague victim.

96 Davies, *The Star to the Wise*, 9.

97 Davies, *The Excommunication out of Paradice* (n.p., 1647) 8–9.

98 Davies, *From the lady Eleanor*, 36.

99 Mary Cary (*The Resurrection of the Witnesses* [n.p., 1648]) and Elizabeth Poole (*A Vision Wherein is manifested the disease and cure of the kingdome* [n.p., 1648]), both writing concurrently with Davies, construct a more linear presentation of their prophetic visions, though Poole's case is an interesting one in that her syntax, originally as involved as Davies's, seems to take on a more generic form once her editor intervenes for the first time, two paragraphs into the tract. Cary's and Poole's writings are no less thematically complicated than Davies's own in their simultaneous need to authorize and instruct. See also Cary's *The Little Horns Doom and Downfall* (n.p., 1651); *A New and More Exact Mappe* (n.p., 1651); and *Twelve humble proposals* (n.p., 1653).

100 Davies, *The Everlasting Gospel*, 4–7.

101 I am borrowing this expression from the title to Suzanne Hull's excellent survey of sixteenth- and seventeenth-century writings for women: *Chaste, Silent, and Obedient: English Books for Women, 1475–1640* (San Marino, CA, 1982).

102 The king's punishment, like Laud's, is apparently personally inspired. Shortly after taking up residence near the royal palace at St. James, Davies is informed that she must leave by the king's command (Spencer, "The History of an Unfortunate Lady," 47). This eviction notice fuels her holy hatred.

103 Davies's writings are "paratactic" in form, downplaying the linear arrangement of ideas within sentences and paragraphs. In contrast, the majority of her contemporaries' works are "hypotactic." While this sort of framing tends to foreground the dramatic and poetic in Davies's language, it makes little attempt to organize points either chronologically or hierarchically. For additional information on paratactic and hypotactic language, see Erich Auerbach, *Mimesis: The Representation of Reality in Western Literature*, trans. Willard R. Trask (Princeton, 1953) 70–75, 99–121.

104 Davies, *The Lady Eleanor, Her Appeal*, A2.

105 In the Geneva Bible (1602), the account appeared as follows: "And Joseph brought unto their father their evil saying [note: 'He complained of the evil wordes & injuries, which they spake & did against him']."

106 Eleanor Davies, *Samsons legacie* (n.p., 1643) 3–4.

107 The relationship is compromised in that Davies's daughter Lucy was removed from her mother's care at the age of ten when she was married to Ferdinando, the next Earl of Hastings. There has been some speculation that the marriage was arranged to keep her from her mother's influence (Antonia Fraser, *The Weaker Vessel* [London, 1984] 155–56), though Cope finds conflicting evidence that identifies Davies as a "principall actor and mover" in the marriage agreement (*Handmaid of the Holy Spirit*, 26).

5 CONNECTIONS, QUALIFICATIONS, AND AGENDAS

1 Thomas Hobbes, *Leviathan*, ed. J. A. C. Gaskin (Oxford, 1996) esp. chapter 13.

2 See, for instance, Susanna Parr, *Susannas Apologie against the Elders* (London, 1659). In this treatise, Parr dramatizes the tremendous spiritual pressure that she faced in defying congregational will to justify her own religious convictions. The simultaneous claims that private will and public morality exert in this account illustrate the paradox.

3 For some of the more familiar voices in this dialogue, see Beilin, *Redeeming Eve*; Brant and Purkiss, *Women, Texts and Histories*; Cerasano and Wynne-Davies, *Gloriana's Face*; Grundy and Wiseman, *Women, Writing, History*; Hannay, *Silent but for the Word*; Haselkorn and Travitsky, *The Renaissance Englishwoman in Print*; Jordan, *Renaissance Feminism*; Krontiris, *Oppositional Voices*; Levin and Watson, *Ambiguous Realities*; Lewalski, *Writing Women in Jacobean England*; Travitsky and Seeff, *Attending to Women in Early Modern England*; and Woodbridge, *Women and the English Renaissance*. For critical studies that attend specifically to the social history of Renaissance women, see also Amussen, *An Ordered Society*; Patricia M. Crawford, *Women and Religion in England*; George, *Women in the First Capitalist Society*; Margaret L. King, *Women of the Renaissance*; Mack, *Visionary Women*; Prior, *Women in English Society*; and Warnicke, *Women of the English Renaissance and Reformation*.

4 I want to remind my readers that histories that appear to be comprehensive – including statistical histories that tally a large number of authors and texts – privilege certain kinds of events and behaviors only by erasing or leaving unspoken countless others.

5 In his introduction to *The Cheese and the Worms: The Cosmos of a Sixteenth-Century Miller*, Carlo Ginzburg reminds us of the methodological difficulties inherent in recovering historical evidence of non-elite European culture:

> Since historians are unable to converse with the peasants of the sixteenth century (and, in any case, there is no guarantee that they would understand them), they must depend almost entirely on written sources (and possibly archaeological evidence). These are doubly indirect for they are written, and written in general by individuals who were more or less openly attached to the dominant culture. This means that the thoughts, the beliefs, and the aspirations of the peasants and artisans of the past reach us (if and when they do) almost always through distorting viewpoints and intermediaries. (trans. John and Anne Tedeschi [Baltimore, 1980] xv)

Ginzburg's warning ought to be compounded further by a recognition of the inherent impossibility of any direct transmission of effect or intent across history and within discourse.

6 Imagining cultural histories for speakers without voice is itself a colonizing and potentially dangerous endeavor, particularly when those hypotheses are then taken for fact and used to justify current marginality.

7 In her essay, "The Tenth Muse," Stephanie Jed discovers/constructs extra-textual documentation to illustrate unwritten colonial economies.

8 For a discussion outlining the connection between social truths, civility and

science in seventeenth-century England, see Steven Shapin, *A Social History of Truth: Civility and Science in Seventeenth-Century England* (Chicago, 1994).

9 *The Midwives Book Or the whole Art of Midwifry Discovered* (London, 1671).

10 *A Mother's Blessing* (London). Two other "mother's legacies" worth scrutiny are Elizabeth Grymeston's *Miscelanea, Meditations, Memoratives* (London, 1604) and Elizabeth Joceline's *The Mothers Legacie to her unborn childe* (London, 1624).

11 Clifford, *The Diaries of Lady Anne Clifford*, ed. D. J. H. Clifford (Stroud, 1990); Mildmay, *With Faith and Physic*. See also Hoby, *Diary of Lady Margaret Hoby*; and the two sets of memoirs in Lady Anne Halkett's and Lady Ann Fanshawe's *The Memoirs of Anne, Lady Halkett and Ann, Lady Fanshawe*, ed. John Loftis (Oxford, 1979).

Bibliography

PRIMARY WORKS

Anderson, James, *Ladies of the Reformation: Memoirs of Distinguished Female Characters Belonging to the Period of the Reformation in the Sixteenth Century*, London, 1855, vol. I.

Anger, Jane, *Jane Anger her Protection for Women*, London, 1589.

Baines, Barbara J. (ed.), *Three Pamphlets on the Jacobean Antifeminist Controversy*, Delmar, NY, 1978.

Bale, John, *The Image of bothe churches after the moste wonderfull and heavenly Revelation of Sainct John the Evangelist*, Wesel, 1541.

A mysterie of inyquyte contained within the heretycall Genealogye of Ponce Pantolabus, Geneva, 1545.

Select Works of John Bale, D.D. Bishop of Ossory, Containing the Examinations of Lord Cobham, William Thorpe, and Anne Askew, and The Image of Both Churches, by Henry Christmas, Cambridge, 1968.

The vocacyon of Johan Bale to the bishoprick of Ossorie in Ireland his persecucions in the same and finall delyveraunce, [Wesel?], 1553.

Bale, John (ed.) *The first examinacyon of Anne Askewe, lately martyred in Smythfelde, by the Romysh popes upholders, with the Elucydacyon of Johan Bale*, Marpurg [Wesel], 1546.

The lattre examinacyon of Anne Askewe, lately martyred in Smythfielde, by the wycked Synagoge of Antichrist, with the Elucydacyon of Johan Bale, Marpurg [Wesel], 1547.

Beaumont, Francis, and John Fletcher, *The Double Marriage*, London, 1620.

Four Plays or Moral Representations in One, London, 1612.

The Prophetess, London, 1647.

The Spanish Curate, London, 1622.

Beilin, Elaine V. (ed.), *The Examinations of Anne Askew*, Oxford, 1996.

Bornstein, Diane (ed.), *Distaves and Dames: Renaissance Treatises for and about Women*, Delmar, NY, 1978.

Boughen, Edward, *Two Sermons: The first Preached at Canterbury at the Visitation of the Lord*, London, 1630.

Brice, Thomas, *Compendious Register in Metre*, n.p, 1559.

Bridge, William, *Babylons Downfall*, London, 1641.

Calamy, Edmund, *Englands antidote against the plague of civil warre*, London, 1645.

Englands Looking-Glasse, London, 1642.

The Noblemans Pattern of True and Real Thankfulnesse, London, 1643.

Cary, Mary, *The Little Horns Doom and Downfall*, n.p., 1651.
A New and More Exact Mappe, n.p., 1651.
The Resurrection of the Witnesses, n.p., 1648.
Twelve humble proposals, n.p., 1653.
Case, Thomas, *Gods rising, his enemies scattering*, London, 1644.
Two Sermons lately preache at Westminster, London, 1641.
Cavendish, Margaret, "Margaret Cavendish: From *A True Relation of my Birth, Breeding and Life, 1656*," in Graham, Hinds, Hobby, and Wilcox, *Her Own Life*.
Challoner, Richard, *Memoirs of Missionary Priests*, Manchester, 1803.
Clifford, Lady Anne, *The Diaries of Lady Anne Clifford*, ed. D. J. H. Clifford, Stroud, 1990.
Conset, Henry, *The Practice of the Spiritual or Ecclesiastical Courts*, London, 1685.
Coppe, Abiezar, *A Fiery Flying Rolle*, n.p., 1649.
Crandall, Coryl, *Swetnam the Woman-Hater: The Controversy and the Play*, Purdue, 1969.
Dabourne, Robert, *The Poor Man's Comfort*, London, 1617.
Davies, Eleanor, *Amend, amend; Gods kingdome is at hand*, Amsterdam, 1643.
Apocalyps, Chap. 11. Its accomplishment shewed from the lady Eleanor, n.p., n.d.
Bethlehem signifying the house of bread, n.p., 1652.
The Everlasting Gospel. Apocalyps 14, n.p., 1649.
The Excommunication out of Paradice, n.p., 1647.
Ezekiel, Cap. 2, n.p., [1647?].
From the lady Eleanor, her blessing to her beloved daughter, London, 1644.
Hells Destruction, [London?], 1651.
I am the first and the last, the beginning and the ending, n.p., 1644[5].
The Lady Eleanor Her Appeal. Present this to Mr. Mace the Prophet of the most High, his Messenger, n.p., 1646.
To the most honourable the high court of Parliament assembled, n.p., [1642?].
The restitution of prophecy; that buried talent to be revived, [London?], 1652.
Samsons legacie, n.p., 1643.
The Star to the Wise, London, 1643.
A Warning to the Dragon, n.p., 1625.
Dekker, Thomas, *The Honest Whore, Parts I and II*, London, 1604–5.
The Noble Spanish Soldier, London, 1623.
The Welsh Ambassador, London, 1623.
Dod, John, and Robert Cleaver, *A Godly Form of Household Governement: for the ordering of private Families*, London, 1598.
Dowriche, Anne, *The French Historie. that is; a lamentable discourse of three of the chiefe and most famous bloddie broiles that have happened in France for the gospell of Jesus Christ*, London, 1589.
Edward, Thomas, *Gangraena*, London, 1646.
Fitzmaurice, James, Josephine A. Roberts, Carol Barash, Eugene R. Cunnar, and Nancy A. Guitierrez (eds.), *Major Women Writers of Seventeenth-Century England*, Detroit, 1997.
Foxe, John, *The Acts and Monuments of John Foxe*, ed. George Townsend, New York, 1965, vols. I, V, VI, and VII.

Fuller, Thomas, *The Church History of Britain; from the Birth of Jesus Christ until the Year 1648*, (1655), new edn., Oxford, 1845, vol III.

Gardiner, Stephen, *A detection of the devils Sophistrie, wherewith he robbeth the unlearned people, of the true byleef in the sacrament of the aulter*, London, 1546.

Geneva Bible: The Annotated New Testament (1602 Edition), ed. Gerald T. Sheppard, New York, 1989.

Graham, Elspeth, Hillary Hinds, Elaine Hobby, and Helen Wilcox (eds.), *Her Own Life: Autobiographical Writings by Seventeenth-Century Englishwomen*, London, 1989.

Greer, Germaine (ed.), *Kissing the Rod: An Anthology of Seventeenth-Century Women's Verse*, London, 1988.

Grosart, Alexander (ed.), *The Complete Works of Sir John Davies of Hereford*, New York, 1967.

Grymeston, Elizabeth, *Miscelanea, Meditations, Memoratives*, London, 1604.

Halkett, Lady Anne, and Lady Ann Fanshawe, *The Memoirs of Anne, Lady Halkett and Ann, Lady Fanshawe*, ed. John Loftis, Oxford, 1979.

Heylin, Peter, *Cyprianus Anglicus: or the History of the Life and Death, of the most Reverend and Renowned Prelate William Laud . . . Lord Archbishop of Canterbury*, London, 1668.

Hobbes, Thomas, *Leviathan*, ed. J. A. C. Gaskin, Oxford, 1996.

Hoby, Lady Margaret, *Dairy of Lady Margaret Hoby, 1599–1605*, ed. Dorothy M. Meads, Boston, 1930.

Hooker, Richard, *The Laws of Ecclesiastical Polity*, London, 1969, vols. I and II.

How a Man May Choose a Good Wife from a Bad, London, 1602.

Joceline, Elizabeth, *The Mothers Legacie to her unborn childe*, London, 1624.

Kempe, Margery, *The Book of Margery Kempe*, ed. W. Butler-Bowden, London, 1936.

Latz, Dorothy L. (ed.), *"Glow-Worm Light": Writings of 17th Century English Recusant Women from Original Manuscripts*, Salzburg, 1989.

Leigh, Dorothy, *A Mother's Blessing*, London, 1616.

The London Prodigal, London, 1604.

Mahl, Mary, and Helene Koon (eds.), *The Female Spectator: English Women Writers Before 1800*, Bloomington, 1977.

Makin, Bathshua, "An Essay to Revive the Ancient Education of Gentlewomen," in Mahl and Koon, *The Female Spectator*.

Marshall, Stephen, *Meroz cursed*, London, 1641[1642].

Marx, Karl, *Capital*, London, 1967, vol. I.

Mildmay, Lady Grace, *With Faith and Physic: The Life of a Tudor Gentlewoman Lady Grace Mildmay, 1552–1620*, ed. Linda Pollock, New York, 1995.

Milton, John, *The Masque at Ludlow*, in *John Milton: Complete Poems and Major Prose*, ed. Merritt Hughes, New York, 1957.

Selected Prose, ed. C. A. Patrides, Columbia, MO, 1985.

Munda, Constantia, *The Worming of a Mad Dogge*, London, 1617.

Mush, John, "The Life of Margaret Clitherow," in Morris, *The Troubles of our Catholic Forefathers*, vol. III.

"Notes by a Prisoner in Ousebridge Kidcote," in Morris, *The Troubles of our Catholic Forefathers*, vol. III.

Parker, Henry, *Observations upon som of his Majesties late Answers and Expresses*, n.p., 1642.

Peck, Francis, *Desiderata curiosa: or a Collection of Divers Scarse and Curious Pieces Relating Chiefly to Matters of English History*, 2 vols., London, 1779, vol. II.

Peele, George, *The Old Wives Tale*, ed. Patricia Binnie, Baltimore, 1980.

Peryn, William, *Thre notable and godley sermons*, London, 1546.

Poole, Elizabeth, *A Vision Wherein is manifested the disease and cure of the kingdome*, n.p., 1648.

A Prophecie of the life, reign and death of William Laud, London, 1644.

Prynne, William, *Sword of Christian Magistracy Supported*, London, 1647.

Rawson, Samuel Gardiner (ed.), *Constitutional Documents of the Puritan Revolution, 1625–1650*, 3rd edn., Oxford, 1962.

Rowley, William, *All's Lost by Lust*, London, 1622.

Sampson, William, *The Vow-Breaker, or the Fair Maid of Clifton*, London, 1625.

Scobell, Henry, *A Collection of Acts and Ordinances of Parliament, 1640–1656*, London, 1658, vol. II.

Sedgwick, William, *Zions deliverance and her friends duty*, London, 1642.

Shakespeare, William, *Measure for Measure*, ed. J. W. Lever, Arden Shakespeare, London, 1986.

Sharp, Jane, *The Midwives Book Or the whole Art of Midwifry Discovered*, London, 1671.

Sheperd, Simon (ed.), *The Women's Sharp Revenge: Five Women's Pamphlets from the Renaissance*, London, 1985.

Sowernam, Ester, *Ester hath hang'd Haman*, London, 1617.

Speght, Rachel, *A Mouzell for Melastomus*, London, 1617.

Stow, John, *The Annales of England . . . untill this present yeere 1592*, London, 1592.

Strype, John, *Ecclesiastical Memorials*, London, 1721, vol. I.

Stubbes, Philip, *Crystal Glas for Christian Women*, London, 1592.

Swetnam, Joseph, *Araignment of Lewde, idle, froward and unconstant women*, London, 1615.

Swinburne, Henry, *A Treatise of Spousals or Matrimonial Contracts*, n.p., 1685.

T.E., *The Lawes Resolutions of Womens Rights*, London, 1616.

Tanner, J. R., *Tudor Constitutional Documents AD 1485–1603 with an Historical Commentary*, Cambridge, 1951.

Trapnel, Anna, *The Cry of a Stone*, London, 1654.

Strange and Wonderfull Newes from Whitehall, London, 1654.

Travitsky, Betty S. (ed.), *The Paradise of Woman: Writings by Englishwomen of the Renaissance*, Westport, 1981.

Tyndale, William, *Tyndale's New Testament*, ed. David Daniell, New Haven, 1989.

Ward, Nathaniel, *A Sermon Preached Before the Honourable House of Commons*, London, 1647.

Whateley, William, *A Bride-Bush, or A Wedding Sermon*, [London], 1617.

Wheathill, Anne, *A handfull of holesome though homely hearbes, gathered out of the godly garden of Godes most holy word*, London, 1584.

Wheatley, H. B., *Of Anagrams*, London, 1862.

Wilson, Thomas, *Jerichoes Down-Fall*, London, 1643.

Wriothesley, Charles A., *A Chronicle of England During the Reigns of the Tudors, from AD 1485–1559*, 2 vols., Westminster, 1875–77.

SECONDARY WORKS

Adorno, Theodore W., *Negative Dialectics*, New York, 1973.

Agnew, Jean-Christophe, *Worlds Apart: The Market and the Theater in Anglo-American Thought, 1550–1750*, Cambridge, 1986.

Alcoff, Linda, "Cultural Feminism versus Post-Structuralism: The Identity Crisis in Feminist Theory," *Signs* 13 (1988): 405–36.

Allison, A. F., and D. M. Rogers (eds.), *A Catalogue of Catholic Books in English Printed Abroad or Secretly in England, 1558–1640*, London, 1968.

Althusser, Louis, "Ideology and Ideological State Apparatuses," in his *"Lenin and Philosophy" and Other Essays*, New York, 1971.

Amussen, Susan Dwyer, *An Ordered Society: Gender and Class in Early Modern England*, Oxford, 1988.

Anderson, Benedict R., *Imagined Communities: Reflections on the Origin and Spread of Nationalism*, London, 1983.

Anstruther, Godfrey, *The Seminary Priests: A Dictionary of the Secular Clergy of England and Wales, 1558–1850*, Ware, Herts., 1969.

Armstrong, Nancy, *Desire and Domestic Fiction: A Political History of the Novel*, New York, 1987.

Aronowitz, Stanley, *The Crisis in Historical Materialism*, New York, 1981.

Auerbach, Erich, *Mimesis: The Representation of Reality in Western Literature*, trans. Willard R. Trask, Princeton, 1953.

Aveling, J. C. H., *Catholic Recusancy in the City of York, 1558–1791*, St. Albans, Herts., 1970.

Aylmer, G. E., *The King's Servants: The Civil Service of Charles I: 1625–1642*, London, 1974.

Rebellion or Revolution? England, 1640–1660, Oxford, 1986.

Baines, Barbara J., "Assaying the Power of Chastity in *Measure for Measure*," *Studies in English Literature* 30 (1990): 283–301.

Ball, Bryan W., *A Great Expectation: Eschatological Thought in English Protestantism to 1660*, Leiden, 1975.

Barnett, Mary Jane, "Tyndale's Heretical Translation: Lollards, Lutherans, and an Economy of Circulation," in *Renaissance Papers, 1996*, ed. George Watten Williams and Philip Rollinson, Columbia, SC, 1996.

Baskerville, Stephen, "Not Peace But a Sword: The Political Theology of the English Revolution," Unpublished typescript.

Beilin, Elaine V., "Anne Askew's Self-Portrait in the Examinations," in Hannay, *Silent but for the Word*.

Redeeming Eve: Women Writers of the English Renaissance, Princeton, 1987.

Belsey, Catherine, *The Subject of Tragedy: Identity & Difference in Renaissance Drama*, London, 1985.

Berg, Christina, and Philippa Berry, "Spiritual Whoredom: An Essay on Female Prophets in the Seventeenth Century," in *1642: Literature and Power in the Seventeenth Century*, ed. Francis Barker, Essex, 1981.

Best, Michael H., and William E. Connolly, "Politics and Subjects," *Socialist Review* 9 (1979): 75–99.

Birje-Patil, J., "Marriage Contracts in *Measure for Measure*," *Shakespeare Studies* 5 (1969): 106–11.

Bloch, Ruth, "Untangling the Roots of Modern Sex Roles: Four Centuries of Change," *Signs* 4 (1978): 237–52.

Bonfield, Lloyd, Richard M. Smith, and Keith Wrightson (eds.), *The World We Have Gained: Histories of Population and Social Structure, Essays Presented to Peter Laslett on His Seventieth Birthday*, Oxford, 1986.

Bossy, John, "The Character of Elizabethan Catholicism," *Past & Present* 21 (1962): 39–59.

The English Catholic Community, 1570–1850, London, 1975.

Bourdieu, Pierre, *Outline of a Theory of Practice*, trans. Richard Nice. Cambridge, 1977.

Boxer, Marilyn, and Jean H. Quataert, "Introduction: Restoring Women to History," in *Connecting Spheres: Women in the Western World, 1500 to the Present*, ed. Marilyn J. Boxer and Jean H. Quataert, New York, 1987.

Brant, Clare, and Diane Purkiss (eds.) *Women, Texts and Histories, 1575–1760*, London and New York, 1992.

Breitenberg, Mark. "The Flesh Made Word: Foxe's *Acts and Monuments*," *Renaissance and Reformation* 25 (1989): 381–407.

Brodsky, Vivien, "Widows in Late Elizabethan London: Remarriage, Economic Opportunity and Family Orientations," in Bonfield, Smith, and Wrightson, *The World We Have Gained.*

Burrage, Champlin, "Anna Trapnel's Prophecies," *English Historical Review* (July 1911): 526–35.

Burstyn, Varda, "Masculine Dominance and the State," in *Socialist Register 1983*, London, 1983.

Bynum, Carolyn Walker, *Holy Feast and Holy Fast: The Religious Significance of Food to Medieval Women*, Berkeley, 1987.

Jesus as Mother: Studies in the Spirituality of the High Middle Ages, Berkeley, 1982.

Camden, Carroll, *The Elizabethan Woman: A Panorama of English Womanhood, 1540–1640*, rev. edn., New York, 1975.

Carroll, Berenice A. (ed.), *Liberating Women's History: Theoretical and Critical Essays*, Urbana, 1976.

Cerasano, S. P., and Marion Wynne-Davies (eds.) *Gloriana's Face: Women, Public and Private, in the English Renaissance*, Detroit, 1992.

Chartier, Roger (ed.), *A History of Private Life*, vol. III, *Passions of the Renaissance*, Cambridge, MA, 1989.

Christianson, Paul, *Reformers and Babylon: English Apocalyptic Visions from the Reformation to the Eve of the Civil War*, Toronto, 1978.

Claridge, Mary, *Margaret Clitherow [1556?–1586]*, New York, 1966.

Clay, C. G. A., *Economic Expansion and Social Change: England 1500–1700*. 2 vols., Cambridge, 1984.

Clifton, Robin, "The Popular Fear of Catholics During the English Revolution," *Past & Present* 52 (1971): 23–55.

Cockburn, J. S., *Crime in England, 1550–1800*, Princeton, 1977.

A History of English Assizes, 1558–1714, Cambridge, 1972.

Collinson, Patrick, *The Birthpangs of Protestant England: Religious and Cultural Change in the Sixteenth and Seventeenth Centuries*, London, 1988.

"The Role of Women in the English Reformation," *Studies in Church History* 2 (1965): 258–72.

Conway, Flo, and Jim Siegelman, *Holy Terror: The Fundamentalist War on America's Freedoms in Religion, Politics and Our Private Lives*, New York, 1982.

Cope, Esther S., "'Dame Eleanor Davies Never Soe Mad a Ladie?'" *Huntington Library Quarterly* 50 (1987): 133–44.

Handmaid of the Holy Spirit: Dame Eleanor Davies, Never Soe Mad a Ladie, Ann Arbor, 1992.

"The Prophetic Writings of Lady Eleanor Davies" (Midday Colloquium) Folger Library, June 20, 1990: 1–19.

Corrigan, Philip, and Derek Sayer, *The Great Arch: English State Formation and Cultural Revolution*, Oxford, 1985.

Corthell, Ronald J., "'The Secrecy of Man': Recusant Discourse and the Elizabethan Subject," *English Literary Renaissance* 19 (1989): 272–90.

Crandall, Coryl, "The Cultural Implications of the Swetnam Anti-Feminist Controversy," *Journal of Popular Culture* 2 (1968): 136–48.

Crawford, Anne, Tony Hayter, Ann Hughes, Frank Prochaska, Pauline Stafford, and Elizabeth Vallance (eds.), *The Europa Biographical Dictionary of British Women: Over 1000 Notable Women from Britain's Past*, London, 1983.

Crawford, Patricia M., *Women and Religion in England, 1500–1720*, London and New York, 1993.

"Women's Published Writings, 1600–1700," in Prior, *Women in English Society, 1500–1800*.

Cross, Claire, *Church and People, 1450–1660: The Triumph of the Laity in the English Church*, Atlantic Highlands, NJ, 1976.

Davies, Kathleen, "Continuity and Change in Literary Advice on Marriage," in Outhwaite, *Marriage and Society*.

De Lauretis, Teresa, *Alice Doesn't: Feminism, Semiotics, Cinema*, Bloomington, 1984.

"The Essence of the Triangle or, Taking the Risk of Essentialism Seriously: Feminist Theory in Italy, the US, and Britain," *Differences* 1(1988): 3–37.

Dickens, A. G., *The English Reformation*, New York, 1964.

Lollards and Protestants in the Diocese of York, 1509–1558, London, 1959.

Dickens, A. G., and John Tonkin, *The Reformation in Historical Thought*, Harvard, 1985.

Dodds, Madeleine Hope, and Ruth Dodds, *The Pilgrimage of Grace, 1536–1537, and the Exeter Conspiracy, 1538*, London, 1971.

Dollimore, Jonathan, "Transgression and Surveillance in *Measure for Measure*," in *Political Shakespeare: New Essays in Cultural Materialism*, ed. Jonathan Dollimore and Alan Sinfield, Ithaca, 1985.

Duffy, Eamon, *The Stripping of the Altars: Traditional Religion in England, c. 1400–c. 1580*, New Haven, 1992.

Eaton, Sara J., "Presentations of Women in the English Popular Press," in Levin and Watson, *Ambiguous Realities*.

Eccles, Audrey, *Obstetrics and Gynaecology in Tudor and Stuart England*, Kent, OH, 1982.

Eley, Geoff, and William Hunt (eds.), *Reviving the English Revolution: Reflections and Elaborations on the Work of Christopher Hill*, London, 1988.

Elliott, Vivien Brodsky, "Single Women in the London Marriage Market: Age, Status and Mobility, 1598–1619," in Outhwaite, *Marriage and Society*.

Elton, G. R., *Policy and Police: The Enforcement of the Reformation in the Age of Thomas Cromwell*, Cambridge, 1972.

Reform and Reformation – England, 1509–1558, Cambridge, 1977.

Emmison, F. G., *Elizabethan Life: Morals & the Church Courts*, Chelmsford, 1973.

Ezell, Margaret J. M., *Writing Women's Literary History*, Baltimore, 1993.

Fairfield, Leslie P., *John Bale, Mythmaker for the English Reformation*, West Lafayette, IN, 1976.

Firth, Katharine R., *The Apocalyptic Tradition in Reformation Britain, 1530–1645*, Oxford, 1979.

Foucault, Michel, *Power/Knowledge: Selected Interviews & Other Writings 1972–1977*, ed. Colin Gordon, trans. Leo Marshall, John Mepham, and Kate Soper, New York, 1980.

"The Subject and Power," in *Michel Foucault: Beyond Structuralism and Hermeneutics*, ed. Hubert L. Dreyfus and Paul Rabinow, trans. Leslie Sawyer, 2nd edn., Chicago, 1982.

Fraser, Antonia, *The Weaker Vessel*, London, 1984.

Frye, Susan, *Elizabeth I: The Competition for Representation*, Oxford, 1993.

"The Myth of Elizabeth at Tilbury," *Sixteenth Century Journal* 23 (1992): 95–114.

Fumerton, Patricia, *Cultural Aesthetics: Renaissance Literature and the Practice of Social Ornament*, Chicago, 1991.

Gadol, Joan Kelly, "Did Women Have a Renaissance?" in her *Becoming Visible: Women in European History*, Boston, 1987.

George, Margaret, *Women in the First Capitalist Society: Experiences in Seventeenth-Century England*, Urbana, IL, 1988.

Giddens, Anthony, *Central Problems in Social Theory: Action, Structure, and Contradiction in Social Analysis*, Berkeley, 1979.

Ginzburg, Carlo, *The Cheese and the Worms: The Cosmos of a Sixteenth-Century Miller*, trans. John and Anne Tedeschi, Baltimore, 1980.

Goldberg, Jonathan, *James I and the Politics of Literature: Jonson, Shakespeare, Donne, and their Contemporaries*, Baltimore, 1983.

Gordon, Ann D., Mari Jo Buhle, and Nancy Schrom Dye, "The Problem of Women's History," in Caroll, *Liberating Women's History*.

Goreau, Angeline, *The Whole Duty of a Woman: Female Writers in Seventeeth-Century England*, New York, 1985.

Greaves, Richard L., "The Role of Women in Early English Nonconformity," *Church History* 52 (1983): 299–311.

Greenblatt Stephen, Introduction to "The Forms of Power and the Power of Forms in the Renaissance," *Genre* 15 (1982): 3–6.

Grundy, Isobel, and Susan Wiseman (eds.), *Women, Writing, History, 1640–1740*, Athens, GA, 1992.

Gunn, S. J., *Charles Brandon, Duke of Suffolk, c. 1484–1545*, Oxford, 1988.

Gurr, Andrew, *Playgoing in Shakespeare's London*, Cambridge, 1987.

Guy, John, *Tudor England*, Oxford, 1988.

Habermas, Jorgen, "Psychic Thermidor and the Rebirth of Rebellious Subjectivity," *Berkeley Journal of Sociology* 24.5 (1980): 1–12.

Hackett, Helen, *Virgin Mother, Maiden Queen: Elizabeth I and the Cult of the Virgin Mary*, New York, 1995.

Hadfield, Andrew, *Literature, Politics and National Identity*, Cambridge, 1994.

Hageman, Elizabeth H., "Recent Studies in Women Writers of the English Seventeenth Century [1604–1674]," *English Literary Renaissance* 18 (1988): 138–67.

"Recent Studies in Women Writers of Tudor England," *English Literary Renaissance* 17 (1987): 409–25.

Haigh, Christopher, *English Reformations: Religion, Politics, and Society under the Tudors*, Oxford, 1993.

"From Monopoly to Minority: Catholicism in Early Modern England," *Transactions of the Royal Historical Society*, 5th ser., 31 (1980): 129–47.

Hall, Catherine, "The Early Formation of Victorian Domestic Ideology," in *Fit Work for Women*, ed. Sandra Burman, London, 1979.

Haller, William, *Foxe's Book of Martyrs and the Elect Nation*, London, 1963.

Halley, Janet E., "Equivocation and the Legal Conflict over Religious Identity in Early Modern England," *Yale Journal of Law and the Humanities* 3 (1991): 33–52.

Hamilton, Don Adam, *The Chronicle of the English Augustinian Canonesses Regular of the Lateran, at St. Monica's in Louvain* (1548–1625), 2 vols. Edinburgh, 1904.

Hannay, Margaret P. (ed.), *Silent but for the Word: Tudor Women as Patrons, Translators, and Writers of Religious Works*, Kent, OH, 1985.

Harding, Alan, *A Social History of English Law*, Baltimore, 1966.

Harding, Davis P., "Elizabethan Betrothals and *Measure for Measure*," *Journal of English and Germanic Philology* 49 (1950): 129–58.

Harris, B. J., *Biographical Dictionary of British Radicals in the Seventeenth Century*, ed. Richard L. Greaves and Robert Zaller, Brighton, 1982.

Harris, Jesse W., *John Bale: A Study in the Minor Literature of the Reformation*, Illinois Studies in Language and Literature, vol. 25, No. 4, Urbana, IL, 1940.

Hartley, T. E., *Elizabeth's Parliaments: Queen, Lords and Commons, 1559–1601*, Manchester, 1992.

Haselkorn, Anne M., and Betty S. Travitsky (eds.), *The Renaissance Englishwoman in Print: Counterbalancing the Canon*, Amherst, 1990.

Heath, Stephen, "The Turn of the Subject," *Cine-Tracts* 8 (1979): 32–48.

Helgerson, Richard, *Forms of Nationhood: The Elizabethan Writing of England*, Chicago, 1992.

Henderson, Katherine Usher, and Barbara F. McManus, *Half Humankind: Contexts and Texts of the Controversy about Women in England, 1540–1640*, Urbana, IL, 1985.

Henriques, Julian, *Changing the Subject: Psychology, Social Regulation and Subjectivity*, New York, 1984.

Hibbard, Caroline M., "Early Stuart Catholicism: Revisions and Re-Revisions," *Journal of Modern History* 52 (1980): 1–33.

Higgins, Patricia, "The Reactions of Women, with Special Reference to Women Petitioners," in *Politics, Religion and the English Civil War*, ed. Brian Manning, London, 1973.

Hill, Christopher, *Change and Continuity in Seventeenth-Century England*, London, 1974.

The World Turned Upside Down: Radical Ideas During the English Revolution, New York, 1972.

Hindle, C. J., *A Bibliography of the Printed Pamphlets and Broadsides of Lady Eleanor Douglas, the 17th Century Prophetess*, Edinburgh, 1934.

Hinds, Hilary, "'Who May Binde Where God Hath Loosed?': Responses to Sectarian Women's Writing in the Second Half of the Seventeenth Century," in Cerasano and Wynne-Davies, *Gloriana's Face*.

Holstun, James (ed.), *Pamphlet Wars: Prose in the English Revolution*, London, 1992.

Houlbrooke, Ralph A., *Church Courts and the People During the English Reformation, 1520–1570*, Oxford, 1979.

The English Family, 1450–1700, London, 1984.

Howard, Jean E., "The New Historicism in Renaissance Studies," *English Literary Renaissance* 16 (1986): 13–43.

Huber, Elaine C., "'A Woman must not Speak': Quaker Women in the English Left Wing," in *Women of Spirit: Female Leadership in the Jewish and Christian Traditions*, ed. Rosemary Reuther and Eleanor McLaughlin, New York, 1979.

Hull, Suzanne W., *Chaste, Silent, and Obedient: English Books for Women, 1475–1640*, San Marino, CA, 1982.

Hunt, William, "Spectral Origins of the English Revolution: Legitimation Crisis in Early Stuart England," in Eley and Hunt, *Reviving the English Revolution*.

Ingram, Martin, "Spousals Litigation in the English Ecclesiastical Courts, c. 1350–1640," in Outhwaite, *Marriage and Society*.

Izard, Thomas C. (ed.), *George Whetstone: Mid-Elizabethan Gentleman of Letters*, New York, 1942.

Jameson, Fredric, *The Political Unconscious*, Ithaca, 1981.

Jed, Stephanie, "The Tenth Muse: Gender, Rationality and the Marketing of Knowledge," in *Women, "Race" and Writing in the Early Modern Period*, ed. Margo Hendricks and Patricia Parker, New York, 1993.

Jessop, Bob, *Capitalist State: Marxist Theories and Methods*, New York, 1982.

Jones, Ann Rosalind, "Counterattacks on 'the Bayter of Women': Three Pamphleteers of the Early Seventeenth Century," in Haselkorn and Travitsky, *The Renaissance Englishwoman in Print*.

"Nets and Bridles: Early Modern Conduct Books and Sixteenth-Century Women's Lyric," in *The Ideology of Conduct: Essays on Literature and the History of Sexuality,* ed. Nancy Armstrong and Leonard Tennenhouse, New York, 1987.

Jordan, Constance, "Gender and Justice in *Swetnam the Woman-Hater*," *Renaissance Drama* 18 (1987): 149–69.

Renaissance Feminism: Literary Texts and Political Models, Ithaca, 1990.

Kamps, Ivo, "Ruling Fantasies and the Fantasies of Rule: *The Phoenix* and *Measure for Measure*," *Studies in Philology* 42 (1995): 248–73.

Kaplan, Cora, *Sea Changes: Essays on Culture and Feminism*, London, 1982.

Kendall, Ritchie, *Drama of Dissent*, Chapel Hill, 1986.

Kieckhefer, Richard, *Unquiet Souls: Fourteenth-Century Saints and their Religious Milieu*, Chicago, 1984.

King, John, *English Reformation Literature: The Tudor Origins of the Protestant Religion*, Princeton, 1982.

"Patronage and Piety: The Influence of Catherine Parr," in Hannay, *Silent but for the Word*.

"Queen Elizabeth I: Representations of the Virgin Queen," *Renaissance Quarterly* 43 (1990): 30–74.

King, Margaret L., *Women of the Renaissance*, Chicago, 1991.

Knott, John R., *Discourses of Martyrdom in English Literature, 1563–1694*, Cambridge, 1993.

Koehler, Lyle, *A Search for Power: The Weaker Sex in Seventeenth-Century New England*, Urbana, IL, 1980.

Kohler, Charlotte, "Elizabethan Woman of Letters, the Extent of her Literary Activity," Ph.D. diss., University of Virginia, 1936.

Krontiris, Tina, *Oppositional Voices: Women as Writers and Translators of Literature in the English Renaissance*, London, 1992.

LaCapra, Dominick, *Rethinking Intellectual History*, Ithaca, 1983.

Laclau, Ernesto, and C. Mouffe, *Hegemony and Socialist Strategy*, London, 1985.

Lake, Peter, "Feminine Piety and Personal Potency: The Emancipation of Mrs. Jane Ratcliffe," *Seventeeth Century* 2 (1987): 143–65.

Lamont, William, *Godly Rule: Politics and Religion, 1603–1660*, London, 1969.

Laqueur, Thomas, *Making Sex: Body and Gender from the Greeks to Freud*, Cambridge, 1990.

Laslett, Peter, Karla Oosterveen, and Richard M. Smith, *Bastardy and its Comparative History*, London, 1980.

Lennon, Thomas M., "Lady Oracle: Changing Conceptions of Authority and Reason in Seventeenth-Century Philosophy," in *Women and Reason*, ed. Elizabeth D. Harvey and Kathleen Okruhlik, Ann Arbor, 1992.

Leonard, E. M., *The Early History of English Poor Relief*, Cambridge, 1900.

Levin, Carole, *"The Heart and Stomach of a King": Elizabeth I and the Politics of Sex and Power*, Philadelphia, 1994.

Levin, Carole, and Jeannie Watson (eds.), *Ambiguous Realities: Women in the Middle Ages and Renaissance*, Detroit, 1987.

Levine, David, and Keith Wrightson, "The Social Context of Illegitimacy in Early Modern England," in Laslett, Smith, and Oosterveen, *Bastardy and its Comparative History*.

Lewalski, Barbara, *Writing Women in Jacobean England*, Boston, 1993.

Leys, Mary D. R., *Catholics in England, 1559–1829: A Social History*, New York, 1961.

Loades, David, *Politics and Nation, 1450–1660: Obedience, Resistance and Public Order*, 4th edn., London, 1992.

Politics, Censorship and the English Reformation, London, 1991.

Lukacs, Georg, *History and Class Consciousness*, Cambridge, 1971.

MacCaffrey, William, *Queen Elizabeth and the Making of Policy, 1572–88*, Princeton, 1981.

MacDonald, Michael, *Mystical Bedlam: Madness, Anxiety, and Healing in Seventeenth-Century England*, Cambridge, 1981.

Mack, Phyllis, "The Prophet and Her Audience: Gender and Knowledge in the World Turned Upside Down," in Eley and Hunt, *Reviving the English Revolution*.

Visionary Women: Ecstatic Prophecy in Seventeenth-Century England, Berkeley, 1992.

"Women as Prophets During the English Civil War," *Feminist Studies* 8 (1982): 19–45.

MacKinnon, Catherine A., "Feminism, Marxism, Method and the State," *Signs* 7 (1982): 515–44.

MacLean, Ian, *The Renaissance Notion of Woman: A Study in the Fortunes of Scholasticism and Medical Science in European Intellectual Life*, Cambridge, 1980.

Macleod, Alison, *The Heretic*, Boston, 1966.

Manning, Anne, *The Lincolnshire Tragedy: Passages in the Life of the Faire Gospeller, Mistress Anne Askew*, London, 1866, reprint, New York, 1966.

Martin, J. W., *Religious Radicals in Tudor England*, London, 1989.

Masek, Rosemary, "Women in an Age of Transition: 1485–1714," in *The Women of England from Anglo-Saxon Times to the Present: Interpretive Bibliographical Essays*, ed. Barbara Kanner, Hamden, 1979.

Matchinske, Megan, "Credible Consorts: What Happens When Shakespeare's Sisters Enter the Syllabus?" *Shakespeare Quarterly* 47 (1996): 433–50.

Maus, Katharine Eisaman, "Proof and Consequences: Inwardness and Its Exposure in the English Renaissance," *Representations* 34 (1991): 29–52.

McEachern, Claire, *The Poetics of English Nationhood, 1590–1612*, Cambridge, 1996.

McEntee, Ann Marie, "'The [Un]Civill-Sisterhood of Oranges and Lemons': Female Petitioners and Demonstrators, 1642–53," in Holstun, *Pamphlet Wars*.

McGowan, John, *Postmodernism and Its Critics*, Ithaca, 1991.

McGrath, Patrick, "The Bloody Questions Reconsidered," *Recusant History* 20 (1991): 305–19.

Papists and Puritans Under Elizabeth I, London, 1967.

McIntosh, Mary, "The State and the Oppression of Women," in *Feminism and Materialism: Women and Modes of Production*, ed. Annette Kuhn and Ann Marie Wolpe, London, 1982.

McQuade, Paula, "'Except that they had offended the Lawe': Gender and Jurisprudence in *The Examinations of Anne Askew*," *Literature & History* 3 (1994): 1–14.

Merchant, Carolyn, *The Death of Nature: Women, Ecology, and the Scientific Revolution*, New York, 1980.

Milsom, S. F. C., *Historical Foundations of the Canon Law*, 2nd edn., London, 1981.

Milward, Peter, *Religious Controversies of the Elizabethan Age: A Survey of Printed Sources*, Lincoln, 1977.

Montrose, Louis A., "*A Midsummer Night's Dream* and the Shaping Fantasies of Elizabethan Culture: Gender, Power, Form," in *Rewriting the Renaissance: The Discourses of Sexual Difference in Early Modern Europe*, ed. Margaret W. Ferguson, Maureen Quilligan, and Nancy J. Vickers, Chicago, 1986.

"Renaissance Literary Studies and the Subject of History," *English Literary Renaissance* 16 (1986): 5–12.

"The Work of Gender in the Discourse of Discovery," *Representations* 33 (1991): 1–41.

Moore, Barrington, Jr., *Privacy: Studies in Social and Cultural History*, Armonk, NY, 1984.

Morely, D., "Texts, Readers, Subjects," in *Culture, Media, Language: Working Papers in Cultural Studies, 1972–79*, London, 1980.

Morris, John (ed.), *The Troubles of our Catholic Forefathers Related by Themselves*, 3 vols., London, 1877.

Mueller, Janel, *The Native Tongue and the Word: Developments in English Prose Style, 1380–1580*, Chicago, 1984.

Mullaney, Stephen, *The Place of the Stage: License, Play, and Power in Renaissance England*, Chicago, 1988.

Nagarajan, S., "*Measure for Measure* and Elizabethan Betrothals," *Shakespeare Quarterly* 14 (1963): 115–19.

Neale, J. E., *Elizabeth I and her Parliaments, 1559–1581*, New York, 1958, vol. II.

Nelson, Beth, "Lady Elinor Davies: The Prophet as Publisher," *Women's Studies International Forum* 8 (1985): 403–9.

Newman, Karen, *Fashioning Femininity and English Renaissance Drama*, Chicago, 1991.

Orgel, Stephen, *The Illusion of Power: Political Theater in the English Renaissance*, Berkeley, 1975.

Orlin, Lena Cowen, *Private Matters and Public Culture in Post-Reformation England*, Ithaca, 1994.

Otten, Charlotte F. (ed.), *English Women's Voices: 1540–1700*, Gainesville, FL, 1992.

Outhwaite, R. B. (ed.), *Marriage and Society: Studies in the Social History of Marriage*, London, 1981.

Oxford English Dictionary, prepared by J. A. Simpson and E. S. C. Weiner, 2nd edn., Oxford, 1989.

Patton, Brian, "The Women Are Revolting? Women's Activism and Popular Satire in the English Revolution," *Journal of Medieval and Renaissance Studies* 23 (1993): 69–87.

Pechter, Edward, "The New Historicism and Its Discontents," *PMLA* 102 (1987): 292–303.

Pollen, John Hungerford, *The English Catholics in the Reign of Queen Elizabeth: A Study of their Politics, Civil Life and Government*, New York, 1971.

Porter, R., *A Social History of Madness: The World Through the Eyes of the Insane*, New York, 1987.

Powell, Chilton Latham, *English Domestic Relations, 1487–1653: A Study of Matrimony and Family Life in Theory and Practice as Revealed by the Literature, Law, and History of England*, New York, 1972.

Power, Eileen, *Medieval English Nunneries, c. 1275–1535*, Cambridge, 1922.

Powers, Alan W., " 'Meaner Parties': Spousal Conventions and Oral Culture in *Measure for Measure* and *All's Well That Ends Well*," *Upstart Crow* 8 (1978): 28–41.

Prest, Wilfred R., *The Inns of Court under Elizabeth I and the Early Stuarts: 1590–1640*, London, 1972.

Prior, Mary (ed.), *Women in English Society 1500–1800*, London and New York, 1985.

Pritchard, Arnold, *Catholic Loyalism in Elizabethan England*, Chapel Hill, 1979.

Purkiss, Diane, "Material Girls: The Seventeenth-Century Woman Debate," in Brant and Purkiss, *Women, Texts and Histories*.

Reed, A. W., "The Regulation of the Book Trade Before the Proclamation of 1538," *Bibliographic Society* 15 (1917–19): 158–62.

Richards, Judith, " 'His Now Majestie' and the English Monarchy: The Kingship of Charles I Before 1640," *Past & Present* 113 (1986): 70–96.

Riley, Denise, *Am I that Name?: Feminism and the Category of "Women" in History*, Minneapolis, 1988.

Roberts, John R. (ed.), *A Critical Anthology of English Recusant Devotional Prose, 1558–1603*, Pittsburgh, 1966.

Rose, Elliot, *Cases of Conscience: Alternatives open to Recusants and Puritans under Elizabeth I and James I*, Cambridge, 1975.

Rostenberg, Leona, *The Minority Press and the English Crown: A Study in Repression, 1558–1625*, Nieuwkoop, The Netherlands, 1971.

Rowbotham, Sheila, *Women, Resistance and Revolution: A History of Women and Revolution in the Modern World*, New York, 1972.

Rushe, Harry, "Prophecies and Propaganda, 1641 to 1651," *English Historical Review* 84 (1969): 752–70.

Scarisbrick, J. J., *The Reformation and the English People*, London, 1984.

Schanzer, Ernest, "The Marriage Contracts in *Measure for Measure*," *Shakespeare Survey* 13 (1960): 81–89.

Shapin, Steven, *A Social History of Truth: Civility and Science in Seventeenth-Century England*, Chicago, 1994.

Sharpe, Kevin, "The Image of Virtue: The Court and Household of Charles I, 1635–1642," in *The English Court: From the War of the Roses to the Civil War*, ed. David Starkey, London, 1987.

Siebert, F. S., *Freedom of the Press in England, 1476–1776*, Urbana, IL, 1952.

Smith, Alan G. R., *The Emergence of a Nation-State: The Commonwealth of England, 1529–1660*, London, 1984.

Smith, Hilda, "Feminism and the Methodology of Women's History" in Carroll, *Liberating Women's History*.

Smith, Lacey Baldwin, *Treason in Tudor England: Politics and Paranoia*, Princeton, 1986.

Smith, Nigel, *Perfection Proclaimed: Language and Literature in English Radical Religion, 1640–1660*, Oxford, 1989.

Smith, Paul, *Discerning the Subject*, Minneapolis, 1988.

Smith, R. H., "Marriage Processes in the English Past: Some Continuities," in Bonfield, Smith, and Wrightson, *The World We Have Gained*.

Smith, Sir Thomas, *De Republica Anglorum*, ed. Mary Dewar, Cambridge, 1982.

Smuts, R. Malcolm, "The Political Failure of Stuart Cultural Patronage," in *Patronage in the Renaissance*, ed. Guy Fitch Lytle and Stephen Orgel, Princeton, 1981.

Somerset, Anne, *Ladies in Waiting: From the Tudors to the Present Day*, New York, 1984.

Sommerville, Johan P., *Politics and Ideology in England, 1603–1640*, London, 1986.

Southern, A. C., *Elizabethan Recusant Prose, 1558–1582*, London, 1950.

Spencer, Theodore, "The History of an Unfortunate Lady," *Studies and Notes in Philology and Literature* 20 (1938): 43–59.

Spufford, Margaret, "Puritanism and Social Control?" in *Order and Disorder in Early Modern England*, ed. Anthony Fletcher and John Stevenson, Cambridge, 1985.

Starkey, David, "Court and Government," in *Revolution Reassessed*, ed. Christopher Coleman and David Starkey, Oxford, 1986.

The Reign of Henry VIII: Personalities and Politics, London, 1985.

Rivals in Power: Lives and Letters of the Great Tudor Dynasties, New York, 1990.

Steen, Sara Jayne, "Women Writers of the Seventeenth Century, 1604–1674," *English Literary Renaissance* 24 (1994): 243–74.

Stone, Lawrence, *The Causes of the English Revolution, 1529–1642*, New York, 1972.

The Crisis of the Aristocracy, 1558–1641, London, 1967.

The Family, Sex and Marriage in England, 1500–1800, New York, 1977.

Tentler, Thomas N., *Sin and Confession on the Eve of the Reformation*, Princeton, 1977.

"The Summa for Confessors as an Instrument of Social Control," in *The Pursuit of Holiness in Late Medieval and Renaissance Religion; Papers from the University of Michigan Conference*, ed. Charles Trinkhaus with Heiko A. Oberman, Leiden, 1974.

Thirsk, Joan, *Economic Policy and Projects: The Development of a Consumer Society in Early Modern England*, Oxford, 1978.

Thomas, Keith, *Religion and the Decline of Magic: Studies in Popular Beliefs in Sixteenth- and Seventeenth-Century England*, London, 1971.

"Women and the Civil War Sects," *Past & Present* 13 (1958): 42–62.

Travitsky, Betty S., "The Lady Doth Protest: Protest in the Popular Writings of Renaissance Englishwomen," *English Literary Renaissance* 14 (1984): 255–83.

Travitsky, Betty S., and Adele F. Seeff (eds.), *Attending to Women in Early Modern England*, Newark, NJ, 1994.

Trimble, William Raleigh, *The Catholic Laity in Elizabethan England, 1558–1603*, Cambridge, 1964.

Trubowitz, Rachel, "Female Preachers and Male Wives: Gender and Authority in Civil War England," in Holstun, *Pamphlet Wars*.

Utley, Francis Lee, *The Crooked Rib; An Analytical Index to the Argument about Women in English and Scots Literature to the End of the Year 1568*, Columbus, 1944.

Valbuena, Olga Lucia, "Milton's 'Divorsive' Interpretation and the Gendered Reader," *Milton Studies* 27 (1992): 115–37.

Wall, Wendy, *The Imprint of Gender: Authorship and Publication in the English Renaissance*, Ithaca, 1993.

Waller, Gary F., "Struggling into Discourse: The Emergence of Renaissance Women's Writing," in Hannay, *Silent but for the Word.*

Warnicke, Retha M., *Women of the English Renaissance and Reformation,* Contributions in Women's Studies 38, Westport, CT, 1983.

Wayne, Don E., *Penshurst: The Semiotics of Place and the Politics of History,* Madison, 1984.

Weeks, Jeffrey, *Sex, Politics and Society: The Regulation of Sexuality Since 1800,* London, 1981.

Weisner, Merry E., "Early Modern Midwifery: A Case Study," in *Women and Work in Pre-Industrial Europe,* ed. Barbara A. Hanawalt, Bloomington, 1986.

Wentersdorf, Karl, "The Marriage Contracts in *Measure for Measure*: A Reconsideration," *Shakespeare Survey* 32 (1979): 129–44.

Wexler, P. "Structure, Text and Subject: A Critical Sociology of School Knowledge," in *Cultural and Economic Reproduction in Education: Essays on Class, Ideology, and the State,* ed. Michael W. Apple, London, 1982.

Wiener, Carol Z., "The Beleaguered Isle. A Study of Elizabethan and Early Jacobean Anti-Catholicism," *Past & Present* 51 (1971): 27–62.

Willemen, P., "Notes on Subjectivity," *Screen* 19 (1978): 41–69.

Willen, Diane, "Women and Religion in Early Modern England," in *Women in Reformation and Counter-Reformation Europe: Public and Private Worlds,* ed. Sherrin Marshall, Bloomington, 1989.

Williams, Ethan Morgan, "Women Preachers in the Civil War," *Journal of Modern History* 1 (1929): 561–69.

Williams, J. A., "English Catholicism Under Charles II: The Legal Position," *Recusant History* 7 (1963): 123–43.

Williams, Penry, *The Tudor Regime,* Oxford, 1979.

Williams, Raymond, "Problems of Materialism," *New Left Review* 109 (1978): 3–17.

Wilson, Derick, *A Tudor Tapestry: Men, Women and Society in Reformation England,* Pittsburgh, 1972.

Wiseman, Sue, "Unsilent Instruments and the Devil's Cushions: Authority in Seventeenth-Century Women's Prophetic Discourse," in *New Feminist Discourses: Critical Essays on Theories and Texts,* ed. Isobel Armstrong, New York, 1992.

Woodbridge, Linda, *Women and the English Renaissance: Literature and the Nature of Womankind, 1540–1620,* Urbana, IL, 1984.

Wright, Louis B., *Middle-Class Culture in Elizabethan England,* Chapel Hill, 1935.

Wright, S. G., "Dougle Fooleries," *Bodleian Quarterly Record* 7 (1932): 95–98.

Wrightson, Keith, *English Society, 1580–1680,* New Brunswick, 1982.

"The Nadir of English Illegitimacy in the Seventeenth Century," in Laslett, Oosterveen, and Smith, *Bastardy and its Comparative History.*

Poverty and Piety in an English Village: Terling, 1525–1700, New York, 1979.

Youings, Joyce, *The Dissolution of the Monasteries,* Historical Problems, Studies, and Documents, London, 1971, vol. XIV.

Ziegler, Georgianna M., "Women Writers of Tudor England, 1485–1603," *English Literary Renaissance* 24 (1994): 229–42.

Index

236

Cambridge Studies in Renaissance Literature and Culture

General editor
STEPHEN ORGEL
Jackson Eli Reynolds Professor of Humanities, Stanford University

Printed in the United Kingdom
by Lightning Source UK Ltd.
116309UKS00001B/132